Rommel, The Desert Fox

ROMMEL,

The Desert Fox

By

DESMOND YOUNG

Foreword by

FIELD-MARSHAL SIR CLAUDE AUCHINLECK

PERENNIAL LIBRARY

HARPER & ROW, PUBLISHERS

New York, Hagerstown, San Francisco, London

Contents

Acknowledgments

My grateful thanks are due to Field-Marshal Sir Claude Auchinleck for writing the foreword to the book and for his unvarying kindness to me during the years I was privileged to serve him; to Field-Marshal Earl Wavell, General Sir Richard O'Connor and Lt.-Gen. Sir Arthur Smith for giving me their appreciations of Rommel as a commander; to Brigadier E. J. Shearer, C.B., Brigadier E. T. Williams, C.B., D.S.O., Brigadier C. D. Quilliam, C.B.E. and Major Digby Raeburn, D.S.O for information regarding Rommel's first appearance in the Western Desert; to Colonel G. H. Clifton, D.S.O., M.C. for the story of his interviews with Rommel as a prisoner-of-war, and to Lt.-Col. R. M. P. Carver, C.B., D.S.O., M.C. for allowing me to quote from his detailed account of the November-December 1941 battle (published in the *Royal Armoured Corps Journal*), and to use his maps. To Chester Wilmot I am deeply indebted for invaluable help about "sources," to Major-General J. F. C. Fuller, Captain B. H. Liddell Hart and Alan Moorehead for advice and permission to quote from their writings, to Lt.-Col. P. Findlay for translating *Infanterie Greift An,* to Dr. Paul Weber of Berne for procuring material in Switzerland, to my friends Mr. and Mrs. Gough of Neuchâtel for driving me about Germany and to Lt.-Col. H. O. Larter of the U.S. Army Historical Section at Frankfurt for helping me when I was there. I am also grateful to Doubleday & Company for permission to quote from General Eisenhower's *Crusade in Europe,* and to the Trustees of Count Ciano's Estate for quotations from *Ciano's Diaries.*

On "the other side of the hill," I received the greatest possible help from Frau Rommel and her son Manfred, from Vice-Admiral Ruge, from Generals Bayerlein, von Esbeck, von Ravenstein and Speidel, from Captains Aldinger and Hartmann, from Dr. Karl Strölin of Stuttgart, who told me the story of Rommel's association with the plot against Hitler, from Baron von Esebeck, war correspondent, military historian and friend of Rommel, who served with him in North Africa and in Normandy, from Wilhelm Wessels, war artist with the Afrika Korps, and from Herbert Günther, Rommel's batman for nearly four years.

Lastly, I owe a great debt to my wife, who suggested the idea to me, kept me up to it and, in the intervals of marketing, cooking and dealing with a litter of puppies, contrived somehow to type what I wrote—and to improve it by criticism.

Cottage du Grand Gondin
Valescure. (Var.)   D. Y.

Foreword

By Field-Marshal Sir Claude J. E. Auchinleck,
G.C.B., G.C.I.E., C.S.I., D.S.O., O.B.E.

In this book is reproduced a letter which I thought necessary to send to my commanders in the field when the name of Rommel was acquiring almost magical properties in the minds of our soldiers. An enemy commander does not gain a reputation of this sort unless he is out of the ordinary and Rommel was certainly exceptional. Germany produces many ruthlessly efficient generals: Rommel stood out amongst them because he had overcome the innate rigidity of the German military mind and was a master of improvisation.

The German junior officers of the Afrika Korps, the platoon, company and battalion commanders, were, it always seemed to me, better grounded in tactics than our own. This was not the fault of our men but of the peculiar tasks laid on our Army in peace and of the lack of any really systematic training. As the war went on, our men found their feet and, more often than not, outmatched the Germans because their natural tactical instinct was developed and forced to display itself by stress of circumstance. But in the higher ranks Rommel remained pre-eminent as a leader on the battlefield. I can testify myself to his resilience, resourcefulness and mental agility and so long as we are still unhappily obliged to train our youth to arms and our officers to lead them into battle, there is much that we can learn from a study of him and his methods.

My own contacts with Rommel were confined to encounters with him and the Afrika Korps in the campaigns of 1941-42 in the Western Desert, but after reading the story of his earlier and later years I find that my idea of him, formed in those strenuous days when the battle was swinging back and forth between Benghazi and Alexandria, does not differ much from the author's considered appreciation. In one respect, however, my conception was wrong. I was surprised to learn how simple and homely he seems to have been. I think that we who were fighting against him pictured him as a typical Junker officer, a product of the Prussian military machine.

That he evidently was not and it may well be that this accounts for his amazing—and it was amazing—success as a leader of men in battle.

Rommel gave me and those who served under my command in the Desert many anxious moments. There could never be any question of relaxing our efforts to destroy him, for if ever there was a general whose sole preoccupation was the destruction of the enemy, it was he. He showed no mercy and expected none. Yet I could never translate my deep detestation of the régime for which he fought into personal hatred of him as an opponent. If I say, now that he is gone, that I salute him as a soldier and a man and deplore the shameful manner of his death, I may be accused of belonging to what Mr. Bevin has called the "trade union of generals." So far as I know, should such a fellowship exist, membership in it implies no more than recognition in an enemy of the qualities one would wish to possess oneself, respect for a brave, able and scrupulous opponent and a desire to see him treated, when beaten, in the way one would have wished to be treated had he been the winner and oneself the loser. This used to be called chivalry: many will now call it nonsense and say that the days when such sentiments could survive a war are past. If they are, then I, for one, am sorry.

The author of this book, Brigadier Desmond Young, has spared no pains to learn the facts of Rommel's life and death from his family and others and I cannot think of any one better fitted to record them. A veteran of the first World War, he was in the thick of the fighting in the Desert until he had the bad luck to be taken at Gazala while the battle was still in the balance. He is an old friend of mine and, after his escape from enemy hands, became one of my staff officers. In Delhi and on long trips in aircraft about the world we have talked about most subjects under the sun. But, lest I be suspected of having inspired his views of military matters on which different opinions may well be held, I should perhaps say that I have never discussed with him the conduct of the war in North Africa. His conclusions about that, as about most other things, are his own, for he is a man of independent mind. As for his book, I read it only after it had already gone to the printers. I did so with the greatest interest and enjoyment, and I am sure that it will prove as fascinating to others as it was to me. That apart, I welcome it because it does justice to a stout-hearted adversary and may help to show to a new generation of Germans that it is not their soldierly qualities which we dislike but only the repeated misuse of them by their rulers.

Prelude

Shambling along in the first, sharp sunshine of a June morning we had just cleared the minefield west of Bir Harmat. It was in and around the headquarters of 10th Indian Infantry Brigade at Bir Harmat that we had been overrun by German tanks the evening before. Like all prisoners who have spent a night in the open, we were a scruffy lot. British and Indian, some shivering in bush-shirts and shorts, some muffled to the eyes in greatcoats, blankets and Balaclava helmets, all unshaven, unwashed, tired, hungry and disarranged inside, we were beginning to realise that what was jocularly known in the Middle East as "going into the bag" was not much of a joke after all. Our guards glanced at us from time to time with the dispassionate contempt with which we ourselves had so often surveyed the endless columns of captive Italians. Terrified, normally, of mines, I trudged along through the fringe of the minefield for easier walking. It was only when a young German soldier called me sharply back to the column that I looked down to see where I was putting my feet—and then I did not very much care.

On the other side of the minefield we passed in front of a German battery in action. Our guns and some tanks, hull-down, were evidently looking for it. Shell from a 25-pounder battery and tracer from the tanks began to fall round the column. A young officer near me had his foot blown off. There were shouts of alarm from up in front. By a common impulse, everyone broke into a shuffling double. I ran for a few yards with the rest and then, because it is just as easy to run into shell-bursts as out of them, dropped back into a walk. Soon I found myself alongside the blond young representative of the Afrika Korps who was bringing up the rear. He motioned to me to run. I took off my cap and showed him my grey hairs. Like a young sheepdog, doubtful whether to pick up a straggler or to keep the rest of the flock together, he hesitated. Then he doubled off in pursuit, beckoning to me to follow.

Since the battery seemed occupied with its own affairs, I strolled off casually to the flank. Fifty yards or so away I found what I was looking for, a slit trench. I slid into it and pulled the spoil down on top of me. Capture in the desert was seldom final. With luck I might lie there until dark and then have a cut at getting through the minefield. Home, by now, might not be until El Adem, but plenty of people had walked much further than that.

Twenty minutes later I was picked up. A German officer, standing up in his truck, spotted me as he passed and stopped. I was hauled out and driven to the head of the column, still under sporadic shellfire. Before I could mingle with the rest of the party a German captain shouted to me in English: "You are the senior officer here?" Perhaps I was. Certainly I was the oldest. "You will go in a staff-car with two German officers under a flag of truce and tell your battery over there to stop firing. They are only endangering your own men." That was true enough. One's natural instinct as a prisoner-of-war is not, however, to do as one is told. I said that I did not think that I could do that. "Then you will detail another officer to do it." I said that I did not think I could give such an order either. (I spent odd moments during the next sixteen months wondering how they would have got me back if I had reached the battery and whether I had not been a fool to refuse.)

At this moment a Volkswagen drove up. Out of it jumped a short, stocky but wiry figure, correctly dressed, unlike the rest of us, in jacket and breeches. I noticed that he had a bright blue eye, a firm jaw and an air of command. One did not need to understand German to realise that he was asking "What goes on here?" They talked together for a few seconds. Then the officer who spoke English turned to me. "The General rules," he said sourly, "that if you do not choose to obey the order I have just given you, you cannot be compelled to do so." I looked at the general and saw, as I thought, the ghost of a smile. At any rate his intervention seemed to be worth a salute. I cut him one before I stepped back into the ranks to be driven off into captivity.

I could hardly have failed to recognise Rommel. But I could hardly have supposed that, only a few years later, his widow would be showing me his death-mask and telling me the story of his murder.

Rommel, The Desert Fox

CHAPTER I

Benghazi (Return)

In the middle of February, 1941, British stock stood sky-high
in Egypt. Those unfailing barometers of our fortunes, the
barmen of Cairo and Alexandria, became so effusive that occasionally they could barely restrain themselves from setting up
a round "on the house." *Suffragis** lost something of their
camel-like air of contempt; even Egyptian taxi-drivers grew
approximately polite. In the higher reaches, fat pashas invited
senior British officers to the Mahomed Ali Club. There were
garden-parties in the gardens of the rich around Gezireh.
Cairo society ceased to practise its Italian. Relations between
the Monarch and His Britannic Majesty's Ambassador were
reputed to verge upon the cordial. In a word, the East (and in
this there is no difference between Near and Middle and Far),
was making its instinctive salaam to success. Only the shop-
keepers of the Kasr-el-Nil, torn between a patriotic desire to
see the last of us and a deeper-rooted reluctance to see the last
of our money, reflected gloomily that the stream of piastres
might soon be diverted to their opposite numbers in Tripoli.

On our side, the personable young women working as tele-
phonists in G.H.Q. or as probationers in the hospitals stared
with open admiration as one of the young lions of the 11th
Hussars sauntered in his cherry-coloured slacks through the
lounge of Shepheard's or the roof-garden of the Continental.
For these were the most famous of the "desert rats" of the
famous 7th Armoured Division. It was they who had struck
the first blow, crossing the frontier wire the night after Italy
entered the war and returning with a batch of Italian
prisoners. Thereafter, for these past eight months, they had
lived in the enemy's pockets, roaming behind his lines in their
armoured cars, watching his every move, shooting him up
along the coast road until he was afraid to stir after dark.
Only the Long Range Desert Group was later to equal their
reputation for daring. Even the escorts of the young women
had to admit that, though the cavalry might be a trifle snob, a
good British cavalry regiment "had something."

* Egyptian hotel servants.

3

In the cloakrooms of the hotels the felt caps of the Rifle Brigade, with their silver Maltese crosses, hung beside those of the 60th with their red bosses and slung bugles. In the bar, the officers of these two almost equally famous battalions of the Support Group reluctantly conceded to each other a common humanity which they were unwilling to recognise in any one else, except, of course, the cavalry and the Royal Horse Artillery.

As for the Australians, strolling through the streets, oblivious of senior officers, or driving, according to their custom, ten up in shabby victorias, they surveyed sardonically the town which their fathers had "taken apart" at the end of the first war. From time to time, they broke into "Waltzing Matilda" or "The Wizard of Oz." The café proprietors, the dragomen, the vendors of fly-whisks and erotic postcards regarded them with a respect born of apprehension rather than affection.

Setting an example to Cairo in turn-out and saluting, "details" left behind by 4th Indian Division, now departed to fresh victories in Eritrea and Abyssinia, moved inconspicuously among the crowds.

If Egypt had a good opinion of the Army of the Nile, the Army of the Nile had a good conceit of itself—and with reason. In the last two months it had advanced 500 miles. It had beaten and destroyed an Italian army of four corps, comprising nine divisions and part of a tenth. It had captured 130,-000 prisoners, 400 tanks and 1,290 guns, besides vast quantities of other material. (Included in "other material" were clean sheets and comfortable beds, silk shirts, elaborate toilet-sets in Florentine leather, scent and scented "hair-muck," becoming blue cavalry-cloaks, *vino* and *liquore* of all varieties, Pellegrino water in profusion, to say nothing of a motor-caravan of young women, "officers for the use of . . ." The Italians went to war in comfort.) When General Berganzoli ("Electric Whiskers") surrendered unconditionally on February 7th, he was joined in captivity in India by more general officers than that country had seen together since the 1911 Durbar.

The army of Graziani which, it had seemed the previous summer, had only to jump into its trucks and drive to Cairo, under cover of a superior air force, and which, indeed, might well have done so, had been swept from the map. Graziani himself, complaining that Mussolini had compelled him to wage war "as a flea against an elephant" ("a peculiar flea," commented the Duce, "with more than a thousand guns"), had posted his will to his wife and retired, first to a Roman tomb, 70 feet deep, in Cirene and then to Italy.

All this had been achieved at a cost of 500 killed, 1,373 wounded and 55 missing, by a force only three divisions strong, of which only two divisions were employed at one time in the operations—7th Armoured Division and 4th Indian Division, the latter relieved after the battle of Sidi Barrani by 6th Australian Division.

The echoes of General Wavell's offensive were soon drowned in the thunder of greater battles on the Russian front. It became the fashion to decry victories won over the Italians. But in the very decision to attack an enemy so overwhelmingly superior in numbers, in the plan whereby our troops were to lie up for a whole day in the open desert within thirty miles of him, penetrate his line of forts by night unseen and then turn and attack them from the rear at dawn, was the first sign of military genius on our side.

Badly officered and with little heart for the war, the Italians crumbled under the shock of surprise, of the discovery that their field-guns could not pierce the armour of our "I" tanks and of the assault of troops whose standard of training was as high as their spirit. Better divisions have done the same before and since. But it is wrong to suppose that these operations were just a glorified field-day. At Nibeiwa many of the Italian gunners served their pieces until the tanks ran over them. General Maletti, already wounded, was killed firing a machine-gun from his tent. At Beda Fomm the 2nd Rifle Brigade alone beat off nine tank attacks, pressed home with determination.

Whether, had he been allowed to try, General Wavell could have gone on to Tripoli, thus turning what had been planned as a five-day raid into a major offensive, is another matter. Would our worn-out tanks and over-taxed transport have been equal to another five hundred miles? Would not the still intact Italian divisions in Tripoli, secure from surprise, have fortified the line Homs-Tirhuana, as General Montgomery expected the Germans to do nearly two years later? Could Benghazi have been used as a supply port under intensive bombing? Above all, would not the Germans have reacted and flown over their reserve airborne divisions from southern Italy? On the whole, it seems that General O'Connor, commanding Western Desert Force, would have found himself "out on a limb," even if he had reached Tripoli. At that time we had not the means to exploit an operation which had already succeeded beyond our wildest dreams.*

Still, Egypt was safe, the Axis power in North Africa broken and British prestige in the Middle East restored. For the first time since the Battle of Britain, people at home had something to celebrate.

Two months later there was consternation in Cairo and British stock slumped as quickly as it had risen. Gradually the details of the disaster filtered through. Benghazi evacuated—that was unfortunate but no doubt "according to plan"; 2nd Armoured Division, recently arrived from England, destroyed as a fighting force, its commander, Major-General Gambier-Parry and his headquarters captured at Mechili; 3rd Indian Motor Brigade overrun there in its first action; 9th Australian Division invested in Tobruk; Lieutenant-General Sir Richard O'Connor, promoted and knighted for his recent success, "in the bag" with Lieutenant-General Philip Neame, V.C. and Lieutenant-Colonel John Combe of the 11th Hussars; Bardia, Sollum and Capuzzo gone; the enemy back on the escarpment east of the frontier wire; the threat to Egypt greater than ever. Not even "a Cairo spokesman" could succeed in convincing the world that this was merely "a propaganda success," not even the honeyed tones of the B.B.C. commentator, Mr. Richard Dimbleby, gloss over it.

Not, at least, so far as the Egyptians were concerned. A cynical and realistic race, especially where their own interests are involved, they saw the red light quickly. The Italians—they had never thought much of them. But these Germans, what soldiers! Real professionals, like our own Egyptian Army. It was to be hoped that they would respect property in Cairo and not play tricks with the currency. Perhaps it would be as well to keep up one's Italian and even to learn a little German. . . . Meanwhile, better continue to be civil to the British, just in case. . . . But no need to overdo it. Neither then nor later did they ever entirely desert Mr. Micawber. There were, however, notable variations in the temperature of their affection for him.

Though the fog of war lay rather unnecessarily thick on our command in the forward areas and there were several "regrettable incidents," there was no mystery about Gen-

* It is fair to say that General O'Connor himself and most German generals take a different view.

eral Wavell's defeat. The seeds of it were sown when the Chiefs of Staff telegraphed to him, immediately after the fall of Benghazi, telling him to be prepared to send the largest possible army and air forces from the Middle East to Greece. When those forces were duly dispatched, he lost "practically the whole of the troops which were fully equipped and fit for operations."

In the last resort, the statement must overrule the soldiers, for they alone see the whole picture. It may be that, for political reasons, the British Government could not have refused to send help to Greece, even though the Greeks showed no great enthusiasm for it, the help was necessarily insufficient and the dispersion of effort made failure on both fronts inevitable. Those who find comfort in "second guessing" may argue that the dispatch of British troops convinced Hitler that there was some secret agreement between the British and Soviet Governments and postponed the invasion of Russia by several vital weeks. The evidence hardly seems to support them. What is certain is that the loss of 57,000 trained men led directly to a major defeat in the Middle East.

General Wavell, or his Intelligence Staff, made one mistake for which he was, characteristically, the first to take the blame. From the information available to him, he calculated that not before May at the earliest could there be a German offensive against Cyrenaica, even if it were a fact, for which there was no direct evidence (indeed, such evidence as there was seemed to contradict it), that German troops were on their way to Tripoli. When, at the end of February, they were reported to be already in Libya, he still considered that no attack was likely before the middle of April and hoped that it might not materialise before May. In fact it was launched on March 31st.

Even this error was very far from being entirely his fault. In 1939 and 1940 the policy of appeasement was still being actively pursued and, because His Majesty's Government "wished to do nothing that might impair their existing relations with Italy" (relations which, on Mussolini's side, were founded about equally on dislike and contempt for the apparently toothless lion), he had not been permitted to set up an intelligence service in Italian territory. In North Africa he had no agents at all before Italy came into the war and it was not possible until long afterwards to "plant" them. Thus the 5th Light Motorised Division was able to land in Tripoli without his knowing anything about it.

Like many another British general before him in the early stages of a war, General Wavell was called upon to shoulder "responsibilities for which my resources were completely inadequate." He shouldered them uncomplainingly and soon had a revolt in Iraq and a minor war against the Vichy French in Syria added to them for good measure. Having dealt successfully with the latter, he was removed from his command. Such, at any rate, was the impression made upon the troops in the Middle East, and explanations, whether well-founded or not, that he needed a rest or was being translated to a sphere of even greater responsibility did not change their feeling that he had been kicked upstairs for having failed to do the impossible in Greece. It was not the last time that, having rendered outstanding services to his country, he was to find himself treated with barely perfunctory politeness by his country's government.

Such were the circumstances of the disaster in Cyrenaica. But if, in the early summer of 1941, one had stopped the first passer-by in the streets of Cairo and asked him the reason for this astonishing reversal of fortune, it is odds-on that he would have replied in one word: "Rommel."

CHAPTER 2

"Our Friend Rommel"

To: All Commanders and Chiefs of Staff
From: Headquarters, B.T.E. and M.E.F.

There exists a real danger that our friend Rommel is becoming a kind of magician or bogey-man to our troops, who are talking far too much about him. He is by no means a superman, although he is undoubtedly very energetic and able. Even if he were a superman, it would still be highly undesirable that our men should credit him with supernatural powers.

I wish you to dispel by all possible means the idea that Rommel represents something more than an ordinary German general. The important thing now is to see that we do not always talk of Rommel when we mean the enemy in Libya. We must refer to "the Germans" or

8

"the Axis powers" or "the enemy" and not always keep harping on Rommel.

Please ensure that this order is put into immediate effect, and impress upon all Commanders that, from a psychological point of view, it is a matter of the highest importance.

(*Signed*)   C. J. AUCHINLECK,

GENERAL,

COMMANDER-IN-CHIEF, M.E.F.*

In any war, the number of generals who succeed in imposing their personalities on their own troops, let alone those of the enemy, is far smaller than generals themselves may like to believe. Take World War I, when it was said with some truth that few British soldiers knew the name of their Divisional commander. How many of the "high brass" meant anything to the "other ranks"? Haig, well, they had heard of him, of course. His "backs to the wall" order in 1918 had a human ring about it. But it was not until the survivors were demobilised and came to learn how he was devoting his last years to their welfare that that remote, solitary and slightly unsympathetic figure made any positive impression. Indeed, in the long span from the Duke of Wellington to Lord Montgomery, the senior British generals who were heroes in the eyes of the private soldier could be counted on two hands and would include some very bizarre figures.

As for World War II, "Monty" himself, "Bill" Slim and "Dickie" Mountbatten all had the common touch in an uncommon degree. So had Alexander, who, one imagines, never gave it a thought. So, in some strange fashion, had Wavell, in spite of his extreme taciturnity. In the U.S Army there were Omar Bradley, "Blood-and-Guts" Patton, and a few more, including MacArthur and "Ike" himself. But the soldier's general remains a rare bird and the general who is known to the rank-and-file of the enemy a still rarer one.

Amongst such, Rommel was a phenomenon, a nonpareil. The instruction quoted at the beginning of this chapter gave rise to much discussion and some derision when it was issued

---

* Although I remember this order very well, as do most people who served in the Middle East, I have been unable to obtain, even from its author, a copy of the original. I have had, therefore, to rely on a retranslation of the translation preserved amongst Rommel's papers by his family. There may be slight verbal discrepancies between the two versions but the sense is the same.

9

in Cairo. Nevertheless it was necessary and, indeed, overdue. For Rommel had so identified himself with the Afrika Korps, had so impressed himself upon his opponents, was getting such a "build-up" from British and American war correspondents, as well as from even pro-British newspapers in Cairo, that he was already the best-known and not far from the most popular figure in the Middle East. Mr. Churchill spoke of him as "a master of war." Our own troops referred to him, half-affectionately, as "that b—— Rommel," which, as I learnt not long ago, was precisely how he was referred to by the Afrika Korps itself. When they added, as they often did, "You've got to hand it to the b——," it needed no psychologist to see that the sporting spirit of the British soldier could easily produce a mild inferiority complex. That did, in fact, occur. Newcomers to the desert and even a minority of the old "desert rats" were inclined to explain: "We bumped into Germans," as though that in itself was a sufficient excuse for failure. To the few who remembered the quite unwarranted accents of pity and comtempt with which we used to speak of "poor old Fritz" in the first war, it seemed that there was a real danger of Rommel and the Afrika Korps securing a moral ascendancy. Perhaps those rather too easy victories over the Italians had not been very good for us after all.

Granted the build-up, it is still hard to see why Rommel so quickly became *"un type dans le genre de Napoléon,"* a bogey to the back-areas and to civilians in Cairo, as well as a more personal and proximate menace to those further forward.

Though he emerged like the Demon King from a trap, unfortunately anticipating his cue, even our Intelligence Staff knew very little about him, either as a soldier or as a man. This was because the British had largely relied upon their French allies for "profiles" of German generals and for those personal details which enable a commander to estimate his opponent. The sudden collapse of France cut them off from this contact and the *dossiers* doubtless remained in the French Ministry of War, to be read by the subjects of them. Thus the War Office was able to supply General Wavell and his staff with only a meagre report about Rommel. From this it appeared that he was a rather impetuous individual who had done well in the first war and as a divisional commander in the invasion of France but was by no means in the top flight of German generals. It was suggested that he was a keen Nazi and that his selection for North Africa was due to party favouritism.

The background was both sketchy and incorrect. Indeed, the most fantastic stories about Rommel's origin and early career are still afloat. For example, in that otherwise well-documented book, *Defeat in the West*, by Milton Shulman, we are told that he was a member, with Goering, Hess, Roehm, Bormann and more of the sort, of the Free Corps, a group of "irresponsible, swashbuckling men" who grew "increasingly more aggressive and brutal in their suppression of disorders" in Germany after the Armistice in 1918 and supplied "the most promising leaders of the bullying gangs of the latter-day Hitlerite S.A. and S.S." Other reports say that he was the son of a labourer and one of the first of the Nazi storm-troopers; others that he was an N.C.O. who rose from the ranks during the first war; others that he was a policeman between the two wars.

The truth is less highly coloured. Rommel was, from first to last, a regular officer and, as is shown by the extract from his *Wehrpass* or record of service, printed at the end of this book, from the day he joined his regiment to the day he died, he was never off the rolls of the German Army. He never belonged to the Free Corps, he was never a policeman, he was never a member of the Nazi Party, still less a storm-trooper, and his connection with Hitler came about quite fortuitously.

The source of some at least of the legends is not difficult to discover. In the summer of 1941 an anonymous article about Rommel appeared in Goebbels' paper, *Das Reich*. This article, which was commended to the attention of the foreign correspondents in Berlin, announced that Rommel was the son of a workingman, that he left the army after the first war to study at Tübingen University, that he was one of the first storm-troop leaders and became a close friend of Hitler and so on and so on.

Rommel saw the cutting in North Africa and reacted violently. What did they mean, he wrote to the Propaganda Ministry, by circulating fabricated stories about him? The Propaganda Ministry tried to get out of it by saying that perhaps Oberleutnant Tschimpke, author of a book about the 7th Panzer Division, which Rommel commanded in France, had supplied the information. Rommel then found time, the battle of Halfaya Pass being over, to turn on the unfortunate Tschimpke. Had he in fact given this information and if so what did *he* mean by it? Tschimpke replied to Rommel denying that he had done anything of the sort. He also wrote to the Propaganda Ministry to ask why they had got him into trouble with the general. The answer, from *Presseabteilung der Reichsregierung, Abt. Auslandspresse, Gruppe: Information, Wilhelmplatz 8-9*, dated October 10, 1941, and signed "Heil Hitler, Dr. Meissner," was one of those comic masterpieces which explain why, in the long run, German propaganda could never be effective. What had been written about General Rommel in the article, said the doctor, could do no harm to the reputation of that excellent man. Indeed, it could only do good, by making him a more familiar and sympathetic figure to the foreign war correspondents. Perhaps, he concluded, it would have been a good thing, from the propaganda point of view, if the statements, though admittedly incorrect, had, in fact, been true.

Tschimpke sent the letter to Rommel, who preserved it amongst his papers. He also preserved a strong dislike and suspicion of any one having anything to do with propaganda or "public relations." The first victim was an unfortunate young officer named Berndt, who came out to join the Afrika Korps after service in the Propaganda Ministry. Reporting to Rommel, to whom he had been personally commended, he was promptly told to go out that evening, his first in the desert, and make a "recce" behind the British lines. Berndt was a brave and intelligent young man and returned from this unpromising assignment with some British prisoners and valuable information. Thereafter Rommel made an exception of him and later used to send him back to Berlin with reports which he did not wish to go through staff channels. But visiting publicists were always suspect.

What were the facts, which Dr. Goebbels' young men could easily have ascertained from the Ministry of War or from Rommel's family, if they did not already know them?

Erwin Johannes Eugen Rommel was born at noon on Sunday, November 15th, 1891, at Heidenheim, a small town in Württemberg, near Ulm. His father, also Erwin Rommel, was a schoolmaster and the son of a schoolmaster. Both father and grandfather were mathematicians of some distinction. Since those were the days when learning was still more highly regarded in Germany than loyalty to a political party, Herr Professor Rommel was much respected in Heidenheim. In 1886 he married Helena, eldest daughter of Karl von Luz, President of the Government of Württemberg and thus a prominent person in those parts. There were five children of the marriage: a son, Manfred, who died young, a daughter, Helena, unmarried and now teaching at the well-known *Waldorfschule* at Stuttgart, Erwin Rommel himself and his younger brothers, Karl and Gerhardt. Karl is almost completely crippled from malaria, caught while serving as a pilot in Turkey and Mesopotamia during the 1914-18 war. Gerhardt supplied the only touch of exotic colour to the otherwise conventional Rommel family by abandoning agriculture to become an opera singer. This profession he still pursues, without any great success and to the mild embarrassment of his relations, at Ulm.

In 1898, Rommel's father became Director of the *Realgymnasium* at Aalen, in other words headmaster of a school in which "Modern Side" subjects rather than classics are taught. In 1913 he died suddenly after an operation. His wife outlived him by twenty-seven years and died only in 1940, when her second son was already a Major-General.

"Tough" is the adjective most obviously appropriate to Rommel of the Afrika Korps but as a small boy Erwin Rommel was the reverse of tough. "He was a very gentle and docile child," says his sister, "who took after his mother. Small for his age, he had a white skin and hair so pale that we called him the 'white bear.' He spoke very slowly and only after reflecting for a long time. He was very good-tempered and amiable and not afraid of any one. When other children used to run away from the chimney-sweeps, with their black faces and top hats, he would go up solemnly and shake hands with them. We had a very sunny childhood, brought up by kind and affectionate parents who taught us their own love of nature. Before we went to school we used to play all day in the garden or in the fields and woods."

School at Aalen did not agree with young Rommel after the freedom of Heidenheim. Finding himself behind the others of his age, he became even paler in the attempt to catch up, lost his appetite and could not sleep. Then he grew lazy and inattentive and made no effort. He was so careless that he became the butt of his class. "If Rommel ever shows up a dictation without a mistake," said the schoolmaster, "we will hire a band and go off for a day in the country." Rommel sat up and promptly turned in a dictation without even a comma out of place. When the promised excursion did not come off, he relapsed into his usual indifference. For several years he remained a dreamy little boy, taking no interest in books or

13

games and showing no sign of that intense physical energy which he afterwards developed.

Then, when he was in his teens, he suddenly woke up. Mentally, he began to give evidence of having inherited the mathematical talent of his father and grandfather. Physically, he started to spend every spare moment in summer on his bicycle and in winter on skis. He passed his examinations with credit. He lost his dreamy abstracted air and reverted to the type of Württemberg, "the home of common sense in Germany." He became hard-headed and practical—and very careful of his money, another Württemberger characteristic. With his great friend Keitel (no relation of the Field-Marshal who subsequently became one of his bitterest enemies), he applied himself to the study of aircraft. Together the two boys built model aeroplanes and then a full-scale glider in which they made repeated but unsuccessful attempts to leave the ground. They began to think about their future careers. Keitel had already made up his mind to become an engineer and find employment at the Zeppelin works at Friedrichshafen. He did so and Rommel would probably have gone with him had his father agreed.

His father opposed the idea and it was then that Rommel decided to join the army. The family had no military tradition, except that Rommel senior had served for a time as a lieutenant in the artillery, before retiring to become a schoolmaster. Nor had the Rommels any influential friends in military circles: they were a respectable Swabian family of moderate means, far removed in education and environment from the Prussian officer class. Rommel was afterwards to have serving under him in Africa generals of aristocratic family, large fortune and military connections which destined them to life in a good regiment from birth and, given ordinary ability, almost assured them of accelerated promotion. Such career as he might have in the army would have to be carved out by himself and there seemed no reason to suppose that he would end up as more than an elderly major, living in retirement on a modest pension in some small town like Heidenheim itself.

On July 19th, 1910, he joined the 124th Infantry Regiment (Koenig Wilhelm I, 6th Württemberg), at Weingarten as an "aspirant" or, approximately, officer cadet, which meant that he had first to serve in the ranks before going to a *Kriegsschule* or War Academy. He was promoted corporal in October and sergeant at the end of December. In March, 1911, he was posted to the *Kriegsschule* at Danzig.

Rommel's time at Danzig was important to him in more ways than one. It was there that he met, through a friend in the War Academy who had a cousin in the same boarding school, the girl whom he was afterwards to marry and who was the only woman in his life. Lucie Maria Mollin was the daughter of a landowner in West Prussia where the family, Italian in origin, had been settled since the thirteenth century. Her father died when she was a child and she was now in Danzig, studying to be a teacher of languages. Rommel fell in love with her at once and she with him and although they did not become formally engaged for another four years there was never any doubt in either of their minds. According to his widow, Rommel at this time was already a serious-minded young man, intensely preoccupied with doing well in his profession. Examinations still did not come as easily to him as the practical side of soldiering and he had to work hard at his books. However, Danzig was a pleasant city in which to be young and in love and, as they both enjoyed outdoor life and dancing, they spent a happy summer whenever, chaperoned by the cousin, they could escape from school.

Rommel duly passed his examinations, if not with great distinction at any rate with marks above the average, and, at the end of January, 1912, received his commission as a 2nd Lieutenant and returned to his regiment. He and Fräulein Mollin wrote to each other every day.

In Weingarten, where the regimental barracks were in the massive old monastery, Rommel was turned on for two years to the training of recruits. He was good at drill and good with men and, like the young Montgomery when he first joined a battalion, was observed to be unusually interested in the minutiæ of military organisation. Otherwise there was nothing to suggest that he was anything out of the ordinary. Physically he was still undersized, though wiry and strong; mentally he was in no way distinguished. Unlike Montgomery, he was not argumentative and preferred to listen rather than to talk, as he did throughout his life. Since he neither smoked nor drank and was already, in his own eyes, engaged, the after-dark amusements of a small garrison town did not appeal to him. The other subalterns found him quiet and too serious for his age but good-tempered and agreeable, always ready to exchange duties to allow the more social to get off, though not prepared to be put upon. One or two of them recognised that he had an independent mind, a strong will and a sense of humour and the N.C.O.s quickly discovered that he would not tolerate anything slipshod. He was thus cut out to be a good regimental officer and, in due course, a good hard-driving adjutant. As an adjutant he would, very properly, be unpopular with the inefficient but it was already clear that he cared less than most young men about popularity. On the whole he seemed a fairly typical Württemberger, shrewd, business-like, careful, with a hard streak in him.

At the beginning of March, 1914, he was attached to a Field Artillery regiment in Ulm and remained with it, enjoying the riding and taking pride in the smart turnout of his battery, until, on the afternoon of July 31st, he returned to barracks to find horses being brought into the barrack-square and orders awaiting him to rejoin his own regiment at once. Next day his company was fitting field equipment. In the evening the colonel inspected the regiment in field-grey, made a stirring speech and, before dismissing them, announced the order for mobilisation. "A jubilant shout of German warrior youth echoes through the ancient grey walls of the monastery," says *Infanterie Greift An*, Rommel's book on tactics, but this and other such comments sound less like Rommel than a gloss by a Nazi propagandist, preparing the 1937 edition for popular comsumption. Had the "warrior youth" been able to foresee the memorial panels to the tens of thousands of officers and men of the Württemberg regiments which still hang in Ulm Cathedral, they might have been less jubilant. Next day the 124th went off to war.

In all armies there is a small minority of professional soldiers (and a few amateurs) who find in war the one occupation to which they are perfectly adapted. Year by year, in the *In Memoriam* column of *The Times*, my eye catches the name of Brigadier-General "Boy" Bradford, V.C., D.S.O., M.C., killed in the Cambrai battle in 1917 at the age of 24, and I remember riding over, unduly conspicuous, I felt, on a white horse, to his brigade headquarters in front of Bourlon Wood and thinking, as I talked to him, that here was someone at last who knew his trade and was equal to any demands that war might make. I remember, too, A. N. S. Jackson, the Olympic runner, my contemporary at Oxford and in the regiment, whom I saw married in 1918 on Paris leave, wearing one ribbon only, the D.S.O. with three bars. There were others like them but not many.

Of this small company of exceptional young men was Rommel, on the wrong side. From the moment that he first came under fire he stood out as a perfect fighting animal, cold, cunning, ruthless, untiring, quick of decision, incredibly brave. At 5 A.M. on the morning of August 22nd, 1914, he went into action against the French in the village of Bleid, near Longwy. He had been patrolling for twenty-four hours, was suffering from food poisoning and was so tired that he could hardly sit in the saddle when he was sent forward to reconnoitre, in thick fog. Having located the village he brought up his platoon. When they were fired upon, he halted them and went on with an N.C.O. and two men. Out of the fog loomed up a high hedge, surrounding a farmhouse. A footpath led past it to another farm. Rommel followed it. As he came round the corner, he saw fifteen or twenty of the enemy standing about in the road. Should he go back and bring up the platoon? That first decision in war is not an easy one to make. Much of a man's future conduct hangs on it. Rommel did what he was to do again and again. Counting on the value of surprise, he collected his three men and attacked, firing from the standing position. The enemy broke and the survivors took cover and opened fire. Rommel found his platoon moving up. Half he armed with bundles of straw, the other half he posted to give covering fire. Then he advanced again. Doors were beaten in and lighted bundles of straw thrown into the houses and barns. House by house the village was cleared. It was a minor action and of no importance except that it was his first and a pattern of the boldness and independence which he showed throughout his service.

Despite his illness and the colossal exertions of the moving warfare of that period, he carried on, sometimes fainting but never reporting sick, until on September 24th he was wounded in the thigh when attacking three Frenchmen in a wood near Varennes, alone and with an empty rifle. By this time his battalion commander had come to rely on him for any particularly tough job and he already had been recommended for the Iron Cross, Class II. Three months later, as soon as his wound was healed, he rejoined the battalion. He came up with it in the middle of January in the Argonne. On January 29th, 1915, he won his Iron Cross, Class I, by crawling with his platoon through a gap in a belt of wire nearly a hundred yards deep, into the main French position, capturing four blockhouses, beating off an enemy attack in battalion strength, retaking one of the blockhouses from which he had been driven out and then withdrawing to his own lines with the loss of less than a dozen men, before a new attack could be launched.

This, again, was only a minor action but it showed Rommel's readiness to exploit a situation to the limit, regardless of the risk involved. It led him time and again into positions of fantastic danger and yet enabled him to win every ounce of advantage, especially against an irresolute enemy.

It was doubtless this willingness to take risks and capacity for individual action which led to his posting, after promotion to *Oberleutnant* (1st Lieutenant) and a second wound in the leg, to a newly-formed mountain battalion, the *Württembergische Gebirgsbataillon* (W.G.B.). This was a unit larger than the normal battalion, consisting of six rifle companies and six mountain machine-gun platoons. It never fought as a unit but rather as a formation, splitting up into two or more Battle Groups (*Abteilungen*) whose constitution varied according to the job in hand. Each battle group was given its task and fought under its own commander, who was allowed wide freedom of action and had merely to report back once a day to the battalion commander. When, after intensive training in mountain warfare in Austria and a peaceful period of nearly a year in a quiet sector in the Vosges, the battalion joined the famous *Alpenkorps* on the Rumanian front, Rommel was quickly entrusted with the command of one of these battle groups which varied in size for different actions from one company to the whole battalion. Meanwhile he had slipped off on leave to Danzig and there, on November 27th, 1916, married Lucie Maria Mollin. Her photograph, taken at this time, shows her to have been a handsome girl, markedly Italian in type, with beautiful modelled features. What it does not show, since the expression is serious, is that she had a great sense of fun, as she still has. Studiousness, courage and strength of character are obvious. She was a good wife for a soldier.

Some of Rommel's subsequent feats in Rumania and Italy would be almost incredible had it not been possible to check them by the statements of others who witnessed and took part in them. In brief, his method was to infiltrate through the enemy lines with a few men, usually laying a telephone line as he went. In mountainous country, where the peaks and the valleys were likely to be held, he worked round the upper slopes, often as steep as the roof of a house and practicable only to skilled mountaineers. Whether in icy fog and deep snow or in the blazing heat of summer he would keep moving at speed by day or night. He had a remarkable eye for country and was proof against heat, cold, fatigue and lack of food and sleep. Once behind the enemy lines he never hesitated to attack, however small his force, for he rightly assumed that the sudden appearance of his men in the rear of their positions and the first devastating burst of machine-gun fire from the back areas would shake all but the best of troops, which the Rumanians and Italians were not. When he took the strongly-fortified Rumanian position of Mount Cosna in August, 1917, he led four companies in single file through the woods between two enemy posts, 150 yards apart, without being detected, and laid a telephone wire at the same time. By the time he reached the summit he had been virtually without sleep for nearly a week and had also been severely wounded in the arm several days before by a bullet fired from far in his rear.

When he took the village of Gagesti in January of the same year, he lay out until ten o'clock at night within the Rumanian outpost line in a temperature ten degrees below freezing. Then, when he judged, correctly, that the Rumanians would be asleep in their billets, he opened up on the village with his machine-guns and half his rifles and led the rest of his troops, cheering, to the attack. As the enemy tumbled sleepily out of the houses he collected them and soon had four hundred of them locked up in the church. His own casualties were negligible.

If he were compelled to make a frontal attack, his practice was to open intense machine-gun fire over the whole sector, with the heaviest concentration at the point where the attack was to be made. Then came an assault with strong forces on a very small front. The attacking troops carried machine-guns, which, as soon as a breach was made, were sited for enfilade fire to the flanks. The remainder of the assault force pressed on, regardless of what was happening in their rear. In other words, he adopted precisely the tactics of penetration in depth which were employed by the German panzer divisions in 1939.

All this time, it was to be remembered, while Rommel was commanding anything up to a battalion, conducting independent operations against the enemy, having his advice sought and taken by senior officers on direction and methods of attack, he was a young man of twenty-five, looking even younger than his age, and in rank only an *Oberleutnant* from a not particularly distinguished line regiment. This in the German army, where seniority counted for more than in our own, where young men were not normally encouraged to air their opinions and where the standard of training was high. That he established an almost unique reputation and was known throughout his division, even before he went to the mountain battalion, is on record. Yet he was not one of those queer personalities who crop up in wars and make an impression by being unusual. He merely had the qualities of courage, boldness, determination and initiative in so exceptional a degree that they could not fail to attract attention. He was a Freyberg rather than an Orde Wingate.

The climax of his career in World War I was reached with the capture of Monte Matajur, south-west of Caporetto, on October 26th, 1917. The Austrians had suffered a series of setbacks at the hands of the Italians and had appealed for German help. In spite of their commitments elsewhere, the German High Command sent the 14th Army, consisting of seven veteran divisions, to take part in an offensive against the Italian positions in the Isonzo valley. The Württemberg Mountain Battalion was again assigned to the Alpenkorps, which was due to attack in the centre, towards Matajur. On the first day the battalion had the task of protecting the right flank of a Bavarian regiment which was to lead the attack. Thereafter it was to follow on after the Bavarians.

To summarise a long and complicated operation, Rommel was not interested in following the Bavarians and persuaded his battalion commander, one Major Sprösser, to allow him to move off to the right of them and attack the Italian positions independently. While the Bavarians were held up, he led two companies before dawn across the Italian front without being detected, and an advance party succeeded in penetrating the Italian front line at first light and capturing an Italian battery position with the bayonet, without a shot being fired at them. Rommel left one company to hold and widen the gap and pushed on with another into the Italian hinterland. He had to return to the help of his first company, which was attacked by an entire Italian battalion. When he took the Italians in the rear they quickly surrendered. He sent back a message to his battalion commander and with it more than a thousand Italian prisoners. On this Major Sprösser came up with four more companies. With six companies under command, Rommel was permitted to proceed with his break-through into the back areas. Finding a road masked from view, he led his whole force along it in single file for nearly two miles while the Italians were still preoccupied with the main battle and bombardment in progress on their front. In open country behind the enemy lines, he sat on the main road leading towards Monte Matajur and captured a ration column, a staff car, 50 officers and 2,000 men of the 4th Bersaglieri Brigade which was moving up. Taking the staff car, he did a preliminary "recce" and decided to cut straight across country to Monte Matajur, the key to the enemy position. Throughout the rest of that day and the whole of the night he drove on his now exhausted troops. At dawn he came upon a camp of the Salerno Brigade. With two other officers and a few riflemen he walked straight into a mass of armed men and ordered them to surrender. After a moment's hesitation, 43 officers and 1500 men laid down their arms, mainly, it would appear, from sheer surprise and the power of the human eye.

When Rommel eventually scaled Monte Matajur from the rear and fired his success rockets from the summit, he had been continuously on the move for fifty hours, had covered twelve miles as the crow flies in mountainous country, had climbed up to 7,000 feet and with never more than six companies under command, had captured 150 officers, 9,000 men and 81 guns. He himself found the lack of fighting spirit in the Italians quite incomprehensible. In the 1937 edition of *Infanterie Greift An* he is made to say that "to-day the Italian Army is one of the best in the world" but here again one suspects a little sub-editing by the army propaganda department.

At any rate, though Rommel could hardly have tried such tricks with success against Lord Cavan's British divisions, it was a remarkably bold operation. For it he was awarded the Pour le Mérite, a decoration usually reserved for senior generals and, when awarded to junior officers, corresponding to the Victoria Cross. He was also promoted *Hauptmann* or Captain. Shortly afterwards, having swum the icy waters of the Piave at night with six men roped together, he attacked, seven strong, the village of Longarone and captured it, with the whole of its considerable garrison, by firing upon it from different points in the darkness and, at dawn, walking in alone, informing the Italians that they were surrounded and ordering them to surrender. He was then sent on leave and, to his disgust, given a staff appointment. This he held until the end of the war.

Leadership in war is not, perhaps, amongst the highest forms of human activity. Yet, whereas a champion of the prize-ring, even a world champion, need be no more than an exceptionally aggressive animal with adequate physique and superlative technical skill, a man to whom other men will unhesitatingly confide their lives in battle must have more to him than that. Thus, soon after I started out on the trail of Rommel, I naturally began to ask myself and others what sort of a person he was, apart from his exploits in action.

From the beginning I ran up against a fundamental difference between the German attitude towards war and our own. For this I was not altogether unprepared. Soon after the first war, I happened to read in translation a book called *Storm of Steel* by one Ernst Jünger and an incident in it had always stuck in my memory, partly because the scene of it was familiar to me. Just after the battle of Cambrai and the successful German counter-attack which followed it, the battalion to which Ernst Jünger belonged was holding the line near Moeuvres, in the neighbourhood of the Hermes Canal. It was a fine, sunny, Sunday afternoon and the officers of his company, having lunched well, were smoking their cigars and drinking their brandy in a dug-out in the front line. "Why not let's go over and raid the English?" someone suggested. It was not a suggestion which one can imagine being made in a British company mess in those days. We were ready enough, if not anxious, to take part in a full-dress attack or an organised raid if we were ordered to do so. A good battalion prided itself on aggressive patrolling and on being in command of No Man's Land at night. But, apart from that, most people were disposed to live and let live and to appreciate a quiet afternoon, with only the odd shell droning over to burst in the back areas, as a Heaven-sent opportunity to read a book or write a letter. Had any one proposed an impromptu raid, "officers only," in such circumstances, he would have been suspected of punishing the brandy too freely and advised to lie down.

In this case the raid was carried out across the fifty or sixty yards which separated the two front lines. Because there was no warning in the way of artillery preparation and because the early afternoon was not the recognized time for raids, it was successful and the company officers returned ten minutes later in triumph, bringing with them two or three prisoners and leaving behind them two or three dead.

The sequel is even more surprising. When the battalion was next out of the line, the officers who took part in the raid presented to the company commander, who had led it, a large silver cup, inscribed "To the victor of Moeuvres."

The German professional soldier has always taken war with a seriousness with which only sport is treated by the British. It is just possible to imagine, though with difficulty, the rest of the side presenting a silver cup to someone who has won the University Rugby match in the last minute by a run from his own 25-yard line. But the cup for "the victor of Moeuvres," solemnly produced with appropriate speeches and filled for a toast to the hero himself—if any one can see that ceremony occurring in a British battalion he must have soldiered in strange company.

This story kept running through my head while I talked in Heidenheim to Hauptmann Hartmann, the first person I met who had served with Rommel in World War I. The Hartmann factory, which makes bandages by the million, had the rather bleak air of extreme impersonal efficiency and almost sterilised cleanliness that only German and Swiss factories seem to attain. Captain Hartmann's office was the typical office of the *Herr Direktor*, gloomy, with its dark panelling, its heavy furniture and its large photographs of former Hartmanns round the walls, not a room in which a file would dare to go adrift or a paper escape from its appropriate tray. Captain Hartmann was, however, by no means so sombre as his surroundings. A dark, good-looking, slightly-built German, he seemed much too young to be Rommel's contemporary (and mine). As he got up from his desk and came across the room to greet me, I saw that he had lost one leg at the hip. Was that in the first war? No, in this, in a glider accident, when he was attached to the *Luftwaffe*. Gliding had been and still was his passion; the first day he came out of hospital after losing his leg he had gone up again. When he spoke of gliding, his face lit up. He was an attractive and sympathetic person with an easy manner.

Then we got on to Rommel. Yes, they had been great friends ever since the first war and until Rommel's death. They served together in the same battalion. He had been with him when he won his Pour le Mérite. He described how Rommel swam the Piave on that December night with his six men and took Longarone. What a soldier! "Where Rommel is, the front is," they used to say in the division. He was always attempting and bringing off things that no one else would have thought of trying. He seemed to have *Fingerspitzengefühl*, a sort of sixth sense, an intuition in his fingers. (It was a word which I was' to hear from every soldier I met who had known Rommel.) Hard, yes, though he never asked any one to do more than he would do himself, or as much, and he was always trying to minimise losses by tactics. He

23

was a tactical genius. Perhaps officers did not like him as much as the men because he always expected more of them and there were very few who could go his pace. But he was "the best of comrades."

"Best of comrades" sounded more promising. After all, they had been young men together and battalions do not spend all their time in the line. Presumably even in Rumania they had their local Amiens to make for when they came out to rest, some equivalent to Godbert or the Cathédrale, where they could settle down in a corner to dine well and forget the war. Such evenings, when one had ridden in along the *pavé* and booked a room and bathed, with bath-salts, and shopped and had a drink with other people from the division, are part of everybody's first war memories, the memories that make one reflect: "Oh, it wasn't too bad after all." (Was it not in the Cathédrale that "Kid" Kennedy, my Brigadier, eyeing the attractive young person who served us, paid her a compliment in terms which I had never heard before, have never heard since and have never forgotten? "By God, Desmond, isn't that lovely?" he said. "You could eat a poached egg off her stomach.")

But when I tried tactfully to switch the conversation from the front line to relaxation and rest and to get some idea of Rommel as a human being as well as a soldier, I came up against a blank wall. Interests? No, Captain Hartmann did not think he had any other interests. When he was not putting his genius for minor tactics into practice, he was working out new plans for embarrassing the enemy. Certainly he never wanted to "beat it up" in the back areas, nor, apparently, to visit them. Was there any change in him, I asked, when he returned to the battalion in 1916 after being married? No, he was just the same, just as tough, just as regardless of danger, just as preoccupied with winning the war on his particular sector. "He was one hundred per cent soldier," said Captain Hartmann, a slightly rapt expression coming over his handsome face, "he was body and soul in the war."

A few days later I tried again, with Hauptmann Aldinger, who had not only served in the same battalion with Hartmann and Rommel during the first war but was Rommel's *Ordonnanzoffizier*, a combination of personal assistant, camp commandant, A.D.C. and private secretary, in France in 1940, in North Africa, and in Normandy in 1944, and was almost the last person to see him alive. Captain Aldinger is a precise little man who might very well be the chief accountant of some large business like Hartmann's bandage factory, in which case the auditors would have an easy job. But in private life he is a designer of gardens, with a considerable reputation in Stuttgart, and an architect of obvious good taste. Perhaps he would see what I was trying to get at and give me a line on Rommel. Here again I made no progress. *Fingerspitzengefühl* came up once more and all the military virtues. A hard man, too hard for many people, particularly officers. "But if Rommel was on your flank you knew you had nothing to worry about on one side at any rate. . . . In those days he believed that every order must be exactly carried out. . . . He had more trust in the Higher Command and in the Staff in the first war than he had in the second. . . ." Other interests? Well, he liked a day's shooting or fishing when he could get it. Reading? Military works mostly. Music or the theatre? No. Food and wine? They meant nothing to him. Was he then entirely serious? Oh, no, he liked to joke with the troops and to talk in the Swabian dialect to people from his part of the country.

It seemed that I was on the trail of that rare and rather colourless creature, the specialist with the single-track mind. The young Montgomery, as he appears in Alan Moorehead's biography, was the nearest parallel to this regular officer with no interests outside his profession. But at least Montgomery had been a notable athlete at St. Paul's, the best-known boy in the school. At Sandhurst he had so annoyed his instructors that he had been told that he was quite useless and would get nowhere in the Army. Rommel had not even that negative distinction.

Life in any army is narrow and limited and nowhere more so than in the old German army, with its class-consciousness and rigid traditions. Thus the outsider, or the man coming into it temporarily from a different world, is inclined to think that the professional who, even in war-time, thinks of nothing but soldiering, must necessarily be narrow and limited also. When General Speidel, Rommel's extremely acute and intelligent Chief of Staff in Normandy, remarked to me that he did not suppose that Rommel had ever read a book in his life that had not to do with war, it was in this mood that I asked whether he was not, then, *"un peu bête."* General Speidel stared at me in astonishment. "Stupid? Good God, no!" he said. "That's the last thing he was."

Eventually I sorted out Rommel to my own satisfaction and related him to my previous experience. But I propose to let

the reader form his own impressions and leave mine until
later.

CHAPTER 3

Between Two Wars

The taste of defeat is always bitter. But the collapse of Germany in 1918 surprised and shook the German professional
soldier much more than the capitulation of May, 1945, which
all but the fanatics of the S.S. had long seen to be inevitable.
Ludendorff, indeed, knew that the great offensive of March was
his final throw. But when the tide of success was checked
and began to turn the other way in the summer, the old type
of German regimental officer as yet had no thought of surrender. The German armies still stood on foreign soil; since the
Russian advances in 1914 no enemy had yet set foot in Germany except as a prisoner. The line might have to be
shortened, as after the battles of the Somme. The whole of
Northern France and Belgium might have to be given up; a
compromise peace might have to be made which would leave
Germany no better off in the West than she was on August 4,
1914. But, outside the General Staff and the Army Commanders, few realised until the last fortnight that there was now
no choice between capitulation and complete disaster. Even
the Allies were preparing to face another winter of trench
warfare and planning their ultimate offensive for the spring of
1919.

In fact, the German armies were squarely beaten in the field
and the blockade had broken the will-to-resist of the German
people at home. Defeat might have been delayed; it could not
have been averted.

Nevertheless, since we all like to attribute our failures to
anything except our own shortcomings, it was natural enough
that the legend of the "stab in the back" should have been
seized upon and swallowed by the returned soldiers. The
Allies, with a strangely faulty appreciation of German psy-
chology, helped to promote and perpetuate it by permitting
them to march back armed across the Rhine bridges, their
bands and colour-parties leading.

They then proceeded to give the Germans a solid, permanent and perfectly legitimate grievance by completely ignoring
the conditions under which the armistice had been arranged.

These, as John Maynard Keynes pointed out at the time, were plain and unequivocal. The Allies had declared their willingness to make peace with Germany on the basis of President Wilson's Fourteen Points, as amplified in his addresses to Congress, and the object of the Peace Conference was to "discuss the details of their application." In fact, they were never discussed and the peace was dictated without the Germans being heard. Moreover, of the Fourteen Points, Four Principles and Five Particulars "only four," says Mr. Harold Nicolson in *Peacemaking*, "can with any accuracy be said to have been incorporated in the treaties of peace." The result was that, although the Treaty of Versailles was certainly not as severe as the sort of peace which the Germans themselves would have devised, no German felt himself bound by it. In particular, no German was prepared to accept the cession of a large slice of West Prussia to Poland, the loss of the city of Danzig and the subjection of some two million Germans permanently to Polish rule. It is against this background that the subsequent behavior of every German officer has to be regarded. The officer class considered that it had been tricked into surrender and it was of no use to argue that, had it continued to fight into 1919, it would have had to accept any terms, however outrageous, which the Allies might have decided to impose.

In 1945 we saw the Germans pulverised and disintegrated like the rubble of their ruined cities, too apathetic for the moment, in their sullen misery, even to hate. In 1918 they still had the spirit to turn upon each other, since the day for turning upon their conquerors was as yet far distant. (That it would dawn, they had no doubt. "Clear out of here and we will hunt the French home with sticks," said a German industrialist to me in Düsseldorff in 1919—and that was four years before the French occupation of the Ruhr.) At the time we were too busy licking our wounds, celebrating our victory, spending our war gratuities and enjoying the beginnings of the short-lived post-war boom to know or care much about what was happening in Germany. Yet the sight of returning officers being seized in the streets or dragged from trains, stripped of their rank badges and, often, butchered was one of the spectacles which impressed the Germans and did much to assure Hitler a welcome in due course. It did much to explain the rise of the Free Corps, its brutalities and the emergence of the Goering, Roehm, Sepp Dietrich type. It also explained why the Socialist Minister of Defence, the ex-basket-maker,

Herr Noske, who was also an ex-N.C.O., turned to the officer class as the only Germans now capable of respecting and restoring the "order" which the German is always trying to impose upon his own people as well as upon others.

There was, however, another side to all this. Through the clouds of economic chaos and confusion of spirit arising from defeat, occupation and civil war, it is hard for any one who was not in Germany at the time to picture German middle-class families living their normal lives, the husbands going down to their bleakly efficient factories and offices, the wives superintending the unceasing scrubbing and polishing, hunting their unfortunate maidservants and preoccupied mainly with the price of food and the difficulties of procuring it. It is harder still to think of a German regular officer relapsing at once into peace-time soldiering, as though he had merely been away on some abnormally lengthy manœuvres.

Yet that, or almost that, is what happened to Captain Erwin Rommel. On December 21st, 1918, he was re-posted to his original regiment, the 124th Infantry at Weingarten, which he had joined in 1910 when he joined the army. On the whole he saw very little of the "troubles." He had to travel through revolutionary Germany in the same month to retrieve his wife from Danzig, where she was seriously ill in her grandmother's house. He was questioned, mildly insulted, since he travelled in uniform, and once nearly arrested, but he brought her safely back to his mother's lodging in Weingarten. (The two women were always the best of friends.) In the summer of 1919 he went for a time to command an internal security company in Friedrichshafen, where he had his first experience of handling Germans who were not prepared to obey orders. He was given a draft of "red" Naval ratings to lick into shape as soldiers. They were a little wild at first, booed Rommel because he wore his Pour le Mérite, demanded to be allowed to appoint a commissar, refused to do the goose-step and held a revolutionary meeting. Rommel attended it, stood on a desk and announced that he proposed to command soldiers, not criminals. Next day he marched them behind a band to the parade-ground. When they refused to drill, he got on his horse and left them. They followed him back to barracks meekly enough and in a few days were so tame that Inspector Hahn, the head of the police at Stuttgart, asked Rommel to select some of them for enlistment in the police, for which they would be paid a special bonus on joining. He also invited Rommel to join with them, which perhaps explains the legend that he was once a policeman. Rommel said that he was going back to his regiment. Most of the men were ready to sacrifice their bonus and go with him. Except when they had to provide a guard over a black-market *Schnaps* factory, perhaps an unfair test of their new-found discipline, he had no further trouble with them. Later he took his company to the Ruhr for internal security duties but had no very exciting experiences there. By January 1st, 1921, after a tour of duty at Schwäbisch-Gemund, he was in Stuttgart, commanding a company in the 13th Infantry Regiment, the 124th having disappeared in the reduction—or renumbering—of the German Army. There he was to remain as a captain for nearly nine years.

How was it that Rommel could thus resume his career and was not driven into joining the Free Corps, that refuge of so many unemployed, disgruntled and truculent ex-regular officers, who knew no other trade but war and did not much care against whom they fought? It was because, in spite of the débacle of November, 1918, and the civil war which followed it, the German Army never ceased to exist, nor was the intention of expanding it at the earliest possible opportunity ever for a moment abandoned. Article 160 of the Versailles Treaty laid down that "by a date which must not be later than March 31, 1920, the German Army must not comprise more than seven divisions of infantry and three divisions of cavalry. After that date the total number of effectives . . . must not exceed 100,000 men, including officers and establishment of depots. . . . The total effective strength of officers . . . must not exceed 4,000."

The intention was to allow Germany a sufficient force for the maintenance of internal order. The effect was to provide the Commander-in-Chief, General Hans von Seeckt, "the man who made the next war," with a hard core of professionals round which he could lay the foundations of the army of the future. They were the reinforcement, the steel frame, on to which the concrete of conscripts could quickly be poured, if and when it became possible to reintroduce conscription, as was done by Hitler in March, 1935.

For such employment Rommel, with his Pour le Mérite and his reputation as a regimental officer, was a "natural." Though he did not know General von Seeckt personally and, indeed, never met him except once or twice on parade, he was exactly the type of man that von Seeckt wanted, a serious-minded young soldier (he was still four days short of twenty-seven at the armistice), and not of the swashbuckling sort which may be effective in war but does not take kindly either to discipline or to the dull grind of training in peace.

For Rommel himself there was really no other choice, even if he had wished for one. The Army was his career and, since he was married and had little or no private means, he was lucky to be able to pursue it. Moreover, he did not find it dull. He was a thinking soldier and liked to fight his battles over again, not in any spirit of nostalgia for war, but to draw from them the correct tactical lessons. He also enjoyed drill and training, as did Montgomery.

That he was perfectly well acquainted with the details and purpose of the vast conspiracy which General von Seeckt set on foot to enlarge and conceal the strength of the army, there is not the slightest reason to doubt. Every one of the four thousand selected officers must have known that his mission was not merely the maintenance of internal security but the creation and training of a new and more formidable force out of the débris of the old. They must all have taken a great deal of pleasure, as we should have done in their place, in the extraordinary ingenuity and persistence with which the object was pursued. I remember reading, in the library of the Rand Club in Johannesburg, the article in the *Quarterly Review* for October, 1924, in which Brigadier-General J. H. Morgan, a member of the Disarmament Commission, described the innumerable subterfuges by which its efforts were being defeated and the whole machinery of mobilisation kept as nearly as possible intact under cover of Demobilisation, Welfare, Pensions Centres and so on. It was as exciting as an Agatha Christie novel and a good deal more alarming. It was a pity that it did not have as large a circulation. For those who were taking an active part in the deception it must have been as thrilling a game as it was possible to play. "If I were a German and a patriotic one," said Morgan himself, "I should bow my head before General von Seeckt as 'the greatest Roman of them all.' Scharnhorst, who turned the disarmament clauses of the Treaty of Tilsit to the discomfiture of Napoleon (and incidentally enabled us to win the battle of Waterloo), was a small man in comparison, for the corresponding clauses of the Treaty of Versailles were drawn with much more care." Regimental soldiering in Germany in the years immediately following the 1914-18 war was not so barren and unprofitable an occupation for a German officer as might have been supposed.

To be stationed in Stuttgart, an agreeable city in his own part of the country, where his family lived, was another piece of luck for Rommel. Thus, although he had to wait until 1933 for his promotion to major, he was far from unhappy. In 1927 he went on leave with his wife to Italy and revisited the scene of his exploits at Longarone, where Frau Rommel discovered in the local cemetery the graves of the Molino family, from which her own family of Mollin was reputed to be descended. (Their exploration of the battlefield was cut short because the Italians of Longarone resented an obviously German officer prowling about a spot which seemed to have agreeable associations for him.)

On another leave, he and Frau Rommel took canoes down the Rhine to Lake Constance. Both expert skiers, mountaineers and swimmers, both good riders, fond of horses and dogs and much preferring country to town life, they got out of Stuttgart whenever they could. They both liked to dance, indeed, but neither was much interested in the theatre or the cinema nor did they care for "parties."

At home, Rommel played the violin in an amateurish fashion but was otherwise easy to live with. He drank very little, never more than a couple of glasses of wine, did not smoke and was not particular about his food. He was extraordinarily handy about the house, could make or mend anything and, when he bought a motor-bicycle, started by taking it entirely to pieces and putting it together again, without, as he said with satisfaction, a nut or a screw left over.

While at Stuttgart, Rommel formed, with Hartmann and Aldinger, an Old Comrades Association of the Württemberg battalion to which they had all belonged. In it there was no distinction of rank. This was one of Rommel's main interests and he spent much of his spare time getting in touch by personal letters with all who had served in the battalion and trying to help those who were having a hard time in post-war Germany. An annual meeting and parade was organised and in 1935, when Rommel was a Lieutenant-Colonel commanding a battalion at Goslar, he returned to Stuttgart for it. General von Soden came to take the salute and invited Rommel to join him at the saluting-base. It was typical of Rommel that he said that he would prefer to march past with his old company.

Thus the years passed pleasantly and uneventfully enough

for the Rommels, the main incident being the birth of their only child, Manfred, on Christmas Eve, 1928, after twelve years of marriage.

Except for the scars of his wounds, war, says his widow, seemed to have left no trace upon Rommel. When he referred to it, which he seldom did at home, it was as a stupid and brutal business, which no sane man would wish to see repeated. But he did not dream at nights, nor did he appear to feel, as did so many young soldiers of all armies after 1918, either that those four years were some strange and bloody hallucination or, conversely, that they alone were real. He remained a serious-minded but good-tempered man of simple tastes, who enjoyed a quiet life and, for the rest, was wrapped up in his profession. That his profession was preparation for war is a seeming contradiction which professional soldiers will more readily resolve than civilians.

On October 1st, 1929, Rommel was posted as an instructor to the Infantry School at Dresden where he remained for exactly four years. His lectures at the school resulted in the publication of his book, *Infanterie Greift An* (Infantry Attacks), based on personal experiences in Belgium, the Argonne, the Vosges, the Carpathians and Italy during the war. It is an excellent little manual of infantry tactics, in which minor operations are vividly described with good sketch-maps and the tactical lessons clearly drawn. It became a textbook in the Swiss Army, whose officers presented Rommel with a gold watch, suitably inscribed. But it also caught the attention of another reader nearer home, with far-reaching effects upon his fortunes.

On October 10th, 1933, Rommel, now a major, was given command of the 3rd Battalion of Infantry Regiment 17, a Jaeger or mountain battalion, in which all ranks were, or were supposed to be, expert skiers. The battalion was at Goslar, there was good snow near-by and, on the day after he took over, the officers suggested that they should all go out together. No doubt they wished to see whether their middle-aged C.O. was up to commanding a battalion of athletes. There was no ski-lift and they toiled up to the highest point. Here they were about to settle down for a drink, a smoke and a rest when Rommel remarked: "I think, gentlemen, that we should be starting down." The descent was made at speed. At the bottom it was acknowledged that the C.O. could ski. "That was very nice, gentlemen," said Rommel, "let's try it again." This was regarded as a sporting effort. But there was very little enthusiasm when he proposed yet a third ascent. By the time they reached the foot of the slope for the third time everyone had had rather more than enough—except Rommel, who observed that the slalom slopes looked good and that they might spend another half-hour or so there. In a British battalion one can often notice officers sliding unobtrusively out of the anteroom when it is a question of making up a four at bridge with the colonel. In the Jaeger battalion, I was told, volunteers for skiing expeditions with the C.O. had to be detailed.

Until Hitler became Chancellor on January 31st, 1933, Rommel had taken little interest in politics. To remain aloof from the "sordid" worlds of politics and commerce had always been the tradition of the German officer class. In the years immediately following the armistice, General von Seeckt set out deliberately to foster it, at the same time that he set out to break down the traditional barriers between officers and men. His purpose was to create a New Model army, but he had no intention of handing it over to the politicians of the Weimar Republic. It would be for the General Staff to decide when the time had come to use it. Meanwhile its allegiance must be only to its own cloth. Thus his orders prohibiting the army from taking any part in politics and even from voting, whilst doubtless reassuring to the Allies, were, in fact, part of a long-range plan which would certainly have alarmed them had they been fully aware of it.

No prohibition was necessary in Rommel's case. He had been brought up in a non-political society in a small German provincial town; he had been educated as a soldier; he had left for the wars when not yet twenty-three. He had been only too glad, when he returned, to escape from the dissensions of post-war Germany to the one world in which he felt at home. "Coffee-housing" was not among his amusements, he read little and he was not in the least politically minded. The only comment which Frau Rommel remembers him making on the Nazis in the early days was that they "seemed to be a set of scallywags" and that it was a pity that Hitler had surrounded himself with such people. For, like 90 per cent of Germans who had no direct contact with Hitler or his movement, he regarded him as an idealist, a patriot with some sound ideas who might pull Germany together and save her from Communism. This may seem a naïve estimate; it was not more naïve than that of many people in England who saw him only as a ridiculous little man with a silly moustache. Both views were founded in wishful thinking. But the Germans, having had a bellyful of defeat and a good taste of Communism, at least had some excuse for believing what they wished to believe. Those who refused to see any danger in that absurd figure, until it was already too late, would not believe what they did not wish to believe, merely because the alternative was too unpleasant to accept.

Moreover, Rommel, though he was a regular officer, was no *hochwohlgeboren*, snobbish Prussian. The idea that an Austrian corporal might prove the salvation of Germany was not as fantastic to him as it was to many senior officers of the *Reichswehr*: he liked corporals. What he did not like were the Brownshirt bullies of the type of Roehm. He had never met Roehm or any of his associates but he suspected, as did most of the army, that they were trying to set up a rival organisation. Moreover, he had seen the Brownshirts about and their hysteria and lack of discipline disgusted him. He was not, therefore, horrified when he heard that Roehm and the rest had been liquidated on the Night of the Long Knives, June 30th, 1934. He believed the story that they had been plotting to overthrow Hitler and seize power for themselves and thought that they had got their deserts. Frau Rommel and others have also assured me that the whole affair caused less stir, at least in provincial Germany, than it did abroad and that details of the killings only gradually leaked out.

Rommel's own first encounter with National Socialism in operation certainly does not suggest that he had any great sympathy with Nazis. He was commanding his Jaeger battalion at Goslar in 1935 when Goslar was chosen as the scene of a thanksgiving ceremony, to be attended by the Führer in person. Everything was to be laid on in style, with bands and banners and peasants from the surrounding districts in their national costumes. Naturally, the battalion would parade. When the details of the parade were being worked out, Rommel was told by a representative of the S.S. that in front of his troops would be a single file of S.S. men, who would be responsible for Hitler's safety. To this he replied that in that case the battalion would not turn out. He was asked to go and see Himmler and Goebbels at the local hotel. They were both exceedingly civil to him and invited him to stay for luncheon. When he explained that he considered the proposed arrangements an insult to himself and his battalion, they agreed that he was quite right. It was just the mistake of an

over-careful subordinate. Of course the orders would be cancelled at once. Rommel returned home, having carried his
point, to report to his wife that he did not much like the look
of Himmler but that Dr. Goebbels was really a very agreeable
and interesting man. That naïve impression remained. Whenever they met in later years, which was not often, Goebbels
went out of his way to be pleasant and to turn on the charm
which he undoubtedly had. Rommel was worth winning over;
if that were impossible, he was worth keeping sweet. With
Hitler, Rommel's first meeting was purely formal. He saluted;
he was introduced; he shook hands; his Pour le Mérite was observed; he was congratulated on the turn-out of his battalion.

On October 15th, 1935, Rommel, now a Lieutenant-Colonel, was posted as an instructor to the War Academy at
Potsdam. It was the first time that he had been near the centre
of things. Earlier he had had the chance of taking his Staff
College examinations and joining the elect. But he was advised that, with his record and his Pour le Mérite, he stood a
better chance of promotion and preferment if he remained
with troops. Since he was by temperament a regimental officer,
the advice tallied with his own inclination. In Potsdam he and
his wife and small son lived quietly near the Academy, mixed
very little in Berlin society and had no friends or even ac-
quaintances amongst the top Nazis. Nor did they even meet
socially the senior officers of the *Wehrmacht*. As in Stuttgart,
their friends were mainly regular officers and their wives of
about their own seniority.

Naturally, however, they knew more of what was going on
in high places than they had ever known before. They knew,
for example, of the growing rivalry between the Nazis and the
General Staff. Relying on the fact that Hitler, on the death of
Hindenburg, had become Supreme Commander of all the
German armed forces and that the officer corps had taken the
oath of allegiance to him, the party bosses were bent upon
making good Nazis of them and incorporating the Wehrmacht
in the "new order." They saw clearly enough that an independent organisation, with traditions rooted in the past, commanding the instinctive loyalty of all Germans except the very
young, might one day turn upon them and take over. Hitler,
who saw it much more clearly, played off the two sides against
each other with supreme cunning.

For its part, the Army, preoccupied though it was from
March, 1935, with its enormous expansion and grateful to Hitler for giving it the opportunity to expand beyond its wildest

dreams, had no thought of subordinating itself to his hench-men. A very few officers of the highest character and ability, like Colonel-General Ludwig Beck, the Chief of Staff, made no distinction between the Führer and his followers and, on moral grounds, regarded both National Socialism and its crea-tor as a national calamity. Beck, though he resigned only in 1938, in protest against the proposal to invade Czechoslovakia, had no illusions from the first. Others, like Colonel-General Werner von Fritsch, the Commander-in-Chief, also disliked and despised both the Nazis and their leader, but mainly, it would seem, because they threatened the supremacy of the Army and because they were the kind of people with whom a German officer really could not associate. Others, again, the Keitels and Jodls, were prepared to sacrifice their professional integrity for promotion, though even they might have hesi-tated if they had known that the day would soon come when Hitler would treat them as uniformed office-boys.

The attitude of the bulk of the General Staff has been de-scribed by General Walter Warlimont: "Gradually the Gen-eral Staff officer found it necessary to acquire some sort of a stabilising influence and he began to look to Hitler, in contrast to his followers, as the new hope for Germany. In addition to the rearmament programme, the peaceful reoccupation of the Rhineland enhanced Hitler's personal reputation within the officer corps, since this move corresponded to the fundamental policy of the Army." This was out of the frying-pan into the fire, had they but known it. But it did not seem so stupid then as it sounds now. Was not Hitler some sort of a soldier him-self, intensely proud of his service in the war? Had he not backed them against the ambitions of Roehm? Did he not know that it was the Army and the Army alone which had kept the military flame alive during the long years of subjec-tion? His Nazi hooligans had helped him to power but could any one suppose that he really preferred them to German officers of the old school? Was he not biding his time until he could afford to get rid of them and rely upon the real protec-tors of Germany?

Such was the view of the General Staff. It percolated down to regimental officers, and Rommel, for one, accepted it, in so far as he thought about such matters at all. There was a clear differentiation in his mind between the Führer and his follow-ers. Until his own bitter experiences opened his eyes, and that was not until after El Alamein, he admired and respected Hitler but had no use for Nazis.

Thus it was with no great enthusiasm that he heard, in 1935, that the Army proposed to take over the S.A. and that he was to be given command of them. He admitted that he would have enjoyed "smartening them up" but he realised that the job would be neither easy nor agreeable. He was not called upon to undertake it. The attempt by the Army to secure control of the S.S. failed. It is unlikely that there was ever any chance of its succeeding.

Rommel, however, was not to escape contact with the Nazis. While still an instructor at the War Academy he was given a special assignment. He was to be attached to the *Hitler Jugend* (Hitler Youth) with the object of improving their discipline. This suited him. He was always fond of boys and at his best with them. Most boys, with their natural instinct for hero-worship, adored him. He was a famous soldier who would stand no nonsense but he talked to them as equals. Here the material was, on the whole, good; physically it was magnificent.

It is interesting to speculate what might have happened to the Hitler Youth had Rommel been given a free hand. They would have been tough and brave, as, indeed, most of them were. In the last days of defeat they would have fought and died gamely, as many of them did, under S.S. *Brigadeführer* Kurt Meyer of the 12th S.S. Panzer (*Hitler Jugend*) Division, at Caen. They might have sprung at our tanks like wolves until, as a British tank commander said, "We were forced to kill them against our will." They would not, it is safe to say, have been the intolerant and fanatical young bullies they became. Certainly they would not have killed prisoners-of-war, as they did under Kurt Meyer's orders. Nor would the survivors now form that hard core of sullen, resentful and dangerous young Germans whom no man in his senses can suppose it possible to convert to our ideas. The Afrika Korps was formed of much the same material; the boys who served in it were tough and brave and confident. They, too, had a good conceit of themselves. But one has only to meet the survivors of the Afrika Korps and of the S.S. to see the difference.

Rommel never had a chance with them, for he quickly ran up against their leader, Baldur von Schirach. The latter, young, handsome, a good speaker, more cultured than most of the Nazis, for he was the son of the Director of the Weimar Theatre and a poet of sorts, has been represented as one of the few idealists of the Party. On the other hand he struck von Hassell as no more than "a bombastic Party ruffian . . . whose countenance reflects baseness." What is certain is that he was of the type to appeal to emotional German youth and that he was slavishly and apparently genuinely devoted to the Führer, to whom he used to send adulatory poems. Not unnaturally he resented the importation of a regular officer who was not even a member of the Party. Rommel and he fell out, however, on an issue which would have been surprising to any one who did not know of Rommel's descent from schoolmasters. So far from wanting to militarise the Hitler Youth, he objected that von Schirach was laying too much stress on sport and military training and not paying enough attention to education and the development of character. He strongly objected, he said, to small boys of thirteen being made into "little Napoleons" and was not at all encouraging to a lad of eighteen who arrived in uniform and a large Mercédes and naïvely confided in him that he "felt like a commanding general." The Hitler Youth were already contemptuous of schools and schoolmasters and refused to be treated as schoolboys. In an attempt to put this right, Rommel arranged a meeting between Baldur von Schirach and Dr. Rust, the Minister of Education. But von Schirach was arrogant and Rust was a fool and nothing came of it. Rommel then told von Schirach that, if he was determined to train the boys as soldiers, he had better first go and learn to be a soldier himself. Von Schirach, though he eventually went, objected that he would lose all his influence with his Hitler Youth if he were seen obeying the orders of a drill-sergeant!

Meanwhile, as soon as he felt able to do so, he set about getting rid of Rommel. Since he was one of Hitler's intimates it was not too difficult to represent that Rommel was not quite a good enough Nazi to be entrusted with the training of the Hitler Youth. Rommel was only attached from the staff of the War Academy and no open dispute between the Party and the Army arose. Rommel returned to Potsdam and was rather pointedly not given the golden badge of the *Hitler Jugend*.

Having finished his three years' tour of duty at Potsdam on November 9th, 1938, he was appointed next day to command the War Academy at Wiener Neustadt. He had been promoted the previous year and had thus risen from captain to full colonel in nineteen years—a rapid enough rise in peacetime but not sensational in view of his record and the enormous expansion of the Wehrmacht since 1935. Such as it was, no one could say that it was due to influence in the higher command of the Army, still less to any favours from the Nazis.

What his record of service does not show is that, before leaving Potsdam, he had been seconded from the War Academy to a temporary job which changed his whole future—for better and for worse. An officer was wanted to command the *Führerbegleitbataillon*, the battalion responsible for Hitler's personal safety, during the march into the Sudetenland in October, 1938. *Infanterie Greift An* had been published in 1937. Hitler had read and admired it. He made the appointment to his escort himself and chose the author. For the first time Rommel was brought to close quarters with the man who was to make him a Field-Marshal and to murder him.

So many buckets have been dropped into the dark well of Hitler's character, so much is known about his treachery, his cruelty, his cunning, his bloodthirstiness, his strange obsessions, his megalomania, that only one mystery now remains: how did he manage to impose so long, not upon the mass of the German people (that is understandable, for to them he was a Voice and a Vision), but upon some quite decent and intelligent men who were in daily contact with him?

Rommel was no trained psychologist, nor was he ever Hitler's intimate. But he was shrewd, a keen observer and a good judge of normal men. At this period he had an opportunity of studying the Führer under stress. The impressions he formed at the time may add little to our knowledge. But they were precise and he made a note of them which his son has preserved. There was no doubt, he said, that Hitler had a magnetic, perhaps an hypnotic power, derived from his evident belief that he was inspired by God or *Vorsehung* (the force which orders all things on earth), to lead the German people "up to the sun." (Rommel even then suspected that, if he could not lead them to victory, he would be equally prepared to lead them to destruction, provided only that the end was dramatic.)

This power was displayed in his handling of a conference. At the start Hitler would have an almost vacant look and appear to be fumbling, like a man idly turning over the pieces of a jig-saw puzzle. Suddenly his sixth sense (Rommel's own *Fingerspitzengefühl*) would come into play and he would listen intently. Then "out of the depths of himself," he would produce an answer which, for the moment at least, would entirely satisfy all those to whom he was speaking.

"At such moments he would speak like a prophet." Rommel realised that "he always acted by intuition, never by reason." But Hitler had, he said, an extraordinary gift of grasping the essential points in a discussion and distilling a solution from them.

This same intuition enabled him to sense the thoughts of any one to whom he was speaking and, when he chose, to say what he knew would please him. His flattery was adroit. Thus, when he had already made up his own mind on a course, he would consult someone who was certain to hold the same views as himself and appear to be convinced by his arguments, even a little unwillingly. When the decision was taken, his consultant, already flattered by being asked his opinion by the Führer, would be doubly flattered at the thought that he had influenced it. (It would be interesting to know whether Hitler had read Mr. Dale Carnegie.)

The next thing that struck Rommel was Hitler's truly remarkable memory. Like General Smuts, he knew practically by heart any book which he had ever read and, as with General Smuts, whole pages and chapters were photographed exactly upon his mind. His grasp of statistics was particularly strong; he could reel off figures of troop dispositions, enemy tanks destroyed, reserves of petrol and ammunition, etc., in a manner which impressed even the highly-trained products of the General Staff.

Baron von Esebeck, the German war correspondent, told me a story, which he had at first hand, to show that Hitler never lost this faculty nor the intuition which had already led the German armies to disaster. In the early spring of 1945 Hitler visited an Army Headquarters on the Eastern Front. "When do you expect the next Russian attack?" he asked the Army Commander. The Army Commander gave a date and his reasons. "No," said Hitler, "it will be a week later," which it was. Then he asked, "How many rounds per gun have you for your medium artillery?" The Army Commander gave a figure. "No," said Hitler, "I sent you more than that: you ought to have so-and-so. Ring up and ask the general commanding your artillery." Hitler was right and the Army Commander was wrong. This is an old trick, well known to visiting royalty and inspecting generals, but Hitler was a master of it and needed no prompting.

Hitler's last quality, which greatly impressed Rommel, who always valued it very highly, was, surprisingly enough, his physical courage. When the Germans were about to enter

Prague on March 13th, 1939, Rommel was again in command of the escort battalion. "What would you do if you were in my place, Colonel?" the Führer asked him. Rommel's answer was in character. "I should get into an open car," he said, "and drive through the streets to the Hradschin without an escort." With the Czechs in the mood they were in, this was advice which few men personally responsible for Hitler's safety would have offered. It was also advice which few men in Hitler's position would have taken. But he took it and the old newsreels show them acting upon Rommel's suggestion.

Of all their stations, Wiener Neustadt, in the mountains southwest of Vienna, gave the Rommels their happiest memories of the time between the wars. Rommel had an independent command. Free from any interference by higher authority, he was doing his favourite job, the training of budding officers in minor tactics and soldierly conduct. With his wife and young son he lived in a charming bungalow surrounded by a large garden. There were endless excursions to be made in a beautiful countryside, endless opportunities for the practice of his latest hobby, photography, in which, as may be imagined, he was technically highly competent but also showed a talent for selection and composition. The rest of the staff were congenial but the Rommels were always content with a domestic life and sufficient to themselves. The summer days slipped pleasantly away. As for the shadow of war, Rommel was not alone amongst Germans in thinking, after Munich and even after Prague, that Hitler would "get away with it somehow." General Thomas, head of the economic branch of the German High Command has, since the war, remarked that "every intelligent German came to the conclusion that the Western Powers saw in Germany a bulwark against Bolshevism and welcomed German rearmament," which shows to what misconceptions appeasement may lead. Even as late as August 23rd, 1939, when Rommel was promoted Major General and posted to the staff of the Führer's headquarters, to be responsible again for Hitler's safety, he was not sure that he was off once more to the wars. An eleventh-hour settlement would not have surprised him half as much as did the alliance with Russia, signed on the same day.

That alliance made war inevitable and, at 4:40 A.M. on September 1st, the German air attack upon Poland was launched. Lloyd George had been proved right when, in his memorandum to the Peace Conference on March 25th, 1919, he said: "The proposal of the Polish Commission that we should place two million Germans under the control of a people of a different race, which has never proved its capacity for stable self-government throughout its history, must, in my judgment, lead sooner or later to a new war in the east of Europe. . . ."

It would be idle to pretend that Rommel had any qualms of conscience over the invasion of Poland. Just as he had welcomed rearmament, whether secret or open, because he felt that Germany could expect little consideration from her conquerors until she was strong enough to speak with them on equal terms, so he had always believed that the Polish Corridor must disappear and Danzig be restored to the Reich, by amicable arrangement if possible but by force of arms if necessary. The fact that his wife's family lived in West Prussia, that it was in Danzig that he had met her, that it was from the War Academy at Danzig that he was first commissioned, may have given him a direct personal interest in the matter, but his opinion was shared by the vast majority of Germans. Moreover, it is fair to remember that in this case, as in the case of the Sudetenland and Czechoslovakia, even the educated German swallowed the propaganda adroitly served up to him by Goebbels because he never had the opportunity of hearing the other side. Men like General Beck and Ulrich von Hassell, who could view European affairs dispassionately and from an international standpoint, were few and far between, as, indeed, they are in any country. This does not in any way excuse German aggression: it merely explains why it did not horrify the German professional soldier as much as it did the rest of the world. In much the same mood must a British regular officer have gone off to the South African War.

From Hitler's headquarters, Rommel had a bird's-eye view of the lightning campaign which overwhelmed Poland in four weeks, before the bulk of the Polish army had even reached its concentration areas. On September 2nd he was at Prusczo, on the 10th at Kielce, on the 13th at Lodz and on October 5th at Warsaw, which had capitulated on September 30th. A day or two later he was on his way back to Berlin. He did not fail to profit by this object lesson in the art of modern war. He saw the importance of close air co-operation with the ground troops and of "ground-strafing" by low-flying aircraft, which the R.A.F. was strangely reluctant to learn. He saw that to spread confusion in the back areas was often more demoralising to the enemy than to inflict casualties. He saw that, in mechanised warfare, what paid was to

push on and exploit success in depth, even at the risk of being
cut off, by-passing points of resistance and leaving them to be
dealt with at leisure by the oncoming infantry. (This was
merely an adaptation to armour of Ludendorff's infiltration
tactics in the March, 1918, offensive and of his own practice in
Rumania and Italy.) He saw that tanks must be used in mass
and not dispersed in "penny packets." Above all, he saw
that, for a man of his temperament, an armoured division was
the one command.

Incidentally, the campaign confirmed his opinion of Hitler's
personal courage. "I had great trouble with him," he told
his wife; "he was always wanting to be right up with the
forward troops. He seemed to enjoy being under fire."
During the invasion of Normandy, Rommel did not find the
Führer conspicuous for courage. But by then he had long
since revised his opinion of him on other grounds.

CHAPTER 4

Ghost Division

To those who took no part in it, the five weeks' fighting that
preceded the fall of France seemed curiously unreal. It was as
though one watched a familiar building, struck by a heavy
bomb, in that split second before it crumbles and subsides into
dust.

I had, I remember, flown back to India by K.L.M. from a
week's hurried leave in England, landing at Jodhpur on the
morning of May 10th. The previous Sunday, a magical spring
day, I had lunched in the Bois, where the chestnuts were in
bloom. Over a cigar and a second brandy I had wondered idly
when, if ever, I should do anything so pleasant again, for
there was no doubt that the "phony" war was coming to an
end. But it was only a vague, personal foreboding, which few
in Paris seemed to share. *"Cette fois on les aura,"* said the
barman in the hotel when I left to catch the night train to
Rome. *"Ça ne sera pas comme en quatorze."* He wore the
ribbon of the Croix de Guerre in his button-hole and seemed
a sensible chap.

As I sat in the U.S. Club in Simla a week or so later and
heard over the wireless the old familiar names, Cambrai,
Marcoing, Péronne, Arras, Bapaume, the La Bassée Canal,

Béthune and, soon, Amiens, Abbéville, Fécamp, St. Valéry, names associated with battles in which, after months of bloody fighting, gains could be seen only on trench-maps, or with back areas where one went out thankfully to rest, it seemed impossible that this could be happening in a country one had known. Were British troops really fighting again over that old, once shell-torn ground? Could it be true that they were being pushed out overnight from places where the line had been held for years?

Dunkirk was different. One could visualise the beaches and the long lines of men stretching far out into the sea. But for me at least the weeks before were like some horrid dream, in which one went abstractedly to work, agreed with someone in the G.H.Q. mess that "It looks damned bad," but from which one expected at any moment to awake.

It was only long after the flood of victory had flowed again over the lost ground, only the other day, in fact, that I began to get the feel of it, to realise what it must have been like to live through those bewildering, hopeless weeks—and that from the other side.

On the red cloth of the dining-room table, in the little house in Herrlingen-bei-Ulm, with a painting of Rommel in uniform looking down at us from the wall, Manfred Rommel and I opened out the huge velvet-covered volume in which the day-by-day and round-by-round story of the 7th Panzer Division, the "Ghost Division," is recorded. Rommel was a great one for records. To Captain Aldinger, his old companion in the Württemberg battalion in the previous war, recalled from retirement and the designing of peaceful gardens to become his *Ordonnanzoffizier* in this, was given the task of collecting the orders and maps and casualty returns for each day that the division was in action and, subsequently, of collating them. Captain Aldinger, as might be expected of him, had done a precise and perfect job. On the left-hand page is a type-written abstract of the orders and war diary, on the right a large-scale map on which the position of the divisional units and of Divisional H.Q. is shown hour by hour. There is not a correction or an erasure. From this book, the only copy in existence, it is possible to see exactly what the division did between May 10th, 1940, when it crossed the Belgian frontier, to 5 P.M. on June 9th, when Cherbourg capitulated to it unconditionally and Rommel accepted, in the Military Prefecture, the surrender of Admiral d'Abrial, with four other French admirals and 30,000 prisoners-of-war.

Nothing, I realise, could be more tedious than to follow its fortunes in such detail. Some day some military historian may do so in the way of duty, though it seems unlikely that the French will care, the British take the trouble, the Americans be interested or the Germans look backwards, to fight these old battles over again. Nevertheless, having spent a week end on the record, page by page, I venture to think that not even General Patton's advances will show armour more boldly handled or a commander more ready to take risks and quicker to exploit success. General von Thoma has said that Rommel was really an infantryman at heart, that he never understood the "technique" of tanks but merely the tactics. (He admits that he was an infantry tactician of the first order.) Since General von Thoma himself fought in 192 tank engagements during the Spanish Civil War alone, many of them against Russian tanks under Marshal Koniev, and, after commanding a tank brigade with great dash and skill in Poland, was Chief Staff Officer of the German Mobile Forces, he ought to know. But when one reads the story of the "Ghost Division" it is not surprising that Rommel taught us a trick or two in Africa about the use of tanks.

On his return from Poland he remained at the Führer's H.Q. and was again responsible for his safety. But he was aching for a fighting command and by this time knew Hitler well enough to ask him for it. Hitler, for his part, had taken a fancy to Rommel, who was not of the aristocratic type of Junker officer with whom he felt ill at ease, however much he bullied them, perhaps because he knew they secretly despised him. "What do you want?" he asked and the reply was naturally "command of a Panzer Division." Rommel took over the 7th Panzer Division at Godesberg, on the Rhine, on February 15th, 1940, succeeding General Stumme, whom he was to succeed again when Stumme died of a heart attack at the beginning of the battle of El Alamein. Frau Rommel remained with Manfred in the house at Wiener Neustadt.

Rommel had just time enough to make himself known to every officer and man in the division and to get to know at least the officers personally, before they were on the move. In two months' intensive training he also had time to work out his own theories of tank tactics on the ground and to apply the lessons he had learnt in Poland. (Both he and Guderian had already studied the writings of General Fuller and Captain Liddell Hart with more attention than they received from most British senior officers.) When the order came for the advance into Belgium, the division was fighting fit and knew that it was under a commander who, whatever mistakes he might make, would make none through hesitating to "have a go."

On May 10th the frontier was crossed about thirty miles south of Liège. On May 13th the division had its first big task, to effect a passage of the Meuse. The Belgians fought well from houses which had been put into a state of defence and from pill-boxes. They had anti-tank guns in concrete positions and plenty of covering artillery. A bridge had to be built under heavy fire and Rommel was up to his waist in water helping to shift baulks of timber. "I'll give you a hand," he said, and stayed with his men until he was sure that the job would be done. Divisional commanders doubtless have no business to be messing about in the front line. But it was a story which did not take long to go round the division. Rommel had already re-earned his old reputation of never asking men to do what he would not do himself. Towards evening the French counter-attacked with tanks and infantry but the attacks were beaten off and by nightfall the first tanks were across, with Rommel's tank leading.

The next day was nearly the end of him. He drove in his tank into a sand quarry and came under heavy anti-tank fire. The tank was put out of action, Rommel was hit in the face and French native troops were advancing to capture him when Colonel Rothenburg, commanding 25th Panzer Regiment, who won the Knight's Cross of the Iron Cross during the operations and was afterwards to die in Russia, came up in his own tank and drove them off.

By May 15th, 7th Division was far ahead of 5th Panzer Division on its right flank and during the night, Rommel, still in front, captured a French battery when it was moving up into what its commander supposed to be a supporting position.

The following night the division broke through the extension of the Maginot line in the fortified zone west of Clairfay. The rearward positions, with their artillery and anti-tank guns under concrete, were smothered with artificial fog and artillery fire; the villages to the flanks were blanked off by the same means. At 11 P.M. the attack was launched by moonlight, the tanks and the motor-cycle battalion leading. The mass of the division followed. The higher command had laid down that tanks should not fire while on the move. Rommel disregarded this order and encouraged his tank crews to do so, saying that loss of accuracy and consequent waste of ammunition were more than compensated by moral effect under such conditions. "We'll do it like the Navy," he said, "fire salvoes to port and starboard." As they broke into and out of Avesnes around midnight, leaving it still occupied by French troops, with French tanks firing wildly in all directions and heavy street fighting continuing, the German tanks fired on the move at batteries on both flanks. A French mechanised division retreating westward along the road, crowded with refugees, and French tanks parked alongside it were overrun before they could come into action. An artillery regiment followed the tanks through Avesnes during the night and captured forty-eight tanks intact. French infantry ran, throwing away their weapons and spreading panic before them. Had all stood fast the Germans would have been in trouble, for the guns of their tanks and the ported anti-tank guns of the motor-cycle battalion could at first do nothing in Avesnes against the heavy armour of the French tanks.

"Vous êtes anglais?" asked a French woman of Rommel, patting him on the arm as he stood beside his tank in a village street beyond Avesnes. *"Non, Madame, je suis allemand,"* replied Rommel, who had a smattering of several languages, though he was no linguist. *"Oh, les barbares!"* cried the woman and, throwing her apron over her head, ran into her house.

Meanwhile all communications were interrupted and even the infantry brigade was not aware of the break-through. Nevertheless, Rommel determined, on his own responsibility, to launch the whole division in an attack towards the west, in an endeavour to reach the Sambre, secure a bridgehead and keep it open. The attack began about 5:30 in the morning (this after a night's continuous fighting), with 25th Panzer Regiment pushing towards Landrécies, where the Guards were first engaged in World War I. They were attacked by motorised columns from both flanks but the French infantry were shocked into surrender by the sudden appearance of the German armour. By 6 A.M. Landrécies was captured, large numbers of French troops were caught in their barracks and a bridge over the Sambre was seized intact. Rommel made the French throw down their arms, over which he drove a tank. The regiment pushed on to Le Cateau, where it was halted by Rommel, for the advance had been made by only two of its battalions, with part of the motor-cycle battalion, and the mass of the division was far behind. While 25th Panzer Regiment took up a position on high ground east of Le Cateau,

Rommel himself went back in an armoured car to bring it up.

All day the 25th Panzer Regiment was heavily attacked by tanks. Behind it, Pommereuil was recaptured by the French, who were thrown out again by the oncoming division. By the evening of May 17th the situation was sufficiently clear to allow the divisional artillery to move up into forward positions and another bridge over the Sambre had been seized at Berlimont, to enable 5th Panzer Division, now completely outdistanced, to come up and cross on the right.

If one looks at the map, one sees that Rommel had pushed forward a narrow salient, thirty miles long and only two miles wide, like a finger pointing into the heart of France. (From Avesnes to Le Cateau alone is nearly fifteen miles.) In doing so he had taken enormous risks; for there were strong French forces on both flanks. But he had broken through the fortified zone and had secured the vital crossings of the Sambre. The operations were rightly regarded as of great importance to the progress of the campaign and for his success and his personal bravery Rommel was given the Knighthood Cross.

That boldness pays is shown by the fact that the Division's total casualties were only 35 killed and 59 wounded, whereas it had taken over 10,000 prisoners in two days, and captured or destroyed 100 tanks, 30 armoured cars and 27 guns.

Though there were great difficulties in bringing up petrol and enemy tank attacks were still continuing on either flank, 25th Panzer Regiment pushed on at the same speed and by 5 A.M. on May 20th, by-passing Cambrai, it had crossed the Canal du Nord at Marcoing and taken up a position south of Arras. On the way, French troops had once more been captured in their barracks. Again the mass of the division was left behind and again Rommel went back to bring it up, taking with him two tanks, his signal section and an armoured car. On the Arras-Cambrai road, at Vise-en-Artois, he ran into the enemy, his two tanks were destroyed and he remained surrounded for several hours.

The fighting round Arras on May 21st is of interest because it was here that, for the first time in either war, Rommel bumped up against the British. It is pleasant to record that he found them a much tougher proposition than anything he had yet encountered. Debouching from Viny to the south and southeast, the 1st Army Tank Brigade attacked him around Achicourt and Agny. They broke through and his 42nd Anti-Tank Battalion was overrun, most of the gun crews being killed, for the Germans found, to their surprise, that they could not penetrate the armour of the "I" tanks, even at close range. The attack was only stopped by artillery fire from an artillery regiment, and from a flak (AA) battery armed with 88 mm. guns—a weapon which doubtless came as an equally unpleasant surprise to us. Even so, Stukas had to be called in before the British armour withdrew again to Arras.

Meanwhile 25th Panzer Regiment which, as usual, had pushed on and reached the high ground south of the Scarpe at Acq, was ordered by Rommel to turn round and attack the British tanks in the rear. In the tank battle which followed near Agnes, though the British lost seven tanks and six A.T. guns, 25th Panzer Regiment lost three Mark IV's, six Mark III's and some light tanks and thus had considerably the worst of it. Rommel, forced to fight a defensive action for once, had another narrow escape, for an officer was killed beside him while the two of them were looking at a map which both were holding.

That this was a harder day is shown by the fact that the division lost 250 in killed and captured alone, whereas its total bag of British prisoners was only 50, though it claimed 43 British tanks destroyed.

The next few days were tough, too. The division crossed the Scarpe on May 22nd but the diary records that British tank attacks were beaten off with difficulty, that mines had to be laid against them, that Mont St. Eloi was captured and lost and captured again and so on. In the advance to the La Bassée Canal on the 24th, British snipers are reported as being active in the bushes and hedges south of the Canal and difficult to dislodge. In spite of them, bridgeheads were secured on both sides of Guinchy on the 26th, the first tanks and guns went over on the 27th, on the 28th the division had taken up a line facing east towards Lille and on the 29th it was ordered out to rest west of Arras. Rommel, with his usual curiosity, celebrated his first day of rest after a fortnight's continuous fighting by driving into Lille. When he saw that the streets were full of British and French soldiers, he realised that he had made a mistake. Since they were as surprised as he, but for a second or two longer, he was able to turn the car round and drive out before any one had the presence of mind to interfere with him. Counting up his recorded escapes from death or capture during this period, apart from the ordinary risks which a divisional commander runs who insists on leading his advanced guard personally into action, one feels that we were a little unlucky to be bothered with Erwin Rommel in Africa.

Within a few days the division was pulled out of rest again and given a special task. The end was now in sight. The French were patently on the point of being driven out of the war and the British had already been driven out of France. Between May 29th and June 4th, more than 300,000 British troops had been embarked at Dunkirk—thanks to Hitler's refusal to allow the German armour to be put in against them. There remained the 51st Highland Division, about to take ship, after a fighting withdrawal, from St. Valéry. It was for Rommel to stop them. He had first to cross the Somme and break through what was left of the Weygand Line.

A race against time was the sort of thing that appealed to him and he wasted none of it. Having made a personal "recce" with his regimental and battalion commanders, he crossed the Somme on the morning of June 6th. That day and the next he met with opposition and had to stage attacks to clear it. Then, right shoulder up, he squared away towards the East of Rouen.

The division moved at night and as the tanks rumbled and clanked through the silent villages, the French peasants, thinking them British, turned out to wish the crews *bonne chance.* They went on their way without speaking. On the night of June 9th they reached the Seine, ten miles south-west of Rouen. Next morning some bolder spirit found the heart to put up a fight at Yvetot. Whoever he was, he was thrust aside. By 2:15 in the afternoon the division had covered the twenty miles from Yvetot to Veulettes and reached the sea, between Fécamp and St. Valéry. This time it was closed up and the divisional artillery was well forward.

At Fécamp, destroyers were lying off the shore when 37th Panzer Battalion appeared and, with its supporting artillery, at once engaged them. A British destroyer promptly closed for action and was straddled at 18,000 yards. A motor-torpedo boat was hit which steamed at 35 knots. So were other vessels and the little harbour was brought under heavy artillery fire. In such conditions, embarkation by daylight was impossible.

St. Valéry was the real prize, for here were the headquarters of General Fortune, commanding the 51st Division, and it was here that the bulk of the division was preparing to embark. During the night of June 10th and the morning of the 11th Rommel seized the high ground to the west, from which he could bring the port under artillery fire. At 3:30 P.M. he himself led 25th Panzer Regiment and part of 6th Infantry Regiment in to the attack, under cover of his guns.

"The enemy fought back desperately, first with artillery and anti-tank guns and later with machine-guns and small arms: there was particularly hard fighting round Le Tot and on the road St. Sylvain-St. Valéry," says the record, and this and the tribute to the British armour around Arras are among the very few entries in which it is admitted that the Ghost Division had found the going hard.

By evening, Rommel had taken about a thousand prisoners and, what was more important, was in a dominating position west of St. Valéry from which his guns could prevent embarkation from the harbour. Nevertheless, in the evening heavy fighting was still going on and first two (Pioneer) battalions and then the rest of the division were ordered up in support. A written demand from Rommel to General Fortune to surrender and march out the 51st Division under white flags to the west was refused and the Germans could see that barricades were being erected on the harbour moles and that guns and machine-guns were being brought into position.

At 9 P.M. a heavy bombardment was opened. The concentrated fire of the whole of the divisional heavy and light artillery was brought to bear on the northern part of St. Valéry and the harbour and 2,500 shells fell in this small area. At the same time 25th Panzer Regiment was again put into the attack, with 7th Infantry Regiment and 37th Pioneer Battalion. The line was advanced nearer to St. Valéry. But "in spite of the heavy fire the tenacious British troops did not give up. They hoped to be embarked during the night but the enemy was prevented by heavy artillery fire from loading. In the early morning hours the British are busy trying to embark from the steep coast to the east of St. Valéry, under cover of fire from warships. But the divisional artillery first hinders this and later makes it impossible. There is a duel between a warship and the 88 mm. A.A. battery. . . . 8th Machine Gun Battalion attacks. . . . Parts of 6th and 7th Infantry Regiments attack and gain more ground near St. Valéry. . . . On the left, Rommel, with 25th Panzer Regiment under Colonel Rothenburg and part of 7th Infantry Regiment, pushes into St. Valéry itself and compels capitulation as the enemy commander sees that further resistance is impossible."

Twelve thousand prisoners were taken at St. Valéry, of

whom eight thousand were British. They included, beside Major-General Fortune himself, the commanders of the 9th French Army Corps and of three French divisions. Tanks to the number of 58, 56 guns, 17 A.A. guns, 22 A.T. guns, 368 machine-guns, 3,550 rifles (there must have been more in the harbour), and 1,133 trucks were amongst the booty. The divisional artillery claimed an armoured cruiser sunk, which would be an unusual victim for a panzer division, but I am advised by the Admiralty that this claim is unfounded.

Rommel never forgot General Fortune of the 51st Highland Division and often spoke of him to Frau Rommel and to his son Manfred as the gallant leader of a good division who had had bad luck. While he was in prison-camp in Germany, General Fortune was given the chance by the Germans of being repatriated to England on the grounds of age and illhealth. Because he felt that he could still do something for the morale of the officers and men of his division by sharing their captivity with them, he refused and remained a prisoner until the end of the war. Rommel came to hear of this and it increased his respect for his former opponent. It would appear that General Fortune also remembered and respected Rommel. Two years or more after the collapse of Germany, a German prisoner-of-war, repatriated from a British prison camp in the Channel Islands, came to Herrlingen to see Frau Rommel. He had met General Fortune in the Channel Islands, he said, after the latter's return from Germany, and the general had asked him to visit her, if possible, when he himself returned home and to express his sympathy with her on her husband's death. I could not check this story with Major-General Fortune before he died but it would appear to be true, since a German soldier could hardly have invented it or, for that matter, have heard of General Fortune. I hope so, for I am one of those old-fashioned persons who regret that chivalry should be among the casualties of "total" war. Fortunately, it dies hard and keeps cropping up in unexpected places, as will be seen later in this book.

The surrender of St. Valéry was on June 12th. On June 17th, the day that Pétain asked for an armistice, three days after the Germans entered Paris, the 7th Panzer Division was pushing up the Cotentin Peninsula to attack Cherbourg. One column moved along the coast through Coutance, another through St. Lô, a name which few could then have pinpointed on the map but which to-day must be as familiar to many Americans as Detroit.

The division met with little opposition. With the exception of a battalion of *Fusiliers Marins,* most of the French, having heard of the request for an armistice, not unnaturally stopped fighting: no man wants to be either the first or the last man killed in a war. A rearguard of "Jocks" of the British 52nd (Lowland) Division, strung across the 20-mile neck of the peninsula by General Marshall-Cornwall to cover the embarkment of 1st Armoured Division and 52nd Division from Cherbourg, compelled the Germans to side-step their positions. But by midnight on June 18th, 7th Infantry Regiment, under Colonel von Bismarck, with two panzer companies, had pushed into the suburbs of the city. During the night the divisional artillery was moved up to begin the bombardment of the forts next morning. It was unnecessary. At "first light" the fortress guns were silent. Only a few odd British guns, on the final covering positions, were still in action.

General Collins of the United States 7th Corps was nick-named "Lightning Joe" for capturing Cherbourg within twenty days of the landing in Normandy. He had to fight for it, however. There was no fight in the senior French officers of both services who were in Cherbourg in June, 1940. It is charitable to suppose that they believed that an armistice was on the point of being accorded. Otherwise there would seem to be no excuse for the fact that they surrendered the fortress and 30,000 men to a single armoured division, barely twelve hours after it had come within range of the formidable fortress guns.

That was what happened. At 2 P.M. on June 19th French naval and military officers came out to offer unconditional surrender and the fighting stopped. At 5 P.M. the formal capitulation paper was signed. In the harbour was the undamaged transport of a British mechanised division.

The division was withdrawn before it could take over and count the arms in the forts. But in the operations from May 10th it had captured:

The Admiral of the French Navy (North) and
4 other admirals.
1 Corps Commander,
4 Divisional Commanders with their staffs,
277 guns and 64 A.T. guns,

458 tanks and armoured cars,
4-5,000 trucks,
1,500-2,000 cars,
1,500-2,000 horse and mule wagons,
300-400 buses,
300-400 motor-cycles,

and the major part of the 97,468 prisoners credited to the
Group to which it belonged. It had brought down 52 aircraft,
captured 15 more on the ground and destroyed 12 more.

There was much more booty which could not be counted
because the division had moved too fast. Nor was there time
to calculate, even approximately, the losses in killed and
wounded which it had inflicted on the enemy. Its own casualties during the period were: 48 officers killed and 77 wounded;
108 sergeants and above killed and 317 wounded; 526 other
ranks killed and 1,252 wounded; 3 officers, 34 sergeants and
above and 229 other ranks missing. It had lost in tanks, Mark I,
3; Mark II, 5; Mark III, 26; and Mark IV, 8.

The figures of casualties and tank losses are small compared
with what was accomplished. At the same time, when one
remembers that Rommel was always properly parsimonious
with men's lives, they are by no means negligible. They prove
that the division had had hard fighting and had not merely
chased a beaten enemy across France.

CHAPTER 5

"None So Blind . . ."

The good fairy who looks after the British had to work over-
time in 1940. She never did them a better turn than when,
despite her deputy, Mr. Churchill, she saw to it that the
French did not continue the war in North Africa. Had they
done so, Hitler must have followed them. Spain would have
come in or been forced to allow the passage of German
troops. Gibraltar would have fallen. The western end of the
Mediterranean would have been closed. French colonial
troops would never have stood against German armour.
Stiffened by a couple of German panzer divisions, even the
chicken-hearted Graziani must have been dug out of his deep
shelter and hustled into Cairo by Christmas. Britain's last base

within striking distance of Europe would have gone. The loss of the Suez Canal would have closed the other end of the Mediterranean. The road to Syria, Iraq, Iran and, ultimately, the Caucasus would have been wide open. Turkey could have been pinched out or coerced into joining the Axis. Such are the contentions of better strategists than I. Had the half of it come off the Good Fairy would have had her hands full.

Only the German Naval Staff correctly appreciated these resplendent possibilities. With no taste for "Operation Sea Lion," the invasion of Britain, Admiral Raeder suggested, on September 6th, 1940, that the best way to strike at her was to exclude her from the Mediterranean. On September 26th he was more explicit. "The British," he said, "have always considered the Mediterranean the pivot of their world-empire. . . . Italy is fast becoming the main target of attack. . . . Britain always attempts to strangle the weaker. The Italians have not yet realised their danger when they refuse our help. . . . *For this reason the Mediterranean question must be cleared up during the winter months.* Gibraltar must be taken. . . . The Suez Canal must be taken. It is doubtful whether the Italians can accomplish this alone; support by German troops will be needed. An advance from Suez through Palestine and Syria as far as Turkey is necessary. If we reach that point, Turkey will be in our power. *The Russian problem will then appear in different light. Fundamentally, Russia is afraid of Germany. It is doubtful whether an advance against Russia from the north will be necessary.* . . . The question of North-West Africa is also of decisive importance. All indications are that Britain, with the help of Gaullist France, and possibly also of the U.S.A., wants to make this region a centre of resistance and to set up air bases for an attack against Italy. . . . *In this way Italy would be defeated.*" If Admiral Raeder is ever visited by the shades of Hitler, Keitel and Jodl he may well greet them with "Don't say I didn't tell you!"

"The Führer agrees with the general line of thought," add the minutes of the meeting. Why, then, did he not follow it out? First, he was not sea-minded. Second, he half believed, even in the late summer of 1940, that Britain would come to terms. Third, if she were obstinate, he hoped to "attract France into the orbit of the anti-British coalition," as Ciano reported after the Brenner meeting on October 4th. Lastly, by the end of September, the Russian bee was already buzzing in his bonnet. Of these deterrents, the first was a disability he shared with Field-Marshal Keitel, Colonel-General Jodl and Colonel-General Halder, his military advisers. The second was a private illusion which Mr. Churchill had done his best publicly to dispel. The French coup he might very well have brought off, had he made a quick and generous peace. The majority of Frenchmen would almost certainly have settled down and, temporarily at least, accepted a German hegemony over Europe. There were no very hard feelings against the German Army. On the contrary, it was regarded with grudging admiration. To-day, even ex-members of the Resistance reserve their hatred for (a) Darnand's *milice* and collaborators generally; (b) the Gestapo; (c) the S.S., in that order. The German Army comes a bad fourth. *"On ne peut dire qu'ils n'étaient pas assez corrects, ces gens-là"* is still commonly said in the part of France where I am writing. As for the last fatal folly, there was no cure for that but the Russian winter and the Red Army.

Obsessed though he was with Russia, Hitler did not altogether forget North Africa. Heavy-handed efforts were made by Ribbentrop to bring Franco into the war. A plan ("Operation Felix") was prepared for the capture of Gibraltar. Goering's pet scheme of a triple thrust into Morocco, Tripolitania and the Balkans was strongly pressed by its author and at least considered. Moreover, though we did not know it at the time, General von Thoma, Chief of the German Mobile Forces at Army Headquarters, was sent in October to see General Graziani and discuss the dispatch of German troops to Libya. General von Thoma reported against the proposal, which was, he says, mainly political—to ensure that Mussolini did not change sides. His contention was that nothing less than a force of four panzer divisions would be of any use, that these could only be maintained with difficulty, if at all, in the face of British sea-power, and that they would have to be substituted for Italians. Graziani and Badoglio would object to any such substitution and, in fact, did not want German troops at all.

General von Thoma added that the African theatre was only suitable for the sort of war that General Lettow-Vorbeck had carried on in East Africa during World War I. He claims that Field-Marshal von Brauchitsch and Colonel-General Halder, his Chief of Staff, agreed with him and were also against sending German troops to Africa, which is very probable. They had both opposed von Manstein's plan of breaking into France through the Ardennes instead of through the Low Countries, and Hitler had overruled them. Hitler lost his temper and von Thoma feels that the reason he was never sent to Africa in command until the war was already lost there (he arrived at El Alamein, where he was captured, on September 20th, 1942), was Hitler's spite.

It does not seem to have occurred to him even after the war that, whether Hitler's motives were political or military, he was right and von Brauchitsch, Halder and he, von Thoma, were wrong. Hitler should, no doubt, have overruled his military advisers, the more so as General von Thoma takes some pride in having pointed out to him, on the strength of his experience in Spain, that the Italian troops were useless, that "one British soldier was better than twelve Italians," that "Italians are good workers but no fighters: they don't like the noise!" and so on. But who, except General von Thoma, could suppose that General Wavell would dare to attack so vastly superior a force or that Graziani's army would crumble as quickly and completely as it did?

When the first golden opportunity was already lost and Graziani defeated, Hitler took action. Having offered Mussolini German anti-tank units after the fall of Sidi-Barrani and suggested (a delicate matter for one dictator to another) placing Italian troops under German command, he woke up completely on the capture of Bardia and told his Chiefs of Staff that he was resolved to do everything in his power to prevent Italy from losing North Africa. . . . "The Führer is firmly determined to give the Italians support. German formations are to be transferred as soon as possible, equipped with anti-tank guns and mines, heavy tanks and light and heavy A.A. guns. . . . Material is to be shipped by sea, personnel by air. . . . Units cannot be transferred until the middle of February and will then take about five more weeks from the time of loading."

At a conference between Hitler, Mussolini and their staffs on January 19th and 20th, the Italians reported that they were bringing their three divisions in Tripoli up to full strength and transferring one armoured division and one motorised division from Italy, the move to be completed about February 20th. They "very warmly welcome the dispatch of the German 5th Light (Motorised) Division." Its move was to be made between February 15th and 20th but equipment could be shipped earlier. At another, domestic, conference on February 3rd, Hitler told his Army Staff that "the loss of North Africa could be withstood in the military sense but must have a strong psychological effect on Italy. Britain could hold a pistol at Italy's head. . . . The British forces in the Mediterranean would not be tied down. The British would have the free use of a dozen divisions and could employ them most dangerously in Syria. We must make every effort to prevent this. . . . We must render effective assistance in North Africa." The Luftwaffe, which had already been ordered to assist the Italians, must intervene still more actively with Stukas and fighters and must strike a blow against the British troops in Cyrenaica, using the heaviest bombs. It must work in co-operation with the Italian Air Force to protect the transports, to disrupt British supplies by land and sea and to combat the British fleet. But first of all attempts must be made to subdue the air base of Malta.

Even if this intervention were enough to bring the British advance to a standstill, the "blocking unit," the 5th Light Division, was still insufficient, said Hitler, and must be reinforced by a strong armoured unit. The dispatch of German troops must be speeded up and air transport used if necessary.

All this was well enough. It will be seen, however, that the thinking was purely defensive. Hitler said as much in a letter to Mussolini on February 28th. "If we are patient for another five days," he wrote, "I am sure that any new British attempt to push on towards Tripoli is bound to fail. I am very grateful to you, Duce, for the fact that you have placed your motorised units at the disposal of General Rommel. He will not let you down and I am convinced that in the near future he will have won the loyalty and, I hope, the affection of your troops. I believe that the mere arrival of the first Panzer Regiment will represent an exceptional reinforcement of your position." The last part of this prediction, at least, was soon to be proved correct.

Hitler thus realised the importance of not losing North Africa. Neither he nor his staff seem to have seen the possibility of conquering it and the far-reaching results that would flow from a successful offensive against Egypt. Halder, for example, never took the North African campaign seriously from the start and never regarded it as more than a political move to keep the Italians in the war. For this the outlay of three or four divisions might not prove too costly. "Of course, if the opportunity for offensive action presented itself we would take it but on the whole we regarded the matter as a fight for time," he said in his interrogation. "I last talked to Rommel about this subject in the spring of 1942. At that time he told me that he would conquer Egypt and the Suez Canal and then he spoke of East Africa. I could not restrain a somewhat impolite smile and asked him what he would need for the purpose. He thought he would want another two armoured corps. I asked him: 'Even if we had them, how would you supply and feed them?' To this question his reply was 'That's quite immaterial to me; that's your problem!' As events in Africa grew worse, Rommel kept demanding more and more aid. Where it was to come from didn't worry him. Then the Italians began to complain because they were losing their shipping in the process. If history succeeds in unravelling the threads of what went on in Africa, it will have achieved a miracle, for Rommel managed to get things into such an unholy muddle that I doubt whether any one will ever be able to make head or tail of it."

Rommel is dead but the unravelling is not so difficult as Colonel-General Halder imagines. Nor is the verdict of history likely to be as favourable to himself as he supposes. History does not rate very highly men in key positions who allow their judgment to be influenced by their personal likes and dislikes. That Halder disliked Rommel is obvious from the tone of his own statement and from the adroit substitution of "two armoured corps" for the two armoured divisions for which Rommel actually asked. It is obvious from the omissions. Halder speaks of a conversation in "the spring of 1942." He refrains from mentioning that it was on July 27th, 1941, that Rommel first sought permission to launch an offensive, with the Suez Canal as its objective and February, 1942, as its target date. Whatever he may have asked for in the spring of 1942, he then asked only for three German divisions, with mixed units amounting to another, and three extra Italian divisions. The Army Command jibbed at providing the extra German units and Halder or one of his staff wrote rude comments on the margin of the plan. Yet if Rommel had had four extra German divisions (two hundred were being employed on the Russian front and the Germans sent three to Tunis in three weeks after the Allied landings in North Africa in November, 1942), it is long odds that he would have reached Cairo and the Canal at the beginning of 1942.

As for supply, Halder again fails to mention what Rommel all along saw, what the German and Italian General Staffs were strangely blind in not seeing until too late, that the key to all supply problems and, indeed, to the control of the Mediterranean, was the capture of Malta.

Lastly, Halder, perhaps naturally, omits to mention that Rommel once called him a bloody fool, or the German equivalent, and asked him what he had ever done in war except sit on his backside in an office chair. It is not to be supposed, however, that he has forgotten it.

The story of the war in North Africa is the story of an unending battle between Rommel, who saw—and proved—the possibility of a major success there and a High Command which refused to take the North African campaign seriously. In that battle Rommel had all the odds against him. He was far away in the desert and *"les absents ont toujours tort."* He was not a General Staff officer and was, therefore, decried by the professionals. On the rare occasions when he saw Hitler, he could seldom see him alone. When he did, he found him, understandably, engrossed in Russia. He was patted on the back and promised support but he felt that any impression he might make would be rubbed out as soon as he left by Hitler's entourage. Above all, Keitel, Jodl and Halder were jealous of his popularity with Hitler and the German public, of his war record and, no doubt, of his good luck in having an independent command beyond the reach of the Führer. The easiest way to "smear" him was to make out that, while he might be a good leader in the field, he was not a man whose views on the larger issues of war could be taken seriously.

Rommel, for his part, had the poorest opinion of Keitel and Halder. In this he was not alone. Prince von Bismarck called Keitel an imbecile; von Hassell found him "stupid and narrow-minded, quite uninformed politically . . . downright servile in his attitude towards the Party." His grateful Führer described him as "a man with the mind of a movie doorman." As for Halder, who appears to have been the sour and superior type of staff officer, he struck von Hassell as early as 1940 as "a weak man with shattered nerves . . . no more than a caddie to Hitler." Beck, his brilliant predecessor as Chief of Staff, thought him merely a competent technician with no personality. His record in the conspiracy against Hitler shows him continually shivering on the brink but never willing to take the plunge. Jodl, who had such brains and character as there were in this Party, treated war as chess. His business was to produce plans, not to question orders. All three were identified with Hitler's ferocious policies in Russia and elsewhere. Keitel and Jodl were tried at Nuremberg and hanged. Halder, who is alleged by von Hassell to have signed the orders for the brutal treatment to be accorded to the Russians, was luckier, perhaps because he had already spent some years in a concentration camp, perhaps because he was so obviously a subordinate, perhaps because he was needed by the Allies as a prosecution witness against his former superiors and so used.

Rommel despised all three of them as "chairborne soldiers." He despised them for their subservience to the Party. When he came to know what had been done under their orders, he detested them for having dishonoured the German Wehrmacht. As will be seen, he was not afraid to protest against atrocities to Hitler himself. If, then, a man is to be judged by his enemies, these three were a good advertisement for Rommel. It was fortunate for the Allies that they were, at this time, so well entrenched at headquarters.

All these headaches and heartaches were, however, in the future when Rommel, in full favour with the Führer, a hero already to the German public and promoted *Generalleutnant* the month before, was appointed to the command of the "German troops in Libya" on February 15th, 1941. The only hint of them was given by Field-Marshal von Brauchitsch at a farewell interview in Berlin (Rommel did not see Hitler). His mission, von Brauchitsch told him, was merely to assist the Italians, who would retain the supreme command of operations in North Africa, and prevent a British advance to Tripoli. The German troops were, in fact, a "blocking unit" and, when he had had a look round, he had better come back and report whether they were really needed. General Schmundt, Hitler's military A.D.C., was to go with him, doubtless to make an independent report to the Führer.

Schmundt proved a good friend to Rommel, though it was perhaps a pity that Rommel liked and trusted him as much as he did. Appointed at the suggestion of Keitel's brother to succeed Colonel Hossbach, an old Prussian officer, who resigned in disgust when Colonel-General von Fritsch was "framed" by Himmler on a false homosexuality charge, Schmundt was a youngish regular officer, very good-looking, very intelligent, very ambitious and · very "smooth." His friends had never known him to be a keen Nazi but, whether from conviction or from self-interest, he became one. That is to say, he became a devoted admirer of Hitler himself. To Rommel, of whom he seems to have been genuinely fond, he drew the distinction which Rommel had always instinctively drawn between the Führer and his followers. Of course Hitler was, unfortunately, surrounded by rascals, he would explain, most of them a legacy from the past. But what a great man! What an idealist! What a master to serve! Living in the closest personal contact with Hitler, and a witness, as he must have been, of many of his outbursts, can he have believed all this? It seems incredible. It was not incredible to Rommel, who was not in the innermost circle and was spared the worst of Hitler's displays of temper and hysteria until much later. Thus, on their way to Africa and while Schmundt remained there, the two struck up a friendship and established a working partnership. Thereafter, when he wished to bring something to the personal notice of the Führer, Rommel wrote directly to Schmundt. Keitel and Halder suspected that they were being by-passed, though they could not prove it. The suspicion naturally did not make them any better disposed towards Rommel.

This relation with Schmundt explains why Rommel so long preserved his illusions about Hitler for, even from Rommel, Schmundt would never hear a word against the Führer. Whatever was wrong was the fault of the Goerings, the Himmlers, the Bormanns, the Keitels, the Jodls, the Halders. Yet only a few days before the attempt of July 20th, 1944, when Rommel was already in trouble with Hitler for his pessimism about the outcome of the war, Schmundt sent him a telegram saying, "Remember, you can always count on me." Schmundt was in the room with Hitler when the bomb exploded and died about two months afterwards. Of his wounds? So it was said. Rommel was never quite sure.

Meanwhile Rommel, like many a junior officer and some senior officers who ought to know better, had defeated security, when he heard of his appointment, by writing to his wife to let her know where he was going. "Now I shall be able to do something for my rheumatism," he wrote. Since Frau Rommel remembered that the doctor who had treated him for rheumatism during the campaign in France had said: "You need sunshine, General, you ought to be in Africa," the inference was not difficult to draw. However, he was able to come home for a few hours after his visit to Berlin. Then he and Schmundt set off for Rome, for Africa and the sunshine. The faithful Aldinger followed with the kit.

CHAPTER 6

Desert Ups and Downs

I. ROMMEL *V.* WAVELL

Rommel was just over two years in North Africa. The graph of his fortunes (and of ours, in reverse) during that period is easy to follow. There is a sharp and spectacular rise for his first victory in April, 1941, followed by a small decline for his failure to capture Tobruk on May 1st. This is rather more than evened off by his defeat of General Wavell's minor offensives in mid-May and mid-June. Then comes a series of rapid ups-and-downs, like the recordings of a demented seismograph, at the end of November and beginning of December, ending in a long drop when he is squarely beaten by Generals Auchinleck and Ritchie and driven back to the borders of Cyrenaica. At the end of the year he is once again on the datum line. There follows another rapid rise when he counterattacks unexpectedly in January and February, 1942, and drives us in turn back to Gazala. On a graph and on the ground he is about two-thirds of the way to the high point he reached the previous April.

At the end of May, 1942, after an initial drop that lasted only a few days but might have been a headlong plunge to disaster, begins that most spectacular rise of all which, in a month, carries him over and past Tobruk, past the Egyptian frontier, past Mersa Matruh, Bagush and El Daba, to Alamein and the very gates of Alexandria. That is the peak. There General Auchinleck holds him and an almost imperceptible but ominous decline begins. General Montgomery's victories at Alam Halfa in August and El Alamein in early November turn it into a descent which proceeds unbroken until May 12th, 1943, when the survivors of the Afrika Korps lay down their arms in Tunisia. Rommel himself has flown off to Germany two months earlier, in a vain attempt to persuade Hitler to allow him at least to save the men.

The graph is easy to follow: the battles are not. Nor, I think, is there much point in attempting to describe them in detail again. Those who want to know where 4th Armoured Brigade was at first light on the morning of November 26th,

1942, can turn to the official historians or to the various divisional histories. Those who want to see the broad picture cannot do better than read or reread Alan Moorehead's *African Trilogy,* or the books of some of the other very able correspondents who accompanied the British forces. Writing under the stress of events, they caught the spirit of the desert war. Yet, since this is the story of Rommel of the Afrika Korps, I cannot altogether omit his battles in North Africa. The reader must be asked to travel what, for those who followed the campaign on the map at the time, will be familiar ground, the same old coast road, the same old desert tracks. It may be a change to go part of the way in a German truck.

When I mentioned to Alan Moorehead that I thought of writing this book, he suggested that it might be useful to get into touch with a German war-artist named Wessels. Wessels was with Rommel in North Africa and Alan considered his water-colour drawings of the Western Desert the best he had ever seen. Unfortunately he had mislaid the address. Before he could find it, I had set off for Germany, to stay with the 10th Hussars at Iserlohn and look around from there. As soon as I arrived, the C.O. of the 10th, also an "old boy" of Campo P.G. 29, our prison-camp in Italy, said that I might, perhaps, like to meet a German war-artist named Wessels who was with Rommel in North Africa. If so, he lived in Iserlohn.

I met Wessels the same afternoon and a very good artist he is, and a very agreeable one. When I told him what I had in mind, he asked if I knew that General von Esebeck, sometime commander of the 15th Panzer Division in the desert, and General von Ravenstein, commander of the 21st, both lived in Iserlohn, within five hundred yards of the house in which I was staying and within twenty yards of each other.

Apart from having served in two wars against them, I have never known many Germans. I had certainly never met a German general, except Rommel, and that professionally and for a few seconds. My prejudice against a class which is largely responsible for my having spent ten years of my life in a sterile and unremunerative occupation is at least as strong as most people's. Nevertheless, I must admit that I found both of them congenial.

General von Esebeck, a quiet, elderly man, living alone in a small bed-sitting-room on the top floor, with seventeenth and eighteenth century paintings of his ancestors round the walls, was a pathetic figure, I thought, a military Mr. Chips.

Wounded in the face by a bomb splinter near Tobruk in 1941 and sent, on his recovery, to the Russian front, he was arrested on suspicion after July 20th, 1944, and thrown into a concentration camp. Lucky to be alive? Perhaps, if a general, frail and prematurely aged, with no pension and no possible career or interests outside the army, is lucky to be alive in Germany to-day.

General von Ravenstein, across the road, was a horse from the same sort of aristocratic stable but one of a very different colour and in very different condition. A lean, good-looking Guards officer, who seemed much younger than fifty-odd, if one had seen him, quietly dressed in his good blue suit and well-polished shoes, a pearl pin in his tie, strolling into the Guards Club or the Cavalry Club in London, one would have placed him at once as a young and successful general. After two disastrous wars, he seemed physically and mentally quite fit enough to command in another. In both he did well. In June, 1918, eighteen months after Rommel, he was given the Pour le Mérite for gallantry in action. Between the wars he retired and became, of all things, head of a news agency in Duisburg, until he was thrown out by the Nazis. Rejoining the army as a colonel in 1939, he commanded a panzer unit in Poland. Then, having fought in Bulgaria and Greece in March and April, 1941, he came out to the desert to command a panzer regiment of 21st Panzer Division. He took over the division before the Halfaya Pass-Sollum battle in June.

It was von Ravenstein who led Rommel's famous break-through on November 24th-25th, 1941. His career in the desert came to an abrupt end when, at first light on November 28th, he inadvertently drove into the middle of the New Zealand Division. "It was terrible," he told me, "because I had on me the Chief of Staff's map with all our dispositions and had no time to destroy it. When I saw that there was no way out, I determined to call myself Colonel Schmidt and hoped that they would not notice my rank badges. But then I was taken up to General Freyberg. You know how we Germans mention our name when we are introduced? I clicked my heels and bowed and before I could stop myself I had blurted out, 'von Ravenstein, General'!"*

* A liaison officer with 6th New Zealand Brigade who drove General von Ravenstein to Divisional H.Q., tells me that he had no doubt about his identity and realised they had caught a bigger fish than "Colonel Schmidt."

65

General von Ravenstein eventually reached Canada. On the way from Suez to Cape Town he organised an attempt, which might easily have been successful, to seize the ship. It was discovered at the last moment by the captain. As an ex-P.O.W., in charge for some time of escaping in a prison-camp, I gave him full marks for it. Though only repatriated in 1948, General von Ravenstein has no complaints. He could not have been better treated. After the war, he was allowed almost complete freedom. "No shortages there," he said. "I can still give you a good Havana cigar: I have a few boxes left." Now, though he has to share it with two other families, he lives in comfort in his own house in Iserlohn. He has some good pieces of furniture and his ancestral portraits also hang on the walls. His wife, a charming Portuguese countess who speaks even better English and French than he does himself, is with him. He also has a job. He is once again head of his news agency in Duisburg. All things considered, General von Ravenstein has not fared too badly. Since he gave 4th Indian Division (and myself) a very uncomfortable time in Sidi Omar just before he was captured, I propose to send him a photograph we took, during his unsuccessful attack on us, of seven of his tanks in flames.

General Fritz Bayerlein, whom I met in more orthodox fashion through the good offices of the U.S. Historical Section at Frankfurt, is something else again. A stocky, tough little terrier of a man, full of energy and enthusiasm, he is still only fifty. In the first war he fought, from the age of sixteen, as a private soldier against the British. He took part in the German attacks round Kemmel in March, 1918, and in the decisive battles on the Somme and about Bapaume and Cambrai in the summer. After the war, he had at first no intention of soldiering. For lack of anything better to do, he rejoined the army in 1921. He was at the Staff College from 1932 to 1935, after which he was posted to panzer troops.

Probably no one on either side, except Rommel himself, saw more continuous active service in the Western Desert than Fritz Bayerlein. He came over to Africa from Guderian's Panzer Army in Russia in October, 1941, and left only in May, 1943, when he was wounded and flown out just before the end. Those nineteen months were months of almost incessant fighting. He was Chief Staff Officer to the Afrika Korps until May, 1942, when General Gausi was wounded and he became acting Chief of Staff to Rommel himself. (Rommel had come out as commander of the Afrika Korps only but was given command of *Panzer Gruppe Afrika,* which included two Italian corps, in the summer of 1941.) This appointment he held until the end, except for five hectic weeks after the capture of General von Thoma at El Alamein, when he commanded the Afrika Korps during the retreat.

Obviously there could be no better authority on the North African campaigns. Yet, as he unfolded, in a hut in the U.S. Interrogation Centre at Ober-Ursel, the familiar map of the desert from Agedabia to Alamein, he told me that this was the first time that he had been asked about Africa and that I was the first British officer he had met who had served there. He was also an authority on Rommel. Not only had he lived with him all those months at close quarters; he had previously known him at the Infantry School at Dresden from 1930 to 1933. We spent a long day together, with a great many "Do you remember's?" I apologise for liking certain German generals. I certainly have no affection for them as a class. But at the end of it I liked General Bayerlein. From these three first and from others later I got a picture of the African campaigns as seen from the German side of the lines.

At the beginning of this book I mentioned that General Wavell or his staff made a miscalculation in a time and space problem when they assumed that Rommel would not be able to attack, in the spring of 1941, as early as he did. The error did not add to the popularity of G.H.Q. There is more excuse for our Intelligence Staff when we know that Rommel surprised not only them but also his superiors in Berlin. He attacked on March 31st. It was only on March 21st that he was told by the Army Command to prepare a plan for the reconquest of Cyrenaica and to submit it for consideration not later than April 20th. It was to be a prudent plan. In the face of substantial British forces, he was not to go beyond Agedabia until 15th Panzer Division arrived. Halder and his staff would doubtless have spent a week or two in examining it with critical and unfriendly eyes. They never had the chance. Nine days before they were due to receive it, Rommel had already reconquered Cyrenaica, with the exception of Tobruk, and reached the Egyptian frontier. He had done much more than he would have been allowed to attempt had he waited for permission. Even his Führer was ignored. On April 3rd, Hitler telegraphed to him telling him to be careful and not to launch any large-scale attack without waiting for 15th Panzer Division. In particular he must not expose his flank by turning up to Benghazi. The last part of the order could safely be disregarded for Benghazi was evacuated the day the telegram was sent. As for 15th Panzer Division, it was already landing in Tripoli and could thus be said to have "arrived."

"It is my belief," writes a very capable officer who was serving with Intelligence in Cairo at the time, "that an ordinary military appreciation was made, taking into consideration the strength of both sides, time and space and all the usual factors. Academically speaking, it was a good appreciation as Rommel's attack should not have succeeded. Unfortunately for us, he gambled and won. By the book, he shouldn't have attacked so soon. . . ." Colonel-General Halder would doubtless have agreed.

The same view is taken by Brigadier Williams, afterwards General Montgomery's chief Intelligence officer but then a troop leader in the King's Dragoon Guards, the "recce" (reconnaissance) regiment of 2nd Armoured Division. "I think personally," he says, "that Rommel began by edging up and found it easy to capture Agheila (that I remember well, because I was in the fort when it was captured and had to make a quick 'get-away'), and that, after that, a well-planned reconnaissance developed into a successful offensive. . . . Certainly Rommel should not have dared to attack us as soon as he did. . . ."

Such was the first appearance of Rommel on the desert stage. The speed with which he overran Cyrenaica was impressive, even to professionals. It impressed still more painfully the public, which measured gains by the map. Yet ground in the desert meant little. It should have been thought of in terms of sea and not of land battles. Once the enemy armour was out of action, the winning tank fleet could cruise across it as far and as fast as its petrol and tracks would allow. What was much more alarming was the vastly superior quality of the German armour. This superiority lasted until the arrival of the Sherman tank, before El Alamein. It was never appreciated either by our General Staff or by the Cabinet, who always thought that quantity could make up for deficiency in quality. In the desert, at least, this theory did not work. Rommel handled his tiny force with remarkable boldness and skill. His greater experience was, indeed, bound to tell. He had already led an armoured division in action and a week of war is worth six months of manœuvres. He was opposed to inexperienced troops and to commanders who had never seen even manœuvres on any sufficient scale, because of our lack of tanks. In a word, he knew more about the business. So did his tank crews. Nevertheless, "With better weapons they were bound to beat us." "I do not believe that he could have been easily stopped," says Brigadier Williams. "We had only 2-pounder anti-tank guns and a lot of worn-out tanks." Even had they been new, they were not in the same class as the German panzers.

In the field of strategy Rommel met his match in General Wavell. The decision to hold Tobruk was a bold one in the circumstances, but "the active defence of its garrison constituted a menace to the enemy's line of communications, which was likely to prevent his advance." In fact, it did so—and probably saved Egypt. Rommel always spoke of Wavell to his son as a commander of the highest order, "a military genius." In his library amongst many presentation volumes about North Africa by Frobenius and others, with uncut pages, I found a well-thumbed copy, in the German translation, of Wavell's pamphlet on the art of generalship, *Der Feldherr, von General Sir A. Wavell* (Zurich, 1942).

It was because Rommel also appreciated the importance of Tobruk that he launched a full-dress attack against it on May 1st, as soon as he had been reinforced by 15th Panzer Division. According to Aldinger, although the Italians possessed the complete defence plans, which they had themselves prepared, they denied having them and did not hand them over. However that may be, 9th Australian Division was not to be overawed by Rommel or any one else. This sort of fighting, where what counted was the tenacity and initiative of sections and individuals, was what Australians were best at. Rommel got "a poke in the nose" and was severely repulsed, with heavy losses in men and tanks. The Army Command profited by the reverse to remind him that "possession of Cyrenaica, with or without Tobruk, Sollum and Bardia is the primary task of the Afrika Korps" and that a continuance of the advance into Egypt was of secondary importance.

In the middle of May, before a consignment of new tanks from England could be unloaded, General Wavell thought he saw "a fleeting opportunity of attacking the enemy forward troops on the Egyptian border near Sollum in favourable circumstances." In a limited operation by a small number of Cruiser and "I" tanks, Sollum and Capuzzo were captured. Next day Rommel brought up his own armour in force and compelled them to retire. On May 27th he pushed us off the Halfaya Pass, the only place, apart from Sollum itself, where tanks can climb the 200 ft. escarpment which runs for fifty miles southeast into the desert, east of the wire marking the Egyptian frontier.

General Wavell was still bent on recovering Cyrenaica, at least as far as Tobruk. Moreover, he was "being urged to attack with the least possible delay," and it is not hard to guess who was prodding him from London. He now had enough new tanks to re-equip 7th Armoured Division, which had been out of the line as a division since the victory over Graziani. The division had been so short of equipment that it had neither the tanks nor the wireless sets to continue its training. Some of the new tanks were of a pattern that had never been seen in the Middle East; many of them required overhaul; all of them had to have sand filters and desert camouflage. "The crews were as strange to each other as they were to their machines."

It was estimated that the Germans had 220 medium tanks and 70 light tanks against our total of approximately 200. The decision to attack was, therefore, a bold one, to say the least of it. Moreover, General Wavell had to try to combine two armoured brigades, one equipped with Cruiser tanks with a speed of 15-20 m.p.h. and a radius of action of 80-100 miles, the other with "I" tanks with a speed of 5 m.p.h. and a radius of action, without refuelling, of only 40 miles. It was like putting a man and a small boy, three-legged, into a hundred-yard sprint. On top of all this, the Germans had something up their sleeve. This was the 88 mm. dual-purpose gun.* An anti-aircraft high-velocity gun which could be used in an anti-tank role with armour-piercing ammunition, it could go through all our tanks like butter. Rommel's record of the Ghost Division definitely states that it was used against British tanks near Arras. British information is equally definite that it was not and that we first ran up against it on June 16th, 1941, in the Western Desert. At any rate it was a most alarming weapon and remained a bogey to tank commanders and others until the end of the war.

In any event, "Operation Battleaxe," after some initial success, was a dismal failure, in which we lost just on a

* See page 49. I have since heard from Major R. von Minden, who stopped our tank attack on May 21st, 1940, with the 88 mm. guns of his flak battery (A.A.Bde 1/61). I have also learnt that the gun was tried out against tanks during the civil war in Spain and that a report on it was sent to the British Ministry of Supply.

hundred tanks. At the time, some of us, without any tanks at all and with no air-cover, were being chased about Syria by the tanks and aircraft of the Vichy French. We were naturally resentful when we heard that six fighter squadrons, four bomber squadrons and two hundred tanks had been employed in what seemed a completely futile operation. It was interesting, therefore, to be told by General von Esebeck, by General von Ravenstein and by Aldinger, independently, that our offensive was taken very seriously by Rommel, and regarded as highly dangerous. General von Ravenstein thinks we made a mistake in trying to attack "the one strong point," Halfaya Pass, particularly with tanks, and that our turning-movement round the southern end of the escarpment should have been much wider. Had we known about the 88 mm. guns dug in there, we should probably have left Halfaya alone; it was the mixed nature of our tanks which made it necessary for the "I" tanks of 4th Armoured Brigade, with their limited range, to turn sharply north to Capuzzo, while the rest of 7th Armoured Division ranged further afield on their flank. At least it is satisfactory to know that "Battleaxe" caused the enemy some anxiety.

From Aldinger I heard a queer story about this period. When we went into Syria it will be remembered that the French hotly denied that they were helping the Germans. They were resisting our advance, they said, merely because we were invading French territory. They would equally have resisted the Germans or any other invader. Having had my truck shot to pieces outside Mezze, near Damascus, I spent three days as a prisoner and heard this explanation given with great vigour and apparent sincerity by various staff officers at French headquarters. What the truth was, I never discovered. The French had, we were told, refuelled German aircraft on their way to Iraq to support Rashid Ali's rebellion: it did not appear at the time that there had ever been more than a few Germans in plain clothes in Damascus or Beirut. Aldinger's story was that, just before or just after "Battleaxe," a French aircraft from Syria landed at Bardia, that the French officer pilot was brought immediately to Rommel, that he spent more than an hour with him and then took off again. If this is so, and Aldinger is positive, he presumably came from General Dentz, Commander of the Vichy French.

The rest of the summer passed quietly, with both sides trying to build up. Here Rommel was at a disadvantage. The

71

eyes of the German High Command were fixed upon Russia and there was no interest in North Africa. Ultimately there might have to be an offensive against the Suez Canal and even against Iran. This, however, could wait until after the defeat of Russia. It would then be opened through Anatolia and the Caucasus. The German army in Libya would play only a supporting part and no new divisions need be expected. Meanwhile, since nothing could be done about his supplies without an operation against Malta, Rommel must restrict himself to planning the capture of Tobruk. If it fell, he was not to advance into Egypt but to stop at Sollum. If the attack failed, he must be prepared to retire to Gazala.

Rommel has often been rated, both by British and by German experts, as a mere military opportunist, a tactician who was not qualified to have any opinions about strategy. That he was a master of "grand tactics" rather than of strategy is probably true. Yet if he were unable to comprehend the broad principles of strategy, it is surprising that he should have been employed as an instructor at Potsdam. It is still more surprising that he should have learnt nothing of them during the years he was there.

In this case, he showed a clearer appreciation than most of the professional strategists. The plan which he put forward officially in July, 1941, for the capture of the Suez Canal has already been mentioned. General von Ravenstein tells me that his ideas in fact went very much further. This advance was to be only the prelude to a further advance to Basra, with the object of stopping the flow of American supplies to Russia through the Persian Gulf. Rommel's own supplies, after the first phase, were to be assured through Syria, though he thought that Turkey might be induced to come in on the German side if all went well both in Russia and North Africa. Alternatively, she might be attacked and collapse.

Before any one dismisses such a scheme as fantastic, as did the German Army Command, who had only seen the first part of it, he should read General Auchinleck's dispatch (38177), covering events in the Middle East from November 1st, 1941 to August 15th, 1942. He will then see how much we had with which to hold Syria, after the Vichy French had capitulated; how much we had in Iraq and Iran; how easily Cyprus could have been captured by airborne troops at any time before the late summer of 1942 and what a constant pre-occupation to him was his northern flank. His fear was, admittedly, an attack through the Caucasus. But, whichever way the attack came, we were too thin on the ground to meet it, had it been made in force. It is also relevant to remember the figures of American supplies which actually reached Russia through the Persian Gulf.

As for Malta, Rommel continually told his staff (and, later, his family) that he could not understand what on earth the High Command were about not to take it. This, he thought, could easily have been done at any time during the summer of 1941 with smoke and airborne troops. Since 35 per cent of his supplies and reinforcement were sunk in August and 63 per cent in October, he had a personal interest in the matter. Yet it was not until the end of 1941, when sinkings had risen to something like 75 per cent, that the High Command woke up to the importance of Malta for the command of the Mediterranean. They then sent U-boats and light surface craft and reinforced the Luftwaffe in Sicily. The result was that, by early 1942, when Rommel had planned to launch his offensive, they virtually controlled the Central Mediterranean. (A share of the credit is also due to the young Italians who made their way into the harbour of Alexandria and sank the only two British battle-ships, *Queen Elizabeth* and *Valiant,* at their moorings.)

By that time they had left it too late to reinforce Rommel with the extra German divisions for which he had asked. Nor, indeed, do they appear ever to have had any idea of doing so. And although they had neutralized Malta and, as Kesselring thought, "eliminated it as a naval base," they had made no attempt to capture it. It was not until the end of April, 1942, under pressure from Admiral Raeder and after a discussion with Mussolini, that Hitler gave permission for a surprise attack on the island with German and Italian paratroops at the beginning of June ("Operation Hercules"). "Even though the postponement of the Malta operation is not a welcome move," wrote the German naval representative at the meeting, "nevertheless I am glad to see the increased interest displayed by the Führer in this important area. . . . The whole business is now assuming importance after having been regarded hitherto as a subsidiary matter in which victories were looked upon as gifts from Heaven but in which nobody bothered to do anything seriously for 'the Italian theatre of war.' "

The attack was twice put off. At the beginning of July, the last minute of the eleventh hour, Hitler finally postponed Operation Hercules until after the conquest of Egypt. He did not consult either the Italians or his own naval command. It is possible that he consulted Keitel and Jodl.

Even in the early summer of 1941, the senior officers of the Afrika Korps, fresh from their first victory, felt that North Africa was regarded by the High Command as a side-show, no more than "picking the chestnuts out of the fire for the Italians." There was, for example, the matter of air support. Why could they not have a few extra fighter squadrons? "I remember Field-Marshal Milch of the Luftwaffe coming over to inspect in May, 1941," said General von Esebeck. "We all prayed that the R.A.F. would favour us with a good heavy raid while he was there. Fortunately the R.A.F. obliged. General Milch was wearing a beautiful white uniform. I could not have been more delighted than when I saw him dive into a slit trench. When he came out, I was even more pleased to see that it was the trench into which the servants had thrown the refuse from the kitchen."

With or without encouragement from the Army Command Rommel was determined to attack. The first objective was clearly Tobruk. "Our freedom from embarrassment in the frontier area for four and a half months," wrote General Auchinleck, "is to be ascribed largely to the defenders of Tobruk. Behaving, not as a hardly pressed garrison, but as a spirited force ready at any moment to launch an attack, they contained an enemy force twice their strength. By keeping the enemy continually in a high state of tension, they held back four Italian divisions and three German battalions from the frontier area from April until November." General Wavell's decision, made in the confusion of a swift and losing battle, had paid off. There could be no advance into Egypt so long as Tobruk held out.

Permission to attack even Tobruk was not, however, easily obtained. Rommel wanted to reduce it in October or November. Hitler, Jodl and Keitel were against his making the attempt until January, 1942. They did not want to stir up anything in North Africa while their hands were full in Russia. The Italians, whose Intelligence, from their agents in Cairo and Alexandria, was better than that of the Germans, knew of General Auchinleck's coming offensive. They, too, opposed any move by Rommel, nominally under their command. The Luftwaffe produced aerial photographs of the railway which was being pushed forward west of Matruh. General von Ravenstein was present when Rommel threw them on the ground. "I will not look at them," he exclaimed petulantly.

Then came a report from Admiral Canaris. A British soldier in hospital in Jerusalem had told the nursing sister, a German agent, that the British were soon going to launch a big attack upon Rommel. On the strength of this, Hitler and Jodl told Rommel that he had better keep quiet, leave Tobruk alone and get ready to meet Auchinleck's attack. (It does not seem to have occurred to them that it would be twice as hard to counter if Tobruk remained in British hands.)

Rommel was determined to take Tobruk. He would not accept the order and flew off with von Ravenstein to Rome to dispute it. Von Ravenstein was in the office of von Rintelen, the German liaison officer with the Italians, when Rommel "blew his top." Having called the unfortunate von Rintelen "a friend of the Italians," he seized the telephone and got on to Jodl himself. "I hear that you wish me to give up the attack on Tobruk," he said. "I am completely disgusted." Jodl mentioned the British offensive. Rommel said that he would put 21st Panzer Division, whose commander he had with him in the office, to hold it off while the attack on Tobruk was in progress. Jodl played for safety. "Can you guarantee," Rommel reported him as saying, "that there is no danger?" "I will give you my personal guarantee!" shouted Rommel. Thereupon Jodl, having covered himself, gave in.

The attack was fixed for November 23rd. Everything was already "laid on" for it and as Countess von Ravenstein and Frau Rommel had joined them, Rommel decided to remain in Rome for his birthday, November 15th. The ladies went sightseeing. Von Ravenstein remembers that they came back to the Hotel Eden for luncheon, full of the wonders of St. Peter's. Rommel listened for some time in silence. Then he joined in the conversation. "You know, von Ravenstein," he said, "I have been thinking again about what we ought to do with those infantry battalions. . . ."

Rommel saw none of the sights of Rome. He did, however, by invitation of the Italian command, see, on his birthday, the film *On from Benghazi,* which depicted the advance of the previous April. It showed the victorious Italians attacking with the bayonet; it showed some very scruffy British officers, played by Italian "bit players," running in panic before them; it did not show a single German soldier in action. "Very interesting and instructive," said Rommel to his hosts, "I often wondered what happened in that battle."

The story has been told how it was only Rommel's absence from his headquarters at Beda Littoria, near Cyrene, which saved him from death or capture. In brief, a British commando party under Major Geoffrey Keyes was landed from a submarine. It was met and guided by a very gallant officer, John Haseldon, afterwards killed. Disguised as an Arab, he had been living behind the enemy lines. "The first building on the right as you enter the village from Cirene," says Major Kennedy-Shaw in *Long-Range Desert Group*, "is a grain silo, then comes a row of bungalows, then, standing back from the road amongst the cypresses, a larger, two-storied building, dark and rather gloomy. In this house, in 1941, lived Rommel. . . . At midnight, Keyes and the two men with him, Campbell and Terry, were at the front door, loudly demanding admission in German. The sentry opened to them but when they were inside, showed fight and was overpowered. At the noise, two officers appeared on the stairs and were shot down. All the lights in the house were then extinguished and silence fell. Keyes started to search the ground floor rooms first. The first was empty but from the darkness of the second came a burst of fire and Keyes fell, mortally wounded. Campbell was also hit and taken prisoner but Terry got away. Major Keyes (who was awarded a posthumous V.C.) is buried at Beda Littoria on a hill a mile south of the village, with four Germans."

Rommel, having flown back from Rome on November 16th, was busy elsewhere, giving the finishing touches to the mounting of his attack on Tobruk. In any case he would not have been caught in the "Prefettura," the gloomy house amongst the cypresses. This was not his headquarters but the headquarters of his Q staff. His own headquarters was in the Casa Bianca at Ain Gazala, near Gambut. He came sometimes to Beda Littoria but never stayed the night there, though a house called "Rommel Haus" was reserved for him and other high-ranking visitors. John Haseldon's information was wrong; the Arabs had either seen Rommel there by day or had confused him with someone else. When the report of the raid reached him, Rommel ordered his chaplain, Rudolf Dalmrath, to drive back to Beda Littoria and give Christian burial to Keyes and to the four dead Germans. Dalmrath drove over rain-soaked roads and through flooded *wadis,* for there had been a cloud-burst, and was 36 hours on the way. He arrived ten minutes before the funeral, in time to preach a sermon and to consecrate the graves, that of Keyes being on the right. Wreaths were laid by an officer of the German General Staff, three salvoes were fired, crosses of cypress

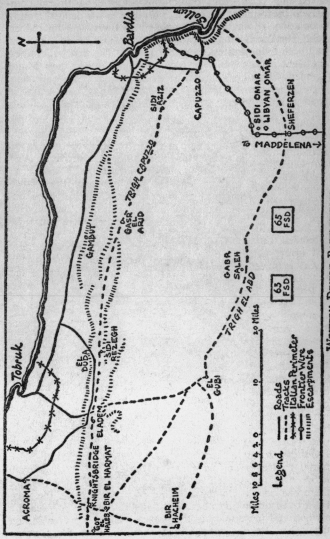

N

Legend
———— Roads
----- Tracks
--·--·-- Italian Perimeter
-o-o-o- Frontier Wire
||||||||| Escarpments

Miles 10 8 6 4 2 0   10   20 Miles

WESTERN DESERT BATTLEFIELDS

Tobruk
ACROMA
EL DUDA
GOT KNIGHTSBRIDGE
EL ADEM
EL HALEB ᵒBIR EL HARMAT
BIR HACHEIM
EL GUBI
SIDI REZEGH
GAMBUT
GASR EL ARID
TRIGH CAPUZZO
SIDI AZIZ
CAPUZZO
Bardia
Sollum
SIDI OMAR
ᵒLIBYAN OMAR
SHEFERZEN
To MADDELENA →
GABR SALEH
TRIGH EL ABD
63 FSD
65 FSD

77

wood were erected and young cypress trees planted. After the war, an account of Geoffrey Keyes' death and of the ceremony, with photographs, was sent by Ernest Schilling, Commander of the German Headquarters in Beda Littoria, and by Dalmrath to his mother, Lady Keyes.

II. "OPERATION CRUSADER"

If we did not surprise Rommel in his headquarters, the opening of General Auchinleck's offensive took him and his troops completely by surprise. When our armoured brigades, with their armoured car screen far in front, swept across the frontier wire at dawn on November 18th, they drove through empty desert to their battle positions on the Trigh-el-Abd.

"Operation Crusader" was the first battle of the Eighth Army. It opened with high hopes. Mr. Churchill even expected a victory comparable with Blenheim or Waterloo. Unfortunately, he said so. Because these hopes were not fully realised and were soon obscured in the fog of subsequent failure, few, outside the Eighth Army itself, ever knew how near it came to complete success. Because only final results count, fewer still can have taken the trouble to compare the figures with those of the battle of El Alamein. Of a total enemy strength of 100,000, 60,000, including 21,000 Germans, were killed, wounded or captured in Operation Crusader. The Eighth Army, 118,000 strong, lost 18,000 officers and men. At El Alamein, 150,000 of the Eighth Army faced 96,000 Germans and Italians and killed, wounded or captured 59,000 of them, including 34,000 Germans.* The Eighth Army losses were 13,500. In November, 1941, we went into action with 455 tanks against Rommel's 412. At El Alamein, General Montgomery had 1,114, against between 500 and 600, more than half Italian. Figures, however, do not tell the whole story. Of General Montgomery's 1,114 tanks, 128 were Grants and 267 Shermans, with 75 mm. guns in completely revolving turrets, all brand new. In November, 1941, we had not a tank that was fit to fight the German Mark III's and Mark IV's. Before our tanks, mechanically unreliable and armed with their pitiful 2-pounder gun, could even begin hitting the enemy tanks effectively, they had to close them by 800

* The German figures are 14,760 German and 21,700 Italian casualties in the winter battle of 1941-42 and 23,000 German casualties in the El Alamein offensive up to December 1st.

yards. While they were doing so, they were all the time under fire of 50 mm. (4-pounders) and 75 mm., against which their armour was no defence. We had no effective anti-tank gun at all.

Why, then, did General Auchinleck attack with one and a half armoured divisions instead of the three he himself considered necessary? First, so long as there were strong Axis forces in Cyrenaica there was a constant threat to Egypt and he could not hope to secure his northern flank against a possible German invasion through the Caucasus. Second, H.M. Government considered it essential to take the offensive in North Africa at the earliest possible moment. "Possible" is an elastic word, especially in London.

The decision accepted, no fault can be found with the general plan. The idea of basing the main force on Girabub, the oasis in the open desert to the south, striking across the desert via Gialo and then turning north to cut Rommel's communications was rightly turned down. The administrative difficulties would have been enormous. Moreover, the flank of the force would have been exposed, during its advance, to incessant air attacks from the coastal airfields in the north. These could have been "stepped up" at will, by reinforcements of the Luftwaffe flying in from Greece and Crete. Our own forces, including the R.A.F., would have had to be split. It would have been necessary to leave a strong covering force to hold the frontier. Otherwise Rommel would have turned the tables on us by coming down the escarpment and making direct for Alexandria. That was, in fact, precisely what he intended to do, had we attacked from the south. The thrust by a brigade group at Gialo was, therefore, merely a deception. It was effective; General Bayerlein told me that that was where they thought the main attack would come.

The plan adopted was to thrust towards Tobruk, while feinting from the centre and the south. The first object was the destruction of Rommel's armoured forces. The two Panzer divisions, 15th and 21st, were the backbone of the enemy's army. What was likely to bring them to battle on ground of our choosing? Clearly, reasoned General Auchinleck, an obvious move to raise the siege of Tobruk. (The relief of Tobruk was, in fact, incidental to the wider object of driving Rommel out of Cyrenaica and, in the next phase, out of Tripolitania. By this plan, the garrison would itself be able to take part in the action.) Since our tanks were inferior to his, we must try to attack his armour with superior numbers.

79

In no case must our single armoured division be caught by the two panzer divisions together. Surprise as to time and the direction of the thrust was essential.

In brief, the main attack was to be delivered by 30th Corps under Lieutenant-General Willoughby Norrie. Including most of the armour (7th Armoured Division and 4th Armoured Brigade Group), with two brigades of the 1st South African (Infantry) Division and the 22nd Guards (Motor) Brigade, it was to concentrate round Gabr Saleh and strike north-east or north-west. When it had defeated the enemy armour, it was to relieve Tobruk. The garrison of Tobruk (70th Infantry Division, an Army Tank Brigade and a Polish Brigade Group, the Australians having been relieved, was to make a sortie when General Norrie considered that the time was ripe.

Meanwhile 13th Corps, under Lieutenant-General Godwin-Austen, comprising the New Zealand Division, 4th Indian Division and 1st Army Tank Brigade, was to pin down and cut off the enemy troops holding the frontier defences. It was then to advance westwards on Tobruk to help 30th Corps. Fourth Armoured Brigade of 30th Corps was to protect its left flank. Eleventh Indian Infantry Brigade, below the Sollum escarpment, and 5th Indian Infantry Brigade, above it, were to contain the enemy frontally and cover our base and rail-head.

Rommel's force was one-third German and two-thirds Italian. It consisted of three armoured, two motorised and five infantry divisions. The two German panzer divisions, 15th and 21st, and the 90th Light (Infantry) Division, formed the Panzer Group, Afrika. Twenty-first Panzer Division was twelve miles south of Gambut, across the Trigh Capuzzo. Fifteenth Panzer Division, with 90th Light, was concentrated round El Adem, El Duda and Sidi Rezegh. Twenty-first Corps, consisting of four Italian infantry divisions, stiffened by three German infantry battalions, was besieging Tobruk. The Italian armoured division (Ariete) was at El Gubi, with its guns dug in. The motorised division (Trieste) was at Bir Hacheim. The frontier defences at Halfaya, Sollum and Capuzzo were manned by German infantry battalions. Sidi and Libyan Omar were held by the Savona Division, with some German guns. Bardia had a mixed garrison of Germans and Italians.

The preparations for the offensive were elaborate. The railway line was pushed forward 75 miles west of Matruh. A pipeline was built from Alexandria and a water-point opened ten miles behind the railhead. Nearly 30,000 tons of munitions, fuel and supplies were stored in the forward area before the battle opened. (This was sufficient to cover the difference between the daily rates of delivery and consumption for one week at most!) The Royal Navy and the R.A.F. for many weeks continually attacked the enemy's supply lines by sea and air. Thanks to the R.A.F. and the Long Range Desert Group, General Cunningham, commanding Eighth Army, under General Auchinleck, Commander-in-Chief, Middle East Forces, had almost exact information about the enemy's dispositions and order of battle. Thanks to the R.A.F. and to first-class administration, camouflage and "security," the enemy knew nothing of ours. The essential surprise was achieved.

The battle that ensued was desperately fought by both sides. On ours there was an exhilaration, a will to victory that I had not seen equalled since the final battles at the end of the first war. "Give me another —— tank," I remember a wounded Scottish sergeant shouting as he leaned out and pointed to his gun, the muzzle drooping like a stick of chewed celery from a direct hit. "Mon, we're doing all right up there; we're giving the b——s hell!" This a hundred yards from the truck of General Willoughby Norrie, commanding 30th Corps, who had just mislaid the whole of his Main Headquarters but remarked that there was a lot to be said for fighting a battle with only an A.D.C.: it saved so much paper. (About the same time, the entire headquarters of the Afrika Korps had been captured by the New Zealanders.)

It was a real soldier's battle, a "proper dog-fight," like those great aerial mix-ups which we used to watch over the lines in 1918. It was fought at such speed, with such swiftly-changing fortune, under such a cloud of smoke from bursting shell and burning tanks, such columns of dust from careering transport, in such confusion of conflicting reports, that no one knew what was happening a mile away. Even to-day it is hard to follow from maps which show the situation, hour by hour. Occasionally, out of the murk, would emerge some heroic figure like "Jock" Campbell, leading his tanks at Sidi Rezegh in an open car, winning his V.C. half a dozen times over. There were hundreds more whose exploits were unrecorded. How many have ever heard how Major-General Denys Reid, commanding the Indian Brigade Group from Girabub, took Gialo by walking into the fort and holding up with his pistol sixty Italian officers at dinner?

81

The heart of the battle was Sidi Rezegh, the key to Tobruk. Here was the hardest fighting of all, tank against tank,
man against man. The "high-spot" was, however, Rommel's
dramatic counter-attack with his armour across the frontier
wire at Bir Sheferzen on the afternoon of November 24th.
Alan Moorehead has vividly described, in *A Year of Battles*,
this raid on our back areas and the resulting stampede of
thousands of soft-skinned vehicles over the desert, like a shoal
of mackerel before a shark.

Why did Rommel suddenly abandon the main battle and
rush eastward with his armour? Had he any plan or was he
merely "stirring up the pot"? Was his move a master-stroke or
a desperate gamble? Major-General Fuller and Lieutenant-
General Sir Giffard Martel, amongst others, have argued the
question and reached opposite conclusions. The answer is
essential to any appraisement of Rommel as a commander.
Again, why, when they passed within a mile or two of them,
did his tanks not pause to set fire to our two main supply
dumps, F.S.D. 63, fifteen miles south-east of El Gubi and
F.S.D. 65, fifteen miles south-east of Gabr Saleh? Without
them, the New Zealand Division could not have been maintained. Without them, 30th Corps would have had to retire
from Sidi Rezegh. There was only the Guards Brigade to protect them.

The second question can be answered first because the answer is easy. Though the dumps were each six miles square,
the Germans did not know that they were there. "God in
Heaven!" said General Bayerlein, "you don't mean to tell me
that?" General von Ravenstein was equally shaken. "And to
think," he said, "that I saw and identified the Guards Brigade
and never bothered to wonder what they were doing there! I
don't think I even fired on them." Both of them returned to the
subject, in the same words. "If we had known about those
dumps, we could have won the battle." They could, indeed,
and whoever was responsible for the concealment and camouflage of those huge quantities of petrol, water and stores
can take some belated credit to himself.* So can the R.A.F.,
for keeping the German reconnaissance aircraft away from
the area.

* I have recently heard that it was Major Jasper Maskelyne. If
so, those famous illusionists, Maskelyne and Devant, never did a
better job.

As to the larger question, General Bayerlein knew exactly what Rommel had in mind. He still meant to take Tobruk but he could not do so while he was himself being attacked. If he turned on 70th Division, it would merely withdraw into the perimeter. The advance of the New Zealand Division along the Trigh Capuzzo had come as an unpleasant surprise to him. If he concentrated all his force against it, he could doubtless destroy it and open up the road to his frontier positions again. But that would give time to what was left of 7th Armoured Division to refit. Meanwhile there was 70th Division on his flank. If he turned on 7th Armoured Division, south-east of Sidi Rezegh (as General Martel thinks he should have done), then the New Zealand Division would join up with 70th Division. If he played safe and retired to Gazala, it would mean abandoning the frontier garrisons, the stores there and his own dumps along the coast. His strength lay in his two panzer divisions. Was there any way in which he could use them, not merely to get himself out of an awkward situation or to pursue a ding-dong battle, but to recover the initiative and turn defeat into victory at one stroke? Yes, he decided—to thrust suddenly eastwards into our back areas and so disrupt our communications that General Cunningham would be glad to call the battle off and withdraw from whence he came. He would then deal with Tobruk, a few days later than he had intended.

"You have the chance of ending this campaign to-night!" he told General von Ravenstein, who was to lead the attack with 21st Panzer Division, when he gave him his orders. They were to push straight through to the frontier wire and beyond, "looking neither to right nor left" and then turn up north to the sea by Sollum. Meanwhile a "combat group" of one motorised battalion with one company of tanks was to attack General Cunningham's headquarters at Maddalena. Another combat group from 15th Panzer Division was to follow up, go down the escarpment and capture the railhead at Bir Habata, where there were large stocks of petrol. If, as Rommel rightly suspected, there was nothing much between the escarpment and Alexandria, then 21st Panzer Division should join it and make at least a rapid raid into Egypt. By that time such alarm and confusion ought to have been caused that Eighth Army would be coming helter-skelter back to its original positions. (There was, in fact, one brigade of the 4th Indian Division behind a large minefield at the foot of the escarpment. After

83

that, there was nothing but the barely trained and badly-equipped 2nd South African Division, which had not yet seen a shot fired. Its nearest brigades were at Mersa Matruh.)

No one can say that his was not a bold plan to have concocted in the middle of a hard-fought battle. Why, then, did it fail? The answer is that it succeeded only too well, up to a point. On November 23rd, General Cunningham already wished to break off the battle. He would undoubtedly have done so next evening had not General Auchinleck flown up from Cairo and forbidden him. In a letter written at Advanced Eighth Army Headquarters on the night of November 24th, General Auchinleck said, after examining the dangers of going on with it: "The second course is to continue to press our offensive with every means in our power. There is no possible doubt that the second is the right and only course. The risks involved in it must be accepted. You will, therefore, continue to attack the enemy relentlessly, using all your resources, even to the last tank. . . ." General Fuller rightly calls it "an outstanding example of the influence of generalship on operations."

Rommel, on the contrary, had to be restrained by a junior officer. As usual, he was up in the forward area. About noon on November 25th General Ravenstein, lying behind Halfaya with some twenty or thirty tanks left out of his original sixty, received orders from Rommel to be ready to attack Egypt. At 2 P.M. came a wireless message: "All orders given to you hitherto are cancelled. 21st Panzer Division is to break through the Indian lines in the direction of Bardia." After his two unsuccessful and, it would seem, rather unnecessary attacks in the morning and afternoon on 7th Indian Brigade (and 4th Indian Division H.Q.) behind their minefields in Sidi Omar, he was doubtful about being able to get through. However, he sent an officer with a column of heavy trucks, which he hoped would be mistaken in the darkness for tanks, to "make a hole" between Sollum and Capuzzo and drove through after them. Next morning, the 26th, he was in Bardia. There he found Rommel sitting up, sound asleep, in his truck. "General," said von Ravenstein, "I am happy to tell you that I am here with my division!" Rommel exploded, "What do you mean, you are here?" he demanded. "What are you doing here? Did I not give you an order to be ready to attack from Halfaya in the direction of Egypt?" Von Ravenstein produced his copy of the countermanding wireless message. Rommel exploded again. "A fake!" he shouted. "This is an order from the British; they must have our code!"

The message in fact came from Lieutenant-Colonel Westphal, later a Lieutenant-General and Chief-of-Staff to Field-Marshal von Rundstedt, but then no more than a G1 (Ops.) left behind in charge of the rear headquarters near Tobruk. He had seen all the air reports, recognised that Rommel's plan of attacking Egypt was impossible to carry out and cancelled the order on his own responsibility. Rommel was a big enough man to congratulate him afterwards. "You did right," he said. "I am very grateful to you." So, it appears, was von Ravenstein.

Meanwhile shouts for help were coming from 90th Light Division, battling desperately to hold off the New Zealanders at Sidi Rezegh. During the night of November 26th-27th Sidi Rezegh was captured. El Duda had been taken by 70th Division that afternoon and, for the first time, the Eighth Army and the garrison of Tobruk joined hands. (General Godwin-Austen moved the headquarters of 13th Corps into Tobruk, whence he is credited with having sent the signal "Tobruk and I both relieved.") On November 27th a wireless intercept told General Ritchie, who had replaced General Cunningham, that the two panzer divisions were hurrying home.

Thus ended Rommel's eastward excursion. In the event, it had done little damage, beyond causing alarm and despondency in the back areas. (Some truck drivers are said never to have drawn rein—or taken their foot off the accelerator—until they reached Cairo. This may be an exaggeration but many were still full of running at Mersa Matruh.) Rommel had failed to recover the general initiative. As he had lost much of his armour, particularly to the artillery of 4th Indian Division at Sidi Omar, his last state was worse than his first. Nevertheless, General Auchinleck admits that his sudden drive "came as a rude shock." Had it succeeded, military historians would have rated it a masterpiece.

For the Germans as well as for ourselves the break-through had moments which are more amusing in retrospect than they were at the time. In the evening of November 24th, Rommel with General Bayerlein and General Cruwell, commanding the Afrika Korps, crossed the frontier wire, Rommel driving "Mammut," the Elephant, his British armoured command truck, a souvenir of an earlier battle, to which he was much attached. It was dark when they tried to turn back and they could not find the gap in the wire, which marked the gap in the mine belt that guarded it. (I remember giving up the attempt to find that gap myself and sleeping peacefully in my station-wagon, to discover next morning that my two front wheels were in the minefield.) Rommel and party slept, perhaps not so peacefully, in the middle of Indian troops and slipped out unchallenged at first light.

The previous afternoon Rommel had visited a field hospital, full of a mixed bag of German and British wounded. Walking between the beds, he observed that the hospital was still in British hands and that British soldiers were all about. It was, indeed, a British medical officer who was conducting him round, having mistaken him, or so he imagined, for a Polish general. The German wounded goggled at him and began to sit up in bed. "I think we'd better get out of this," whispered Rommel. As he jumped into "Mammut," he acknowledged a final salute.

General von Ravenstein also told me how Rommel tried to capture what he insisted was General Cunningham and his staff. "I had no time to take prisoners," he said. "In fact, when I drove through some British units and numbers of men, seeing the tanks on top of them, tried to surrender, I had to call out, 'Go away! I'm not interested in you!' What could I have done with prisoners? Then Rommel joined me. On a piece of rising ground east of the wire we saw through our glasses a group of staff officers with their maps. 'General Cunningham!' said Rommel. 'Go and take him!' While I was collecting a tank or two he became impatient. 'Never mind, I'll go and take them myself!' Standing up in his car, his sun glasses pushed up on his forehead, waving and shouting, he dashed off with three unarmoured staff cars and about twenty motor-bicycles, in a cloud of dust. However, General Cunningham (if it was General Cunningham) saw them coming and, being unarmed, I suppose, and without an escort, he and his staff jumped into their cars and made off."

(I still cannot find out what became of the "combat group" from 15th Panzer Division which was supposed to attack Maddalena. General Neumann-Silkow, son of a Scottish mother, then commanding the division, was killed ten days later and no one else seems to know. Had it turned up, it would have found Eighth Army Headquarters in a state of considerable "flap," busy trying to organise a defence force of tanks with scratch crews and no ammunition. An essential part of the plan thus miscarried.)

The dog-fight round Sidi Rezegh was resumed. Everything turned on whether 1st Brigade of 1st South African Division could get up to the support of the New Zealanders in time. The division was new to desert war. Its 5th Brigade had been overrun and almost completely destroyed a week earlier in a well-conceived and brilliantly executed German attack. Major-General "Dan" Pienaar, a foxy last-war veteran, was understandably cautious about moving across country and perhaps being caught by enemy armour in the open. His advance was slow and hesitating. When 15th and 21st Panzer Divisions arrived, having fought an action against the concentrated tank strength of 7th Armoured Division on the way home, General Freyberg was unable to hold on. The New Zealanders were driven off Sidi Rezegh. By December 1st Tobruk was once again isolated. Nevertheless, General Ritchie and General Auchinleck, who had joined him at Maddalena, rightly guessed that Rommel's bolt was shot. They resolved to give him no rest. In fact, he made two more efforts. In an attempt to reach his frontier garrisons, he sent two strong armoured columns eastward, one along the coast road, the other along the Trigh Capuzzo. Both were defeated, the first by 5th New Zealand Brigade, the second by 5th Indian Brigade. Next morning, December 4th, he launched a heavy attack on the Tobruk salient. Backed by 88 mm. guns brought up to close range, it was very nearly successful. Had it been resumed next day, it might have been completely so, for deep penetrations had been made into our positions. But that night Rommel, knowing that the Eighth Army was about to attack him again, began to withdraw.

The withdrawal was never a rout. Aided by a surprisingly gallant defence of El Gubi by the Italians, it became a fighting retreat, conducted by easy stages. Behind a screen of anti-tank guns, the German armour was handled with great skill and resisted all attempts to outflank and roll up the main force. When an opportunity offered, it struck back. I still remember that grey December afternoon, the 15th, when I stood by a 5th Indian Brigade truck near Alam Haza and heard the last telephone message come through from the C.O. of The Buffs as his battalion was overrun by German tanks. For all that, Rommel was gradually forced out of every position in which he tried to stand. Now greatly outnumbered in tanks and short of petrol, thanks to the destruction by 4th South African Armoured Car Regiment of one of his main dumps near El Gubi, he could do no more than fight a series of delaying actions. By January 11th he had taken refuge in an immensely strong defensive position round Agheila where "a broad belt of salt-pans, sand dunes and innumerable small cliffs stretches southwards for fifty miles, its southern flank resting on the vast expanse of shifting sands of the Libyan Sand Sea." The Eighth Army had nothing left with which to dig him out.

"To those who watched it anxiously from afar," writes Lieutenant-Colonel Carver of 7th Armoured Division, "the changes and chances of the battle were inexplicable; they only knew the disappointment of hopes buoyed up, to be dashed again and again, so that when victory came at last and Rommel's hold on Cyrenaica collapsed, they failed to appreciate the lion-hearted determination and persistence which had won through at last. To those who took part, a bitter taste remained; those who fought in tanks cursed those who sent them into battle, inferior in armour and armament and in tanks which broke down endlessly. The infantry, with a sprinkling of useless anti-tank guns, looked to the tanks to protect them against enemy tanks and were bitter at their failure to do so. The armoured commanders, hurrying from one spot to another to protect infantry from the threat of enemy tanks, which did not always materialise, blamed the infantry for wearing out their tanks and crews by such a misuse of the decisive arm in desert warfare."

To this I would add a footnote of my own. Though it is mentioned in General Auchinleck's despatch, no one who did not serve in the desert can realise to what extent the difference between complete and partial success rested on the simplest item of our equipment—and the worst. Whoever sent our troops into desert warfare with the 4-gallon petrol tin has much to answer for. General Auchinleck estimates that this "flimsy and ill-constructed container" led to the loss of thirty per cent of petrol between base and consumer. Since the convoys bringing up the petrol reserves at one time themselves required 180,000 gallons a day, the overall loss was almost incalculable. To calculate the tanks destroyed, the number of men who were killed or went into captivity because of shortage of petrol at some crucial moment, the ships and merchant seamen lost in carrying it, would be quite impossible. Not only did the 4-gallon tin lead to "a most uneconomical use of transport," as General Auchinleck mildly remarks; it also encouraged the grossest extravagance. What to do with a leaking tin if your tank was full? "Chuck the b—— over the side," was the answer of the always improvident British soldier—and his practice. Yet when I went back to India at the beginning of 1942, there was a factory outside Cairo still turning out these abominations. This at least partly disposed of the current rumour that someone in the Ministry of Supply had ordered x-millions of them and insisted that they be delivered. It did not dispose of the statement made to me by a very distinguished American engineer with whom I discussed the matter in New Delhi, that he had seen, in the railway workshop at Gwalior, stamps suited to the mass production of the admirable German "Jerrycan," with which everyone in the desert who could lay hands on them had already equipped himself. When I asked him what they were being used for, he said that they were stamping out steel ovens for Italian prisoners of war! Meanwhile "the progress of our armour was first retarded by the enemy rear-guards and finally brought to a standstill by lack of petrol." How many millions of gallons had gone into the sand?

Under such handicaps, with a bare numerical superiority of ill-armed, ill-armoured, unreliable tanks; with a far inferior system of tank recovery; compelled, for lack of anti-tank guns, to use 25-pounders to hold off the panzers; with one division untrained to the desert; with a total strength little more than that of the enemy, the Eighth Army had defeated Rommel and driven him out of Cyrenaica. With one hundred Sherman tanks it would have destroyed him and the war in North Africa would have been over. The survivors of this battle cannot wear an "8" on their Africa Star. For some reason it was assumed by the authorities responsible for such things that the Eighth Army sprang into being only on October 23rd, 1942, at the battle of El Alamein. They can, however, be proud that they fought with it through some of its greatest days.

CHAPTER 7

To the Gates of Alexandria

If Rommel had an outstanding quality, it was resilience. Like one of those weighted toy figures, no sooner was he knocked down than he was on his feet again. By January 11th, 1942, he was licking his wounds behind El Agheila. The same day, more than three hundred miles to the eastward, the South

Africans captured Sollum. Bardia had fallen at the beginning of the month. On January 17th the garrison of Halfaya, cut off from their water-supply ..nd exhausted from lack of food, at last surrendered. The frontier strongholds were reduced at leisure and at small cost. Their fate was certain from the moment that Rommel began his withdrawal.

Two-thirds of the Axis armies had been destroyed. Of the Afrika Korps, barely half had escaped death, capture or disablement. The morale of the remainder can hardly have been at its highest. As for the Italians, any fighting spirit that ever existed in the infantry divisions had sunk to zero during the long walk back from Tobruk. (The Germans, they complained, took all their transport.) The two German panzer divisions, or what was left of them, had been withdrawn to be re-equipped. Of Rommel's 412 tanks, 386 were lying, burnt out, blackened wrecks around the battlefields. Over 800 of his 1,000 aircraft had been shot down or destroyed on the ground. No new German formations could be expected for some time. It seemed that all he could hope for was to stand at Agheila until he was driven out by the Eighth Army or forced to withdraw by difficulties of supply. General Auchinleck estimated that not until the middle of February could he himself overcome his own administrative problems and concentrate enough troops to resume the offensive.

On January 21st, Rommel attacked. "The improbable occurred: without warning the Axis forces began to advance."

As on March 31st, 1941, Rommel may at first have intended no more than a large-scale reconnaissance. Yet it needed a man both morally and physically tough to think even of that at the moment. For Rommel, like our own commanders, had had two months of incessant fighting. Like them, he had slept in or beside his truck, never undisturbed for more than an hour or two. Like them, he had eaten what and when he could. Like them, he had faced bitter cold and rain and blinding dust-storms. Even more than they, he had spent most of his days and nights bumping at speed across the battlefield. During the long retreat he had had neither the thrill of pursuit nor the prospect of victory to make him forget fatigue. When he reached Agheila he was, in fact, exhausted. Yet, to the men of the Afrika Korps, he assigned no limited objective. They were to take three days' rations and to follow him as far and as fast as they could. Reinforced, but with no more than a hundred tanks, some of them light, and with virtually no fighter cover at all, he set out with three columns. The weak and widely dispersed covering forces were quickly brushed aside. "As usual," says General Auchinleck, "Rommel rapidly and skilfully made the most of his initial success." The reconnaissance developed at once into an offensive. First Armoured Division, which had just replaced the veteran "desert rats" of 7th, was new to desert warfare. It lost 100 of its 150 tanks and many guns. The Eighth Army was caught off balance. By February 7th, at the cost of only about thirty of his own tanks, Rommel had hustled it back to the line Gazala-Bir Hacheim. It was bold and brilliant generalship, by any standard.

Not only in Cyrenaica was the barometer falling for the British. From the Far East a chill wind was blowing; the breath of impending calamity was in the air. The Japanese were sweeping at speed through the "impenetrable jungles" of Malaya. The "impregnable fortress" of Singapore was about to be attacked from the side whence no attack could come. In Burma, two weak divisions were faced with the prospect of withdrawing across country—if they could. Nearer home, the Axis High Command had at long last come to see the strategic importance of Malta and the Mediterranean. Incessant air attacks were launched against the island; as the result, Rommel lost not a single ton of his supplies in January. Aircraft and submarines closed the Central Mediterranean to our own convoys. Heavy losses were inflicted on our naval forces; Admiral Cunningham was left with only three cruisers and a few destroyers. His flagship sat on the bottom in Alexandria.

These events started a series of chain reactions. Just as General Wavell had had to discard from weakness to assist the foredoomed campaign in Greece, so General Auchinleck was prevented from building up his strength by demands for reinforcements for the Far East. Already in December, before Rommel had been driven out of his Gazala position, the 18th Division had been diverted from the Middle East to Malaya. (It landed in Singapore just before the capitulation and two of its brigades, after a spirited but hopeless resistance, disappeared into Japanese prison camps.) Simultaneously, the dispatch of 17th (Indian) Division had been stopped. Tanks, fighter aircraft, guns had also to be sacrificed.

Yet, because it seemed certain that Malta must fall unless we could secure the airfields of Western Cyrenaica and give cover to the island and to the relieving convoys, the Cabinet was insistent that an offensive be staged at the earliest possible moment. What was the earliest possible moment? "Now, if not sooner," was the view of the Prime Minister. "When there is some chance of it being a success," said General Auchinleck. A premature offensive might result in the piecemeal destruction of the new armoured forces which he was trying to create. Then, in an attempt to save Malta, he might lose Egypt and the whole Middle East. The vicious circle was completed by the fact that every day that passed with Malta unable to interfere with Rommel's "build-up" reduced the chances of attacking him successfully. In February, a convoy carrying a large number of tanks had already reached Tripoli.

Long-distance arguments, like long-distance telephone calls in India, leave the exasperated participants with the impression that there must be a half-wit at the other end of the wire. Especially is this the case when both, from their own angle, are right. Fortunately Sir Stafford Cripps and General Nye, Vice-Chief of the Imperial General Staff, were persuaded to come out to Cairo, since General Auchinleck could not be persuaded to leave the Middle East and go to London. There the Commander-in-Chief was able to convince them that his strength both in tanks and in the air was altogether too small to offer even a reasonable prospect of an immediate offensive's being successful.

By agreement, the offensive was fixed for the middle of May. Rommel meanwhile received so many tanks that it was doubtful whether we would even then have numerical superiority. The War Cabinet, however, was determined that, to save Malta, the risk of losing Egypt must be accepted. General Auchinleck was ordered to launch his attack not later than the middle of June. In the event, Rommel attacked first, on May 27th, with tanks about equal in number and greatly superior in quality, even to the new American "General Grants." The airfields of Western Cyrenaica were not captured; Malta did not fall, thanks to Hitler's folly in postponing the airborne assault on it, but we very nearly lost Egypt.

The disasters of June, 1942, came as a staggering blow to the British public. Nothing shook them more than the fall of Tobruk which, in fact, it was not intended to hold if things went wrong. (The decision was altered at the eleventh hour for fear of the effect on public opinion at home. By then many of the mines had been lifted and Tobruk became a staging camp for retreating troops rather than a garrison fortress.) South Africa, because of the surrender of her troops there, and Australia, because of old associations, were equally appalled. Even the Eighth Army, which had sensed victory in the first few days, could not understand how it had slipped from its grasp. Thus it has never been generally realized how close was Rommel to defeat—and to capitulation.

"It all turned on the 150th Brigade box at Got-el-Ualeb," said General Bayerlein. "We never knew that it was there. Our first attacks on it failed. If we had not taken it on June 1st, you would have captured the whole of the Afrika Korps. By the evening of the third day we were surrounded and almost out of petrol. As it was, it was a miracle that we managed to get our supplies through the minefield in time."

The Gazala position consisted primarily of minefields, stretching from Gazala on the coast to Bir Hacheim, forty miles to the south in the open desert. Minefields alone will not stop tanks; lanes through them can quickly be cleared. There must be something behind them. It was impossible to dig and man a continuous trench system, as in the 1914-18 war. Moreover, such a system would have been useless, for, however far it stretched, its left flank must always be in the air. General Auchinleck and General Ritchie therefore devised a series of "boxes" or strongholds, the first at Gazala, the last at Bir Hacheim. Wired and mined in and prepared for all-around defence, they were, in effect, castles. Their garrisons were supplied to stand a siege and had their own complement of artillery inside the boxes.

These boxes had a double function. In the first place, they were to guard the minefields and prevent the enemy cutting lanes through them at leisure. In the second place, like castles in the Middle Ages, they were points of resistance which a prudent enemy must try to reduce. Otherwise, the garrisons could sally out and take him in the rear or harass his communications. While he was involved with them, our armour, kept well away outside the boxes, would fall upon him. Having thus forced him to give battle on ground of our own choosing, we could, when the right moment came, take the offensive ourselves. A solid defensive system from which to launch it and on which to fall back if necessary, the Gazala position would be a sort of Scapa Flow for the Eighth Army.

Rommel's first objective, as General Auchinleck rightly assumed, must again be Tobruk. He dare not advance into Egypt until he had captured it. To attack Tobruk, he had only two choices. He could smash his way through the minefields and boxes and make direct for it or he could skirt the whole

Gazala position, come round by Bir Hacheim and then strike north. Rommel chose the second course. The Italian armoured division, the Ariete, was to capture Bir Hacheim the first night if possible. In any case the Afrika Korps was to make straight for the sea. It was, in fact, to take Tobruk on the third day, having meanwhile defeated the British armour! The Italian divisions were to hold the front and prevent us breaking out westwards from the Gazala position. One of them, Trieste, was to cut a gap through the minefield where it was crossed by the Trigh-el-Abd track. This was a precaution, to shorten the supply line in case Bir Hacheim did not fall at once. It was behind this minefield that the 150th Brigade box was situated.

"I never liked this plan," said General Bayerlein, "and, as Chief of Staff of the Afrika Korps, I told Rommel so continually. It seemed to me altogether too risky to go on without first knocking out Bir Hacheim. Six weeks before he asked me 'What would you do with your armour if you were General Ritchie?' I told him that I would keep it well away to the eastward, somewhere about El Adem, refuse battle at first and then strike at our flank when we were inside the Gazala position. 'You're crazy,' he said, 'they'll never do that!' though it was just what he would have done himself. As a matter of fact, I think General Ritchie's dispositions were excellent. The American 'General Grant' tanks, too, with their 75 mm. gun, came as a great surprise to us and 15th Panzer Division lost 100 tanks the first day.

"General Cruwell, commanding the Afrika Korps, was shot down and made a forced landing in the 150th Brigade box, where he was taken prisoner. General Gausi, Chief of Staff to Rommel, was wounded. General Nehring took over the Afrika Korps and I took over from Gausi. When we had failed to capture Bir Hacheim and failed to get a passage through the minefield, both of us begged Rommel to break off the battle but he wouldn't hear of it. That was, I think, on the evening of May 31st. We were in a really desperate position, our backs against the minefield, no food, no water, no petrol, very little ammunition, no way through the mines for our convoys, Bir Hacheim still holding out and preventing our getting supplies from the south. We were being attacked all the time from the air. In another twenty-four hours we should have had to surrender."

That bore out exactly a story which I first heard in Barce prison camp only a few days after these events. On the first day of the attack the 3rd Indian Motor Brigade was overrun. An officer of the 10th Hussars, an old friend of mine, had his tank destroyed soon afterwards and found himself amongst the Indian prisoners, near Rommel's headquarters east of the minefields. Ringed round by 88 mm. guns to keep off our armour, Rommel was making desperate attempts to capture 150th Brigade box and get his supplies through. The Indian prisoners were dying of thirst and fighting for the few drops of water that were served out to the wounded. Major Archer-Shee, an officer of imposing presence, demanded to see Rommel and, to his surprise, was taken to him. He spoke enough German to make his protest. If the prisoners could not be given food and water, then the Germans had no right to keep them and should send them back to the British lines. Rommel was reasonable and even sympathetic. "You are getting exactly the same ration of water as the Afrika Korps and myself," he said: "half a cup. But I quite agree that we cannot go on like this. If we don't get a convoy through to-night I shall have to ask General Ritchie for terms. You can take a letter to him for me. . . ."

It was, it seems, as near as that, though one cannot quite picture Rommel going meekly off into captivity. But General Auchinleck, back in Cairo, saw before General Ritchie that the capture of 150th Brigade box changed everything. "I am glad that you think the situation is still favourable to us and is improving," he wrote on June 3rd. "All the same, I view the destruction of 150th Brigade and the consolidation by the enemy of a broad and deep wedge in the middle of your position with some misgiving. I feel that if he is allowed to consolidate himself . . . our Gazala position, including Bir Hacheim, will become untenable eventually, even if he does not renew his offensive. . . . Situated as he is, he is rapidly becoming able to regain the initiative which you have wrested from him in the last week's fighting. . . ."

What went wrong? It is easy to be wise after the event. In this case I am on record as having been right at the time. In *A Year of Battle*, Alan Moorehead recalls my telling him on June 2nd or 3rd, that I was afraid we had already missed the boat by not launching an attack with 5th Indian Division, under General Briggs, when Rommel was pinned against the minefield. Such an attack had, indeed, already been discussed. At intervals on June 2nd, I saw General Briggs, a deceptively mild officer with two bars to his D.S.O. Together we deplored the delay. At one moment we were going to attack: at another

95

the whole division was going to go south round Bir Hacheim and start on a non-stop drive to Derna. In the end we hung about and did nothing. When the attack was at last put in on June 5th, it was three days too late. One hundred and fiftieth Brigade box had fallen: a lane through the minefield had been cleared. The Afrika Korps was itself again, with petrol, food, water and ammunition, with plenty of 88 mm. guns in position and with tanks behind them in the salient. In the belated attack, 10th Brigade of 5th Division had some initial success but our armour failed to exploit it. In the evening the German tanks and lorried infantry slipped round behind the brigade. Germans in British carriers overran the single battalion protecting the flank before they were recognized. The tanks and lorried infantry followed. Brigade headquarters and the tactical headquarters of the division went up in the smoke of burning tents and trucks. General Briggs and General Messervy of 7th Armoured Division, returning from a "recce," managed to slip through. Brigadier Boucher, the brigade commander, making his way back to his headquarters, and I, waiting for him there, were less lucky.

That night, sitting amongst the German tanks in the open, it was easy to see that Rommel was on the move again. He had, indeed, recovered the initiative which General Ritchie had wrested from him and had no intention of giving it up. June 5th was the turning-point of the battle, though the chance of winning it outright went three days earlier.

Rommel now did what he ought to have done at the start. He sent General Bayerlein off to put Bir Hacheim finally out of business. It took a week of unceasing artillery bombardment and Stuka attacks. Even then the gallant Free French were still holding out. But they could not hold out much longer and General Ritchie told General Koenig to abandon Bir Hacheim on the night of June 10th and try to break through. He got away with a large part of his force, driven out by a British girl driver.

With Bir Hacheim off his back, Rommel at once reverted to his original plan of taking Tobruk. By midnight on the 11th, 90th Light Division was a few miles south of El Adem. The armoured divisions were echeloned on its left. There followed two days of great and decisive tank battles. Rommel threw in all his armour. But he threw it in behind a screen of anti-tank guns, of which he now produced more than it was ever suspected that he had. The British armoured brigades, weakened by the loss of most of the Grants, had to try to break through the screen to get at the German tanks. The guns took heavy toll of them. The tanks fell upon the remainder. By nightfall on June 13th most of our armoured strength was gone. Moreover, the enemy had possession of the battlefield and could recover his damaged tanks: ours were lost to us.

It was now clear that the Gazala position would have to be abandoned. But both General Auchinleck and General Ritchie were reluctant to believe that the Eighth Army was beaten. It had lost its armour but much of its infantry was intact. The New Zealand Division had been ordered from Syria. A new armoured division, the 10th, was on its way out from England. There were about 150 tanks under repair in the workshops. We should soon again have more tanks than Rommel. We were still superior in the air, as we had been throughout. The decision was taken to give up Gazala but to hold a line from the western perimeter of Tobruk to El Adem and Belhamed. At the same time a mobile force was to be maintained to the eastward and a new striking force built up near the frontier. This meant that Tobruk, or part of it, would again be invested, which was contrary to plan, since the Navy had said that it could not be supplied. However, a temporary and partial investment was different from a sustained siege.

In General Bayerlein's opinion, this decision was fatal. "To my mind," he said, "General Ritchie ought to have gone straight back to the frontier after we captured Bir Hacheim and were astride the Gazala position. In any case he should never have tried to hold Tobruk with the defences in the state they were and with an improvised garrison. If he was going to hold it, as we assumed he was, then he should have prepared to do so from the start, laid new minefields, got his guns into position and so on. Above all, he should have put an experienced general in charge. If someone like General Morshead or General Gott or General Freyberg had been there, things might have been different. As it was, a few units fought well. I remember a Scottish battalion (the Cameron Highlanders) which went on fighting long after General Klopper had surrendered. But there seemed to be no proper defence plan at all."

Fatal the decision certainly proved. Having captured Sidi Rezegh on June 17th and heavily defeated our armour on the same day, Rommel attacked Tobruk from El Duda on June 20th, exactly as he had proposed to attack it on November 23rd of the previous year. Using his Stukas to dive-bomb the minefields and clear a passage, he quickly broke into the fortress from the south-east. Inside, all was soon confusion. General Klopper, bombed out of his headquarters, his signal communications gone, had lost all touch and all control. As the German tanks fanned out from the gap in the perimeter and drove straight to the harbour, some troops fought on. Some broke out to the eastward, a battalion of the Coldstream Guards naturally in good order. The South Africans, holding the western and south-western side of the perimeter, hardly knew what was happening until 90th Light Division took them in the rear. Suddenly at dawn next morning they obeyed General Klopper's order to surrender. In prison camps for many months afterwards they were bitterly resentful and ashamed. The fortress which had held out for nine months in 1941 had been taken in a day. Inevitably they would be blamed. Inevitably they blamed General Klopper.

During the last hours and for long afterwards, Tobruk was covered with a funereal pall of black smoke from the dumps fired just before the capitulation. Millions of pounds of petrol and stores were burnt. Nevertheless, there was enough left to enable Rommel to drive on to Egypt.

It was now too late to stand on the frontier. General Ritchie sought permission to retire to Mersa Matruh. Reluctantly General Auchinleck agreed, though with misgivings. For without armour, Mersa Matruh was no more easily defensible than the frontier. By the evening of June 23rd, Rommel was again on the frontier wire.

Should he have gone on? General von Thoma says that he disobeyed a specific order from Mussolini, conveyed through Marshal Badoglio, to stop on the frontier after the capture of Tobruk. General Bayerlein denies this. A conference was held west of Bardia on June 22nd, he says. He himself only came in when it was nearing the end, but Rommel told him afterwards that General Bastico, his immediate superior, had been of the opinion that an advance into Egypt should not be attempted. There was, however, no order to that effect either from the Italian or the German High Command and General Bastico gave way when Rommel told him that he had been assured by Marshal Kesselring that he would get all the supplies he wanted. The point is clarified, if that is the word, by two extracts from Ciano's Diaries. On June 22nd he says that "a restraining telegram has already been sent from Rome advising Rommel that he should not venture beyond the line Fort Capuzzo-Sollum." Next day he writes, "From some intercepted telegrams from the American observer in Cairo,

Fellers, we learn that the British have been beaten and that if Rommel continues his action he has a good chance of getting as far as the Canal Zone. *Naturally Mussolini is pressing for prosecution of the attack. . . ."*

The decision was, then, Rommel's, the indecision was not. To a man of his temperament it was inevitable. He had the Eighth Army on the run. Was he to stop and let it re-form and then start the whole business over again from the line where he had halted fourteen months before? With the glittering prize of Egypt and the Suez Canal almost within his grasp, both the German and the Italian High Command must realise what was at stake and give him the extra support and supplies he needed. "No one could have guessed," says General Bayerlein, "that the British would so quickly regain control of the Mediterranean and be so successful in stopping our shipping." Still less could any one have guessed that Hitler, with his famous intuition, and Keitel, Jodl and Halder, with their trained staff minds, would not even see the opportunity that lay open before them. Of course he must go on. The Afrika Korps was, indeed, exhausted. But to Rommel, with his tremendous vitality, no soldier was ever too exhausted to fight the last round of a winning battle—or, for that matter, of a losing one.

Go on they did, and at speed. By the evening of June 24th (four days from the fall of Tobruk), Rommel was up to Sidi Barrani. Next day his columns were within forty miles of Mersa Matruh. That evening General Auchinleck personally took over command of the Eighth Army. At once he resolved that no part of it should be shut up in the Mersa Matruh defences, which he had not enough troops to man. The Tobruk mistake was not to be repeated. Rommel must be stopped, if possible, in the area between Matruh and El Alamein. But 30th Corps was to occupy the El Alamein position as a precaution. On the evening of June 26th, the German tanks broke through the minefields south of Charing Cross. Next day they bumped the New Zealand Division, fresh and, as always, full of fight. They lost heavily but pressed forward along the coast and succeeded in cutting the road twenty miles east of Matruh. Fiftieth Division and the newly-arrived 10th Indian Division had to fight their way out at night, leaving much of their ammunition and equipment behind. There was now nothing for it but to withdraw to the position which General Auchinleck had long before prepared. On June 30th Rommel came up to the El Alamein line. Alexandria was 65 miles away. He had, General Bayerlein assures me, just twelve German tanks left.

CHAPTER 8

The Enemy in Africa

I. "DESERT-WORTHY"

On the morning of June 21st, Rommel was able to report that Tobruk was in his hands. Next day he learnt by wireless from Hitler's headquarters that he was a Field-Marshal, at forty-nine the youngest in the German Army. That evening he celebrated his promotion—on tinned pineapple and one small glass of whisky from a bottle which his staff had procured from the Tobruk Service stores. After dinner he wrote to his wife: "Hitler has made me a Field-Marshal. I would much rather he had given me one more division." Still, he was in unusually high spirits, as well he might be when he looked back on his fourteen lean years as a captain and reflected where the next ten had brought him.

This was the peak of his professional career and of his success in North Africa. He had reached it in sixteen months from landing in Tripoli, with the modest mission of preventing the British capturing Tripolitania. He had had to adapt himself, not only to a new type of warfare but to the strange and exacting life of the desert. It would be infelicitous to say that he took to it like a duck to water, but he quickly became as "desert-worthy"* as a Bedouin. "Rommel may not have been a great strategist," said General Bayerlein, "but there is no doubt that he was the best man in the whole of the German Army for desert war."

It was a young man's war. Rommel was no longer a young man. Thanks to years of skiing and mountaineering he was, however, physically in his prime. "He had the strength of a horse," said a young German paratroop officer, himself a skiing champion. "I never saw another man like him. No need for food, no need for drink, no need for sleep. He could wear

* "Desert-worthy" was a term first used for vehicles fit for the desert. It came to be more widely applied, to formations, to units and even to individuals.

out men twenty and thirty years younger. If anything, he was *too* hard, on himself and everyone else."

There was, indeed, a Spartan strain in Rommel which made him take pride in being impervious to discomfort and fatigue. Neither heat nor cold nor hard lying affected him. Even the *ghibli*, as the Germans called the *khamseen*, the blinding sandstorm which reduced all in the desert, Arabs and camels included, to a common misery, he professed to regard as an exaggerated annoyance. Piloting his own Storch, he insisted on taking off in one during his first desert battle. When he had nearly killed himself, coming in to land with visibility *nil,* he admitted that it had been "difficult to see what the British were up to." No doubt they were merely up to their eyebrows in driving sand.

Like Napoleon, Rommel could snatch a few minutes' sleep, sitting up in his truck or with his head on a table, and wake completely refreshed. I asked Günther, his batman, now a pastry-cook in Garmisch, whether he minded being disturbed when he was having a night in. "Not at all," said the stolid Günther, who was with him for four years. "He always seemed quite pleased and was wide-awake in a second. He slept with one eye open: if a message came, he usually woke before I called him " Günther added that he was a very even-tempered man who never took it out on his batman and was easy to satisfy. (His generals saw a different side of him.)

Food, Rommel had never cared much about. He was quite content to set off for a day in the desert with a small packet of sandwiches or a tin of sardines and a piece of bread. Once he invited an Italian general to lunch with him in the open. "It was rather awkward," he remarked afterwards: "I had only three slices of bread and they were all stale. Never mind, they eat too much." Realising that the more one drinks in the desert the thirstier one becomes, he carried only a small flask of cold tea and lemon and often brought it back untouched.

In the evening he would dine alone in his caravan with his old friend Aldinger. He insisted on being given the same rations as the troops. They were not very good. "One of the reasons we had so much sickness, especially jaundice," said von Esebeck, the war correspondent, cousin of the general, "was that our rations were too heavy for the desert. Our black bread in a carton was handy but how we used to long to capture one of your field bakeries and eat fresh, white bread! And your jam! For the first four months we got no fresh fruit or vegetables at all. We lived all the time on Italian tinned meat. The tins had a big 'A.M.' on them: the troops used to call it *'asinus Mussolini.'* "

To a young officer of the Afrika Korps who ventured to say that, while he had no complaints, the food was not too appetising, Rommel replied genially: "Do you imagine that it tastes any better to me?" In fact he never noticed how it tasted. His only recorded taste, a negative one, was that he disliked tea and coffee made with brackish water. (He cannot have enjoyed his visit to Girabub, where the water has the exact consistency of Epsom salts. Of Girabub, they used to say: "Here Mr. Eno would have starved to death and Mr. Bromo made a fortune.")

After the evening meal, which lasted twenty minutes at the most and at which he drank his one glass of wine, Rommel would turn on the wireless. He listened only to the news. Then he would write his daily letter to his wife. In action, when he had no time to write, it was Günther's duty to write for him. He also carried on a continuous correspondence in his own hand with survivors of his first-war battalion. No letter from one of them ever went unanswered. Official papers took up the rest of the evening until bedtime. If he read at all, it was a newspaper or a book on a military subject. He had some interest in the history of North Africa and was mildly curious about the ruins of Cirene. But the story that he had kept up his classics and was a keen archæologist who spent his scanty leisure in digging for Roman remains was a production of the propagandists. Von Esebeck was responsible for it. "Some of us had been scratching about and had turned up some bits of Roman pottery," he told me. "We were looking at them when Rommel came along. What he actually said, when we showed them to him, was: 'What the hell do you want with all that junk?' But you can't tell that from the photograph!"

In the morning, Rommel was up and about by six. A stickler for turn-out on a parade, he let the Afrika Korps dress as they pleased in the desert. Usually they followed the Australian fashion and wore shoes, shorts and their peaked caps. He himself was always shaved and in uniform. Sometimes he wore shorts but more often breeches and boots and invariably a jacket. His tropical helmet he threw away, like the rest of us, soon after his arrival: he never put on a tin hat. His only eccentricity, perhaps borrowed from the British, was a check scarf round his neck in winter. Under it, according to the German custom, he wore his Iron Cross. He was thus consid-

erably more dressy than our own commanders who, in their
short, zip-fas ed, camel-hair coats and corduroy slacks,
could only be di tinguished by their red hats and rank badges
—when they wore them. (General Messervy, temporarily captured when commanding 7th Armoured Division, succeeded
in passing as a private soldier. "A bit old for this, aren't you?"
asked a German officer. "Much too old," agreed General
Messervy: "Reservist: they had no right to call me up.")

By 6:30 A.M. Rommel had started on his daily round of his
positions. Sometimes he went by air, flying the aircraft himself. Though he had no ticket, he was a confident pilot and an
excellent navigator. In battle, he generally used "Mammut,"
his British armoured command truck. Often he drove himself
about in a Volkswagen, finding his way unerringly across the
desert from the first. No post was too isolated for him to turn
up at it. When he descended on the back areas, it was an
unlucky senior officer whom he caught in bed after seven.
"You damned lazy fox," he said to one unfortunate colonel
who came out to meet him in his pyjamas. "I suppose you
were waiting for me to bring you your breakfast?" To Aldinger he remarked afterwards: "It's a great thing to be a
Field-Marshal and still remember how to talk to them like a
sergeant-major."

His visits to the forward area were no mere perfunctory
inspections. With his keen eye for country and his great mas-
tery of minor tactics, he missed nothing—a machine-gun
badly sited, transport in the wrong *wadi,* mines too obviously
laid, an uncamouflaged O.P. If he were not satisfied with a
position, he would drive out alone a mile or so into the desert,
to look at it with the enemy's eyes. Not infrequently he drew
fire. Then he would return to a flank, so as not to give the
position away. Crawling towards the fort at Acroma, he was
fired on when he was half-way through the minefield. "That
comes of being in a hurry," he said. "I should have moved
more slowly." His attention to their own small problems, his
fertility of tactical ideas, his skill in desert navigation, these
impressed the young officer and the young soldier. He was
one of themselves, a "front-line type."

Moreover, he could talk to them, for he had a great affection for youth. "He was always gay when he was speaking to
young men," said von Esebeck. "He had a smile and a joke
for everyone who seemed to be doing his job. There was
nothing he liked better than to talk with a man from his own
part of the country in the Swabian dialect. He had a very

warm heart," added von Esebeck reflectively, "and more charm than any one I have ever known." This last, from a well-read and sophisticated man, who had seen much more of the world and of "society" than Rommel, was a surprise.

In battle, Rommel was at his best. He was a natural leader and he relied, both instinctively and deliberately, upon personal leadership. As was remarked at the time, he was the first to identify desert war with war at sea, the first to understand that "no admiral ever won a naval battle from a shore base." He had an exceptionally quick brain and an exceptionally quick eye for a military situation. But the reason that he was able to catch so many fleeting opportunities, the secret of his early successes, was that he did not have to wait for information to be filtered back to him through the usual channels of command. He was up to see for himself, in his aircraft, his tank, his armoured car, his Volkswagen or on foot. It was thus that he was able, without any appreciable interval for planning, to turn his reconnaissances in April, 1941, and January, 1942, into victorious offensives. It was thus that he was able to emerge from defeat and almost certain disaster at the end of May, 1942, and to swing the issue of the battle as soon as his supplies were assured. So far as one man can in modern war, he contrived to "ride in the whirlwind and direct the storm."

He has been criticised, by Captain Liddell Hart amongst others, for "dashing about the battlefield" and being too often out of touch with his headquarters. There is some truth in that. Yet Captain Liddell Hart himself admits that he had "a wonderful knack of appearing at some vital spot and giving a decisive impetus to the action at a crucial moment." Major-General Fuller has fewer doubts. "In rapidity of decision and velocity of movement," he writes, "the Germans completely outclassed their enemy and mainly because Rommel, instead of delegating his command to his subordinates, normally took personal command of his armour . . . It was not that the British Generals were less able than the German. It was that their education was out of date. It was built on the trench warfare of 1914-1918 and not on the armoured warfare they were called upon to direct." Rommel was twice defeated when General Auchinleck took over in the forward area and gave his orders on the spot. He escaped defeat in June, 1942, because decisions and communications on our side were too slow.

No one in the desert doubted that personal command paid. But it would be a mistake to picture Rommel as a modern

Prince Rupert, always waving his hat and leading his tanks in headlong charges against the enemy. On the contrary, he was a canny fighter who, more often than our own commanders, refused action except on his own terms. His main contribution to tank tactics was, indeed, his use of a screen of self-propelled anti-tank guns. Behind it, his panzers advanced; behind it, they would withdraw or refuel; through it, they would be launched to the attack, when his guns had taken toll of our armour. Repeatedly our tanks were entrapped and led on to the guns in their attempts to close. Repeatedly, with his own armour concentrated, he caught ours dispersed. He was artful in other ways. His first order on landing in Tripoli was for the construction of dummy tanks. He constantly used his transport to create dust and suggest the presence of his panzer divisions. He started by dragging tarpaulins behind trucks but soon got the idea of fitting propellors behind them. The streams of coloured flares which lit the desert at night were often for our benefit. Captured trucks and carriers were freely employed, not only because the Germans were short of transport but also to create confusion during an advance.

Nor was his system of command so haphazard and slipshod as has been supposed. He did not merely rush about the battlefield giving impromptu orders to individuals or minor formations. Had he done so, he could never have controlled forces of 100,000 men with the success he did. His orders were often given verbally. In the heat of battle, when he thought that the enemy would not have time to profit if they picked them up, he sometimes gave them over the air in clear. But Aldinger assures me that a shorthand note was always taken and that they were confirmed in writing, whenever time allowed. In any case they were short and unequivocal. Rommel never had any doubt about what he wanted and left none in the minds of his subordinates.

Inevitably, he took great personal risks in battle. Again and again he was close to death or capture. Once both his driver and his spare driver were killed alongside him and he had to drive the truck out himself. Rommel was an exceptionally brave man and completely imperturbable under fire but our senior commanders would have done the same had it been the custom. No one could have been braver, on a lower level, than Generals Freyberg, or "Jock" Campbell or "Strafer" Gott. Rommel, like Napoleon and Wellington, took risks because he had to, if he were to direct the battle in person. They were merely occupational hazards. He was the more easily able to accept them because he was comfortably convinced that it was impossible for him to be killed in action.

So were his subordinates. They, however, attributed his immunity to his *"Fingerspitzengefühl,"* that innate sense of what the enemy was about to do. "At noon on November 25th," said General Bayerlein, "we were at the headquarters of the Afrika Korps at Gasr-el-Abid. Suddenly Rommel turned to me and said, 'Bayerlein, I would advise you to get out of this: I don't like it.' An hour later the headquarters were unexpectedly attacked and overrun. The same afternoon we were standing together when he said, 'Let's move a couple of hundred yards to a flank: I think we are going to get shelled here.' One bit of desert was just the same as another. But five minutes after we had moved the shells were falling exactly where we had been standing. Everyone you meet who fought with Rommel in either war will tell you similar stories." Everyone did.

It is easy, in considering, academically, Rommel's method of command, to forget its main purpose and its main effect— the encouragement in his troops of a will to win. On that hangs, in the last analysis, the issue of all battles. Battles may, indeed, be lost by bad generalship or bad staff-work. But no generalship, however good, and still less staff-work, can outweigh lack of morale in the fighting man. *"A la guerre les trois quarts sont des affaires morales,"* said Napoleon, and others have put it higher. Rommel's continual prowling about their forward positions may have been an irritation to his subordinate commanders. It is possible that he could sometimes have been better employed in studying maps and messages at his headquarters than in dashing into the dust and confusion of a desert "dog-fight." That it was his personal inspiration and the physical sight of that stocky, confident figure in action which made the Afrika Korps what it was is certain.

At the time we believed that the Afrika Korps was a *corps d'élite,* hand-picked from volunteers and specially toughened and trained for desert warfare. It was not so. The men were not volunteers. "Otherwise the whole of the German Army would have volunteered," said General von Ravenstein. Nor were they individually selected. They were recruited from depots and units in the usual way and it is not to be supposed that German commanding officers were always more scrupulous than our own in sending their best for extra-regimental duty. There was no special training, except that some of the officers were privileged to be attached to the Italians for instruction. Otherwise the Afrika Korps was just the run-of-the-mill of the Wehrmacht. The young German soldier was strong, willing and well-trained in the use of his weapons. He was disciplined, patriotic and brave. Physically he was not particularly well-suited to the desert. The very young and the very blond could not stand the heat; nor could the veterans of the first war. On the whole, the Germans did not adapt themselves to desert conditions as easily as did the Australians, the New Zealanders, the South Africans, the Indians or the British. Few of them, either officers or men, had ever been out of Europe. They did not understand Africa. For example, it was hard to make them realise that all water was not fit to drink. "There was no proper water purification system," said von Esebeck, "and we suffered much from dysentery as well as from jaundice. Our doctors did not know nearly as much as yours about keeping troops fit in a tropical climate. German field hospitals were inferior to yours and there was, at first, no plasma for blood transfusions. It took us a long time to learn to look after ourselves in the desert."

On the credit side, the Afrika Korps had better weapons, though less transport, and knew better how to use them. It had better prospects of leave. It was better supplied with newspapers, such as its own *Oase*. It was homogeneous, whereas the Eighth Army was always a very mixed bag. It arrived in Africa in good heart. All this admitted, it was Rommel who, almost at once, by personal influence and example, by force of character, by taking more risks than his troops, converted it into that tough, truculent, resilient fighting force we knew. Rommel *was* the Afrika Korps, to his own men as well as to his enemy. It was he who made them bold, self-confident and even arrogant in battle. It was he who taught them to pull the last ounce out of themselves and never to admit that they were beaten. It was because they were the Afrika Korps that, even when they were taken prisoner, they marched down to the docks at Suez with their heads high, still whistling "We march against England to-day." In Germany in 1949 they still carry their palm-tree brassard in their pocketbooks. If you ask them whether they were in North Africa they take pride in answering: "Yes, I was in the Afrika Korps: I fought with Rommel." Good-luck to them, for they fought well and, as the Germans say, the next best thing to a good friend is a good enemy. It is a pity they were not fighting in a better cause.

Idolised by the Afrika Korps, Rommel was revered some way this side of idolatry by his generals. From all their accounts, he was a hard and difficult man to deal with. In battle he put out the most sensitive antennae to the reactions of the enemy: he was not so sensitive to the feelings of his senior officers. He had a rough tongue and could be brutal. He was impatient. He would not see what he did not want to see. He would not have his orders questioned. He could not bear to be told that anything was impossible. He had a bad habit of going over the heads of commanders and giving orders direct to subordinates. A still worse one was that of dragging his Chief of Staff with him wherever he went and leaving no one at headquarters with authority to make a decision. In action he was inclined to occupy himself with details, such as the capture of General Cunningham, which did not strictly concern a supreme commander. Out of the line he was unsociable. "Of course he had not had quite the same early advantages as most German Field-Marshals," explained, deprecatingly, one of his generals, around whom one could still detect a lingering aura of cavalry messes and country estates, of full-dress uniforms and balls and the visits of minor royalty.

Such was the criticism. The grounds for it were inherent both in Rommel himself and in his method of command. He was a man who insisted on "running his own show." It was inevitable that he should often overrule his subordinate commanders. It was his nature to do so with little ceremony. It was equally inevitable that senior German officers should dislike a system practised in the past by Napoleon but outmoded in modern war, if only because in modern war direct personal command is seldom possible. To do them justice, the criticism was invariably and immediately qualified. Rommel was the bravest of the brave; he had a sixth sense in battle; he was wonderful with troops; when he had quieted down it was always possible to talk to him; if he gave orders over one's head he would apologise afterwards; he was generous with praise and would admit when he had been wrong. Could they think of any one better for desert war, I asked them. No, they all agreed, nor of any one half as good.

II. NOSTR'ALLEATI ITALIANI

The Afrika Korps was homogeneous. The Axis forces in North Africa were not entirely so. There were also the Italians. Poor Italians, they have almost taken the place in military legend of our own "oldest allies" in the first war. Rommel naturally had his stock of stories which were retailed to Manfred, with additions by Aldinger. There was, for example, the story of the attack which the Italians were persuaded to launch at Tobruk. When they were half-way across and out of reach of the Germans, they dropped their arms and put their hands up. Suddenly they turned about and came scampering back. *"Mamma mia!"* they explained breathlessly, "those aren't English, they're Australians!" Again, Rommel was visiting their trenches when the Australians made a local attack. *"Santa Maria!"* cried the Italians and fell on their knees. "I'm going to give you a bit of advice," said Rommel to the Italian officer in command. "Stop them praying and persuade them to shoot. . . . This is where I leave you. Good-bye!"

The story that the Australians had sent back Italian prisoners with the seats cut out of their breeches and a message to the Germans to replace them with an equivalent number of the Afrika Korps, I regarded with some distrust. I remembered that the Germans were said to have done exactly the same with our oldest allies after an attempted raid in 1918 at Merville. In that case, however, their backsides were painted blue and the message from the Germans was to the effect that when they wanted specimens they would come and collect them. The British need not, therefore, bother to send them over. There was a suspicious similarity about those stories and I should not be surprised if they are as old as war itself.

On the whole Rommel agreed with the Italian soldier who said to him: "Why don't you Germans do the fighting, General, and let us Italians build the roads?" But he never thought that they were all cowards. The Ariete Armoured Division fought very well at El Gubi and elsewhere: Brescia was not too bad. There was a good battalion commanded by a Major Montemuro. The pioneers were all good and worked well, even under fire. Properly officered, given decent equipment and a prospect of home leave, he felt that something might have been made of them. (General Speidel told me that the northern Italian divisions of General Garibaldi's 8th Italian Army, to which he was Chief of Staff, fought well in Russia under much worse conditions.) The equipment, like the officers, was worthless. The early Italian tanks were only "sardine-tins" and many tanks and armoured cars had no radio sets and had to communicate by flags. Since this must have been known to Mussolini and since, as appears from Ciano's Diaries, he had the profoundest comtempt for his unfortunate fellow-countrymen and for all his generals, it remains a mystery how he expected them to "live like lions." Nevertheless, though no lions, some of them had a slightly pathetic admiration for Rommel. At a meeting of his Council of Ministers on February 7th, 1942, Mussolini, after his usual attack on the Italian generals, described how "the Bersaglieri are enthusiastic about Rommel. They give him their feather and carry him in triumph on their shoulders, shouting that with him they are sure to reach Alexandria." The incident may have been embellished for the occasion. Nevertheless, Rommel had a paternal way with Italian "other ranks" which made him *simpatico* to them.

To the Italian High Command and to Italian officers he was not *simpatico* in the least. The officers as a class he considered contemptible. He was especially horrified to learn that there were three scales of rations for Italian troops in the desert, one for officers, one for N.C.O.s and one for other ranks, in sharply descending order. That the officers did not attempt to look after their men, he attributed to the fact that they had "no military tradition." But that did not excuse, in his eyes, their too evident reluctance to acquire one. (He made an exception of the Air Force, which produced some dashing fighter-pilots.) For their part, Italian officers regarded him as a rough, rude man, always demanding impossibilities.

Since he was always nominally under Italian command, disputes on the higher levels were inevitable. General Garibaldi, with whom he first had to deal, he found a genial old gentleman, quite a good soldier and, what was more important to Rommel, prepared to let him have his way. General Bastico, whom he christened "Bombastico," was more troublesome. Though General Bayerlein described him as "nix" and "nul," Bastico had ideas of his own. After the Sidi Rezegh battle in December, 1941, he came over with Kesselring to Gazala and quarrelled with Rommel about his intention of withdrawing to Agedabia. It would have a very bad effect in Italy and might cause a revolution. Rommel replied that he could guarantee only one thing, that he was going to get the Afrika Korps out. If the Italians liked to stay where they were, that was their affair. Conversely, there was Bastico's attempt to prevent the advance into Egypt, already mentioned in the last chapter.

Then there was General Count Ugo Cavallero, Chief of

Staff after the resignation of Badoglio in December, 1940. Because he spoke German as well as Italian and gave the impression of a competent staff officer, Rommel was at first inclined to trust him. He was also dependent on him for his supplies. Ciano paints Cavallero's portrait with the loving care which one Italian gangster is always ready to lavish on another. "A perfect bazaar-trader who has found the secret way to Mussolini's heart and is ready to follow the path of lies, intrigue and imbroglio. He must be watched; a man who can bring great trouble to us. . . . Among the many insincere individuals that life puts into circulation every day, Cavallero easily carries off the palm. . . . To-day, with his artificial, hypocritical and servile optimism, he was unbearable. . . . A shameless liar. . . . He would bow to the public lavatories if this would advance him. . . . A dangerous clown, ready to follow every German whim without dignity . . . the servant of the Germans . . . deliberately deceiving the Duce." When Mussolini proposed, after Rommel's promotion to Field-Marshal, to make Cavallero one also, because otherwise he was "between Rommel and Kesselring, like Christ between the thieves," Ciano protested. "Bastico's promotion," he said, "will make people laugh, Cavallero's will make them indignant."

Lastly came the Duce himself. To any one still inclined to suppose that only dictatorships can get things done, because only dictators know their own minds, it is instructive to study Mussolini's attitude towards Rommel, as recorded by Ciano. In May, 1941, having read an order of the day which Rommel is said to have addressed to the Italian divisional commanders, threatening to denounce them to military tribunals, he is considering a personal protest to Hitler. On December 5th, 1941, he is "so proud of having given the command to the Germans. . . ." On December 17th, when the battle went wrong, "he blames Rommel who, he believes, spoilt the situation with his recklessness." By February 7th, 1942, after Rommel's counter-attack, he "extols Rommel, who is always in his tank at the head of his attacking columns." On May 26th, "Mussolini now interests himself only in the coming offensive in Libya and he is definitely optimistic. He maintains that Rommel will arrive at the Delta unless he is stopped, not by the British but by our own generals." On June 22nd, he is "in very good humour and preparing to go to Africa. In reality he was the man behind the decisive attack, even against the opinion of the High Command. Now he fears that they may not realise the magnitude of the success and therefore fail to take advantage of it. He only trusts Rommel. . . ." Four days later he is "pleased over the progress of operations in Libya but angry that the battle is identified with Rommel, thus appearing more as a German than an Italian victory. Also Rommel's promotion to Field-Marshal, 'which Hitler evidently made to accentuate the German character of the battle,' causes the Duce much pain. Naturally he takes it out on Graziani 'who has always been seventy feet underground in a Roman tomb at Cirene, while Rommel knows how to lead his troops with the personal example of the general who lives in his tank.'" On July 21st, he is in a good humour and is so certain of reaching the Delta that he has left his personal baggage in Libya. Still, he has "naturally been absorbing the anti-Rommel talk of the Italian commander in Libya." On the 23rd, he has "realised that even Rommel's strategy has its ups-and-downs." By September 9th, he is "angry with Rommel," who has accused Italian officers of revealing plans to the enemy. On September 27th, he is "convinced that Rommel will not come back. He finds him physically and morally shaken." By January 5th, 1943, he has "only harsh words for Cavallero and for 'that madman Rommel, who thinks of nothing but retreating in Tunisia.'"

No Cavallero, Rommel was hardly up to dealing with dictators. He liked Mussolini when he first met him, precisely because he seemed to be a man who knew his own mind and could give an order. Naïvely he imagined that Mussolini was his friend. He did not realise how quickly Il Duce's friendship shifted with the breeze of fortune. Fortunately Rommel could see a joke, even against himself. In 1942 he was summoned to Rome to discuss supplies. When he entered that enormous room in the Palazzo Venezia he spotted, lying on the immense desk, the insignia of the Italian order for valour. Rightly he guessed that it was intended for him. The discussion grew heated. When Rommel rashly said something disparaging about the Italian navy, Mussolini glared at him. Then he seized the order, pulled open a drawer, flung it in and locked the desk. "It was a beautiful thing," said Rommel ruefully. "Why couldn't I have kept my silly mouth shut for another ten minutes? He couldn't very well have asked me to hand it back."

There was something to be said on the Italian side, however. Tact was not Rommel's strong point. When he was about to make his counter-attack in January, 1942, he did not tell his Italian superiors about it, for fear there should be a "leak." He merely instructed his "Q" staff to pin up the orders for it in the Italian back-area messes after the advance had started. Since this was the first news the Italian General Staff had had of it they were understandably indignant. Rommel was sent for. He replied that he was in the front line but would be glad to see General Bastico there. General Bastico did not appear. Some days later Rommel was told that he proposed to withdraw all Italian troops. Rommel said that it was all the same to him if he did. This cost him his first decoration—and the affection of General Bastico.

Feeling also ran high on the Italian side over the delicate matter of the division of loot. There was in existence an official agreement, drafted, one can only suppose, by Cavallero, under which the Italians were to hand over to the Germans everything they captured in Russia while the Germans were to surrender to the Italians the spoils of war in North Africa. It is unlikely that the first head of the agreement was often invoked: the Italians complained bitterly of the non-observance by their allies of the second. "There is violent indignation against the Germans because of their behaviour in Libya," writes Ciano in the summer of 1942. "They have grabbed all the booty. They have thrust their claws everywhere, placed German guards over the booty and woe to any one who comes near." No one can squeal more shrilly than the hijacked mobster and it was fortunate for Rommel that he was too much of a big shot and too well protected to be taken for a ride. What made Ciano even more furious was that "the only one who has succeeded in getting plenty for himself is Cavallero. . . ."

The Axis allies were not, therefore, the best of bedfellows. Nevertheless, in summing up the Italians to Manfred, Rommel made a not ungenerous and refreshingly un-German remark. "Certainly they are no good at war," he said. "But one must not judge everyone in the world only by his qualities as a soldier: otherwise we should have no civilisation."

We English told much the same stories against the Italians. We were naturally bitter about having been stabbed in the back by our allies of the first war and were not inclined to differentiate between the Italian people and the regime under which they lived. In battle we regarded them as the "poor relations" and camp-followers of the Germans. But officers of the Indian divisions remembered that they had fought well at Keren. Later, many thousands of us who were "on the run" in

Italy and were sheltered, fed and helped on our way by the *contadini*, at the risk of their lives, formed a very different opinion of the courage of individual Italians and their wives and daughters and felt that it would not be long before the tradition of friendship between our two countries would be restored. I, for one, shall never forget Frederico and Antonio Alberici, in whose house, a mile from the prison-camp, I lived gaily and happily for weeks, mostly under the wine-casks, *nella cantina*, while the Germans passed the front door and Farinacci, over the radio, nightly threatened death to any Italians who should befriend us. Nor shall I forget the enchanted summer, our first in Europe since the war, that we spent at Tremezzo and the friends we made there. The Italians may not be a military nation but they have a lively intelligence, gaiety and good hearts. Rommel was right to see that it is such qualities which constitute civilisation—though a rougher soldiery may still be needed to defend it.

III. CIVIL WAR

Towards his enemy, Rommel's attitude was one of friendly if sometimes suspicious hostility. Like all Germans, he resented at first our employment of Indian divisions against Europeans, until he encountered 4th Indian Division and discovered that the Indian soldier was at least as well-disciplined and "correct" as any in the desert. He could not resist a mild sneer, for propaganda purposes, at the "coloured English" who accompanied the South Africans, though he knew very well that they were non-combatants. The Australians he considered rough, particularly with the Italians, but it was the sort of roughness which amused him and did not show "a bad heart." He ranked Australians highly as individual fighting-men but thought that they were inclined to get out of hand. He would have liked a division of them but remarked that an army of Australians would not be an easy command. The South Africans he considered good material but too raw, though he gave credit to their armoured cars and acknowledged that they later fought very well at Alamein. For the New Zealanders he had a great and lasting admiration. They were, he always maintained to Manfred, Aldinger and others, the finest troops on our side.

The British he respected—as promising amateurs. He even went so far as to admit that, for small, independent operations, requiring great personal initiative, such as those of the

Long Range Desert Group and the S.A.S. (Special Air Service), they were better than the Germans, who would not have had the same confidence or shown so much enterprise far behind the enemy lines. (It is fair to recall that the L.R.D.G. contained a high proportion of New Zealanders though it was organised and commanded by British regular officers.) British regular formations were, he thought, stubborn and brave in defence but insufficiently trained. He made an exception of 7th Armoured Division, particularly of the two Rifle battalions of the Support Group, the 11th Hussars and the artillery. Nevertheless he thought that in tank actions our armoured units and even single tanks were far too much inclined to go bald-headed into the attack. His criticism that we used armour in penny packets and thus invited its destruction in detail has been echoed by British military critics. The British system of command he naturally thought too slow, involved and clogged with paper. In spite of many inquiries I cannot discover that he expressed any opinion about any individual British general except General Wavell, whose campaign against the Italians would, he declared, always be studied as a supreme example of bold planning and daring execution with small resources. His assessment of his opponents was thus strictly professional and unemotional. He certainly did not hate or even dislike them: for New Zealanders, individually and collectively, he had almost an affection.

"The war in North Africa was a gentleman's war," said General Johann Cramer, last commander of the Afrika Korps, to a correspondent of *The Times,* when it was all over. Rommel also took pride in the clean record of his troops (and of ours), for he had strong views on correct conduct and the observance of the soldier's code. There was nothing remarkable about that. They were shared by the great majority of German regular officers, particularly those who were serving before 1933. In the higher ranks, there were only a few exceptions, the Keitels and the Jodls, who had sold out so completely to Hitler that they were prepared to transmit, even if they did not approve, his most outrageous orders.

To us this survival of chivalry came as a surprise. Knowing nothing of the feud between the Party and the Wehrmacht, of the Nazis' jealousy of the Army, of the contempt of the officer class for the "brown scum," of the long, if weak-kneed, opposition of many generals to their Führer, we naturally lumped all Germans together. In war it was perhaps as well to do so. Nations, by and large, get the governments they deserve. If they put up with Hitlers and Mussolinis they must take the consequences. Their enemies cannot be expected to draw nice distinctions between the wearers of different varieties of the same uniform. Nevertheless it can now be conceded that, whatever it may have done in Poland and Russia, the regular German Army in Africa fought a clean war. Strangely enough, it fought a cleaner one than in 1914-18. Perhaps because there was less hand-to-hand fighting, perhaps because the officers were on better terms with their men, perhaps because General von Seeckt and his successors had established a better tradition, there was, in the desert, none of the killing of prisoners which one remembers, on both sides, in World War I. (The fact that it was much easier to be taken prisoner in the desert, through no fault of one's own, may also have had something to do with it.)

At any rate, it was quickly discovered by the British that the Afrika Korps proposed to fight according to the rules. For this the whole credit was given to Rommel. Since the Afrika Korps looked up to him for an example in everything, he undoubtedly deserved a large share of it. However, he was lucky. "Thank God, we had no S.S. divisions in the desert," said General Bayerlein, "or Heaven knows what would have happened: it would have been a very different sort of war." He went on to tell me, what I for one had not realised, that, while a German general might have control of S.S. troops in the field during actual operations, he had no powers of discipline over them whatsoever. His only remedy, even against an "other rank," was to report him, through the usual channels, to Himmler in person. The result was likely to be unsatisfactory. "Had the July 20th plot succeeded," he added, "there would have been civil war between the S.S. divisions and the Army in Italy."

The Afrika Korps did not beat up prisoners. On the contrary, after the first rough pounce, it treated them with almost old-world courtesy. At Gambut, soon after the opening of the May, 1942 battle, I met an Army Film Unit photographer, a Scot, who had just managed to escape after an hour or two in enemy hands. He was newly arrived from England, this was his first experience of action and he was highly indignant. "What like of people are these bluidy Germans, sir?" he asked me. "I wad never ha' credited it. A German officer, an officer Ah'm tellin' ye, actually took ma camera off me an' wouldna give it back. . . . Never mind," he added more cheerfully, "Ah hae his receipt for it." So he had, on the back of an envelope, with name, rank and date. He proposed to look for the Oberleutnant after the war.

This was my favourite story, until I had the misfortune to be captured myself. I could then cap it with the young German who, after searching me, politely handed back a gold cigarette-case which he found in the pocket of my bush-shirt. He apologised for taking my field-glasses but explained that these were *Militärgut* whereas the cigarette-case was *privat*. Comparing notes with others in a prison-camp I found that no one had any serious cause for complaint until after being handed over to the Italians. Since I still have my cigarette-case, I must have been lucky in my Italians also. I tried, however, not to expose them to the same temptation.

Misunderstandings there were from time to time between Rommel and ourselves and some of them had unpleasant repercussions upon prisoners. Such misunderstandings were quite genuine and the fault was not always on the German side. For example, we published an order to the effect that prisoners should not be given a meal before being interrogated. The intention was innocent enough. A prisoner is usually somewhat shaken when he is first captured and if he is interrogated immediately he may give away information of value. If, however, he has a meal and perhaps a cigarette, he has time to collect himself. The order meant no more than that the meal should be postponed until after the investigation. The assumption was, I presume, that this might involve a delay of an hour or two.

It was nevertheless unwise to put such an order on paper and still more unwise to circulate it in forward areas where it might fall into German hands. I did not realise quite how unwise until I reached Tmimi aerodrome, having spent twelve hours standing up in a truck, under a hot sun, without food or water. Having been captured twenty-four hours earlier and having had nothing to eat or drink for six or seven hours before that I was looking forward to an evening meal and above all to water. We were paraded and addressed by a German officer in English. "I regret, gentlemen," he said, "that we are unable to give you anything to eat or drink. As your orders are that German prisoners shall be starved and deprived of water until they reach Cairo for interrogation, I am obliged to treat you in the same way. You will get nothing until you reach Benghazi and have been interrogated, unless the British Government see fit to cancel the order. They have been asked to do so." Presumably the British Government did, since we were given a meal and a drink at Derna next morning.

More serious might have been the consequences of an order found on a British commando officer captured during an unsuccessful raid on Tobruk in August, 1942. Whatever its intention, as translated into Italian it gave the impression that, if prisoners could not conveniently be removed, they were to be killed. I have not seen the original text. I can only assume that it stressed that the infliction of casualties on the enemy was more important than the capture of prisoners. The distinction is a little subtle, even in English. Staff officers who draft such orders should remember that fine shades of meaning do not always survive translation. They should also remember that all orders are liable to fall into enemy hands and that those who suffer are their own countrymen in captivity. Many were manacled for months after the Dieppe raid, when our own orders for the handcuffing of German prisoners were captured.

Hitler's famous or infamous order of October 18th, 1942, was at least unequivocal:

From now on [said paragraph 3], all enemies on so-called Commando missions in Europe or Africa challenged by German troops, even if they are to all appearances soldiers in uniform or demolition troops, whether armed or unarmed, in battle or in flight, are to be slaughtered to the last man. It does not make any difference whether they are landed from ships and aeroplanes for their actions, or whether they are dropped by parachutes. Even if these individuals, when found, should apparently be prepared to give themselves up, no pardon is to be granted to them on principle. . . .

This order does not apply [said paragraph 5], to the treatment of any enemy soldiers who, in the course of normal hostilities (large-scale offensive actions, landing operations and airborne operations), are captured in open battle or give themselves up.

I will hold responsible under Military Law [added the final paragraph], for failing to carry out this order, all commanders and officers who either have neglected their duty of instructing the troops about this order or acted against this order where it is to be executed.

The order was signed "Adolf Hitler" and was, therefore, "top level."

On June 18th, 1946, General Siegfried Westphal was questioned about it at Nuremberg:

Question: You were on the African front?
Answer: More than a year and a half.
Question: How was the war conducted there?
Answer: I can answer in a sentence: it was conducted in a chivalrous and irreproachable manner.
Question: Who was your chief?
Answer: Marshal Rommel.
Question: Did he ever order or sanction violation of the rules of war?
Answer: Never.
Question: What position did you hold with him?
Answer: I was the head of the Operations Section and afterwards his Chief of Staff.
Question: You were, then, always in contact with him?
Answer: I was in contact with him always, both personally and on service matters.
Question: Do you know the order issued by Hitler on October 18th, 1942?
Answer: Yes.
Question: Did you receive this order?
Answer: Yes, we received it in the desert near Sidi Barrani, from a liaison officer.
Question: How did Marshal Rommel behave on receipt of this order?
Answer: Marshal Rommel and I read it standing beside our truck. I then immediately proposed that we should not publish it. We burnt it at once, where we stood. Our reasons were as follows: The motives of the order, which I think you will find in the introductory paragraph,* were clear in themselves. We knew the Brit-

* "1. Our enemies have for a long time been adopting methods, in carrying on the war, which are not in accordance with the International Conventions of Geneva. Particularly brutal and stealthy is the behavior of the members of the so-called Commandos which, as has been proved, are themselves in part recruited from circles of released criminals in the enemy countries. Captured orders prove that they are instructed not only to shackle prisoners, but even to simply kill defenceless prisoners the moment they think that, in the future pursuit of the mission, these prisoners constitute a burden, or otherwise an inconvenience. Finally orders have been found in which the killing of prisoners has been ordered as a matter of principle."

ish orders for hand-to-hand combat. We knew the slogan of El Alamein: "Kill the Germans wherever you find them" and various other aggravations of the war. We had also captured an order, issued by a British armoured brigade, according to which prisoners must not be given anything to drink. Nevertheless, we did not wish this order to reach our troops, for that would have led to an aggravation of the war of which it would have been impossible to foresee the consequences. That was why the message was burnt ten minutes after it was received. . . . But it was only on another continent that one could have got away with so blatant an act of disobedience. I do not think that one could have done it in the east or the west.

In fact, Rommel was very far from being the only German general who ignored this and similar orders.

General Westphal was then questioned about the strange case of "the nephew of Field-Marshal Alexander":

Question: Could you briefly run through the case of the commando action in which the nephew of Field-Marshal Alexander took part?

Answer: In the autumn of 1942, a close relation of Field-Marshal Alexander was taken prisoner behind the German lines. He was wearing an Afrika Korps cap and was armed with a German pistol. He had thus put himself outside the rules of war. Marshal Rommel gave the order that he should be treated like any other prisoner. The Marshal thought that he did not understand what might have been the consequences of his conduct.

(What Rommel actually said when someone proposed that this officer should be shot, as he could legitimately have been, was: "What, shoot General Alexander's nephew? You damned fool, you might as well make a present of another couple of divisions to the British Army!" The officer in question, who was not a nephew but a cousin of General Alexander [now Field-Marshal Lord Alexander], and bears the same name, tells me that he relied on the Junker tradition of the solidarity of the military caste and took the view that a German general was unlikely to order the execution of a close relation of another general. Though Rommel was no Junker, the event proved him right.)

There are endless anecdotes about Rommel's treatment of

our prisoners, all, so far as I have heard, to his credit. For perhaps the best I am indebted to Brigadier G. H. Clifton, D.S.O., M.C., at the time of his encounters with Rommel a captured New Zealand brigade commander.

Brigadier Clifton, christened "the flying kiwi," was a born escaper. When he joined us in Campo PG 29 he at once evolved a very bold plan which came tragically near to success. He lowered himself at night out of a second-storey window into the smallest possible patch of shadow in the angle of a wall. The wall was actually on a sentry's beat. He stood face to the wall until the sentry moved away and then slid across the yard on his stomach and under a barbed wire fence. Travelling at high speed across country, he reached the nearest railway station, Ponte d'Olio, and took the first train in the morning to Milan. From the main station he crossed over by tram to the north station for the Como line and arrived in Como some time before he was missed at morning roll-call. At Como he made his fatal mistake. He proposed to follow the road past the Villa d'Este, as I did myself later on, and then cross over the mountains into Switzerland. To save time he hired a carriage at the station. When he was paying it off, there was a dispute about the fare. Two carabinieri, who had already been watching him with some suspicion, strolled over. That evening he was brought back to us.

Removed to Campo PG 5, the "Straf" camp for inveterate escapers, we heard that he had been seen standing on the roof, fired at by sentries from all sides. On his way to Germany, seated between two guards in a railway carriage, he contrived to dive through a window while the train was running. He was shot at by the guards, severely wounded in the thigh and spent many months in a hospital, where he was well cared for by a German doctor who still writes to him. On March 22nd, 1945, he escaped again from a camp in Silesia and on April 15th, having been flown across the Pacific by the United States Air Force, he was back home in Auckland, New Zealand. When I met Rommel's widow, almost the first question she asked me was, "Did you know Brigadier Clifton? Where is he and did he manage to escape? My husband always hoped he would get out of Italy. He had a great opinion of him."

Here, then, is Brigadier Clifton's story:

"In the early hours of September 4th, 1942, I drove out into 'No-man's-land' south of Alameyil Ridge, to tidy up someone else's night battle which had gone astray. It was before first light and a most confusing situation. As a result, we drove up to the wrong people, while looking for a forward company of my own brigade. The enemy concerned were Italian parachutists from the Folgere Division and, for a few minutes, it looked as though we might return with fifty Italians instead of staying as their prisoners. The argument was settled against us, however, by the intervention of a German artillery officer who was acting as F.O.O. about 100 yards away. He came down, told the Italians not to be so-and-so fools and we went 'into the bag.'

"About two hours later I arrived back at my old headquarters in the Kaponga Box, now occupied by a swarm of Italians and a German paratroop battalion in reserve. It was only 7 o'clock in the morning but it seemed a lifetime since I left, expecting to return for breakfast.

"Ten minutes later there was great excitement and an Intelligence Officer came across and told me that Rommel was arriving. Sure enough, three or four reconnaissance vehicles came round the corner, headed by an enormous staff car, with Rommel in person sitting up at the back. He stepped out to much saluting and clicking of heels. I noticed that he addressed himself first to the Italian colonel who was the senior officer in the area.

"After a short discussion he then summoned the German major commanding the paratroops and a few minutes later I was called over and so met the famous Rommel for the first time. He was a short, stocky figure, running to waistline and obviously rather sensitive about it, but full of self-assurance and drive. Speaking in German, although he evidently understood English, he proceeded to harangue me about the 'gangster' methods of the New Zealanders. It appeared that we had bayoneted the German wounded at Minqarqaim in the night battle behind Matruh and he was very much annoyed about it. He said that if we wanted to fight rough, so could they, and that any further action of this sort on our part would be answered by immediate reprisals.

"As the nearest New Zealander available for such reprisals, it became a rather personal matter to me. I was, however, able to explain our point of view over the occurrences of that famous night-attack. Our first wave, going through in the dark, caught the Germans by surprise. Some of them, lying on the ground, had fired or thrown bombs after the first company had passed. As a result, the supports following on simply stuck every man who failed to stand up and surrender. It is quite likely that some of the Germans were bayoneted several times by people in passing.

"I explained what had happened. Whether it was the way I put it across I do not know but Rommel said, 'Well, that is reasonable and could happen in a night battle but . . .' He then went on to describe an incident in which a German wounded officer had been thrown into a burning truck.

"After some discussion on this alleged incident he asked, 'Why are you New Zealanders fighting? This is an European war, not yours. Are you here for the sport?' Realising that he really meant this, and never having previously faced up to putting into words the self-evident fact that if Britain fought we fought too, I held up my hands with the fingers closed and said, 'The British Commonwealth fights together. If you attack England you attack New Zealand and Australia too.' 'What about Ireland?' asked Rommel quickly. I had the answer to that one. A week or so earlier we had been given the figures of Southern Ireland volunteers in the fighting services. I believe their percentage to total population equalled any nation in the Commonwealth.

"Rommel did not comment on this, wished me good luck and off he went to the battle, where his last offensive in Egypt was being very roughly handled. Six days later I escaped from Matruh but that is another story of a long walk and bad luck, which finished when I was recaptured on September 15th by three young panzer officers hunting gazelle ten miles west of the front at El Alamein. In due course, after being shot up by our own Hurri-bombers, a most embarrassing interlude, I was dumped at Rommel's headquarters for the second time.

"The Marshal deigned to see me again, accompanied by the three lads who had picked me up and were expecting seven days special leave to Germany as a reward. (Incidentally, they were disappointed.) Rommel once more opened the conversation with strong comments on our 'gangster' methods, occasioned this time by a Flying Fortress high-level bombing attack on a hospital-ship leaving Tobruk. He then said, 'I do not blame you for attempting to escape, it is your duty and I would have done the same if I were in your position.'

"Appreciating his increasing waistline and tight boots and breeches, I replied: 'I am quite sure you would try, sir, but I do not think you could have walked as far as I did.' (More than 100 miles in less than five days on one can of water.) Rommel came back very quickly with, 'No, I would have had more sense and borrowed a motor-car.' Trick to him. 'So would I, but with only twenty seconds start there was not much time, though we had a suitable vehicle marked down.' He then added that I was a nuisance and that any further attempt at a break would finish by my being shot while escaping. However, he decided to get rid of me quickly by plane from Daba early next morning direct to Rome.

"Germans are literally minded, in addition to having a tragic lack of humour. Rommel impressed me as an outstanding exception and that impression grew stronger with every senior German officer I had the misfortune to meet. On the occasions when he met our troops either as prisoners or wounded he greeted them as one soldier meeting others and treated them very fairly. Brigadier Hargest, who was captured at Sidi Azeiz in late November, 1941, and was taken into Bardia by Rommel, formed the same impression. I think he comments on it in his book, *Farewell Campo 12*." (Brigadier Hargest was pulled up by Rommel for not saluting. "That did not prevent him from congratulating me on the fighting quality of my men," he wrote.)

Clifton's story is creditable to both sides. There is a somewhat macabre footnote to it which shows that Rommel was not the only German with a rough sense of humour. During the first interview, while Clifton was being interrogated, the interpreter, Major Burchardt, who spoke excellent English, himself intervened. "You were in Crete, I think, Brigadier Clifton?" he said. "So was I, with the German paratroops. At the end of an action I came across the body of one of your native soldiers, Maoris you call them, don't you? Alongside it were 27 ears, on a string. They *may*, of course, have been British ears; they *may* have been Cretan ears. But *we* were inclined to believe that they were German ears." Burchardt smiled. Clifton did not. The anecdote may have been well-founded but he felt that it was ill-timed.

Hospital-ships were a sore point with Rommel. He was indignant when he heard that the Royal Navy was pulling them into Malta for examination, furious when it was reported that they had been attacked by the R.A.F. at sea. Drafting a strong note of protest, he was somewhat shaken to learn that an Italian general, frightened of flying the Mediterranean, had taken a passage in a hospital-ship as a stretcher-case and had been removed, unwounded, at Malta. His final disillusionment came at a conference in July before El Alamein. Rommel was complaining bitterly about being halted for lack of petrol. Three tankers had just been sunk in two days. Cavallero reassured him. Other means had already been adopted to keep him supplied. Petrol was being sent over in the double-bottoms of hospital-ships! Rommel turned on him. "How can I protest against British interference with hospital-ships when you do things like that?" he demanded. Cavallero was surprised and hurt.

To sum up the spirit in which the desert war was fought, I may quote General von Ravenstein. "When I reached Cairo," he said, "I was received very courteously by General Auchinleck's A.D.C. Then I was taken to see General Auchinleck himself in his office. He shook hands with me and said: 'I know you well by name. You and your division have fought with chivalry. I wish to treat you as well as possible.'

"Before I left Cairo I heard that General Campbell had been awarded the Victoria Cross. I asked and obtained permission to write to him. I still have a copy of my letter if it would interest you."

The letter read:

Abbasia, February 10th, 1942

DEAR MAJOR-GENERAL CAMPBELL,

I have read in the paper that you have been my brave adversary in the tank battle of Sidi-Rezegh on November 21-22, 1941. It was my 21st Panzer Division which has fought in these hot days with the 7th Armoured Division, for whom I have the greatest admiration. Your 7th Support Group of Royal Artillery too has made the fighting very hard for us and I remember all the many iron that flew near the aerodrome around our ears.

The German comrades congratulate you with warm heart for your award of the Victoria Cross.

During the war your enemy, but with high respect.

VON RAVENSTEIN

"Jock" Campbell was killed soon afterwards, when his car overturned near Buq-Buq. But he lived long enough to receive the letter and to have copies of it posted on battery order boards, soon after the presentation parade at which he received the V.C.

There are two opinions on the question of chivalry in war. General Eisenhower holds the other. "When von Arnim was brought through Algiers on his way to captivity," he writes in *Crusade in Europe*, "some members of my staff felt that I should observe the custom of bygone days and allow him a call on me. The custom had its origin in the fact that mercenary soldiers of old had no real enmity towards their opponents. Both sides fought for the love of a fight, out of a sense of duty or, more probably, for money. A captured commander of the eighteenth century was likely to be, for weeks or months, the honoured guest of his captor. The tradition that all professional soldiers are comrades-in-arms has, in tattered form, persisted to this day.

"For me, World War II was far too personal a thing to entertain such feelings. Daily as it progressed there grew within me the conviction that, as never before in a war between many nations, the forces that stood for human good and men's rights were this time confronted by a completely evil conspiracy with which no compromise could be tolerated. Because only by the utter destruction of the Axis was a decent world possible, the war became for me a crusade. . . .

"In this specific instance, I told my Intelligence Officer to get any information he possibly could out of the captured generals but that, so far as I was concerned, I was interested only in those who were not yet captured. None would be allowed to call on me. I pursued the same practice to the end of the war. Not until Field-Marshal Jodl signed the surrender terms at Rheims in 1945 did I ever speak to a German general and even then my only words were that he would be held personally and completely responsible for the carrying out of the surrender terms."

General Eisenhower is a wise and generous man, with whom no one would willingly disagree. His attitude is a perfectly logical and intelligible one. Nevertheless, there are some who feel that even tattered traditions may be worth preserving if, when wars are over, victors and vanquished still have to live and work together in the same world.*

* Not long before his death, the late Field-Marshal Earl Wavell sent to Frau Rommel a copy of his lectures on generalship, inscribed "To the memory of a brave, chivalrous and skilful opponent." As such he would have treated Rommel had he fallen into his hands, for that was our experience of Rommel in Libya. But no one who knew Lord Wavell would suppose that his detestation of the flag under which Rommel served was any less deep than that of General Eisenhower—or my own. Both points of view are defensible and interminably arguable. I happen to agree with Field-Marshals Wavell and Auchinleck. But I am ready to admit that General Eisenhower may be right.

CHAPTER 9

To Tunis and Surrender

We left Rommel, at the end of June, knocking, not very peremptorily, at the gates of Alexandria. He was now up against something hitherto unknown in the desert, a position that could not be turned. The British right flank rested on the sea, its left, forty miles south, on the "impassable" quicksands of the Qattara Depression. (Randall Plunkett of the Guides Cavalry found himself unpopular with the planning staff in Cairo when he succeeded in bringing his armoured cars across them from Siwa during the retreat.) Moreover, the position had been more thoroughly prepared for defence than the Germans imagined.

The Eighth Army was, however, very far from being entirely on the defensive. The general impression in England, even to-day, seems to be that, having fallen back completely routed from the frontier, it remained cowed and cowering at El Alamein while a panic-stricken staff in Cairo burnt mountains of paper and made ready for a retreat into Palestine or East Africa. Then, so runs the popular legend, General Montgomery arrived out of the skies and, having re-created or, indeed, created it, at once turned defeat into victory. The legend is unfair to the Eighth Army: it is also contrary to the facts. At the beginning of July there was certainly "a bit of a flap." On what was locally known as Ash Wednesday, papers were indeed burnt. Some civilians and women were evacuated. The fleet left Alexandria, where it would have been too much exposed to bombing. In common prudence, preparations were made for the defence of the Delta, in case the Germans should succeed in breaking through the Alamein defences. There were even plans for a fighting retreat southwards up the Nile or into Palestine and, if necessary, Iraq, should the Delta go too. Plans against any eventuality are always prepared by planning staffs. That is what they are there for. There were doubtless plans for the continuance of the war from Canada, had it been necessary for the British Government to leave England.

General Auchinleck, however, had no more intention of abandoning El Alamein than had Mr. Churchill of leaving

London. On the contrary, throughout July the Eighth Army continually attacked the enemy in an endeavor to recover the initiative from him and, if possible, to destroy him where he stood. The first attack was made on July 2nd, after Rommel had unsuccessfully attacked El Alamein itself on July 1st. Close fighting continued for several days and it was only lack of reserves which brought the advance of 13th Corps to a standstill. On July 10th, 9th Australian Division captured the important position of Tel-el-Eisa, west of Alamein, and held it against heavy and repeated counter-attacks. On July 14th, the New Zealand Division and 5th Indian Infantry Brigade put in a night attack and gained ground on the vital Ruweisat Ridge. On the night of July 16th, the Australians captured the El-Makh-Ahad ridge to the south. Rommel reacted strongly, for we had created a salient in his position. His attacks on the Ruweisat Ridge on July 18th and 19th were, however, repulsed.

On July 21st, while the Australians attacked in the north, the New Zealand Division, supported by armour, was launched in the centre in an attempt to cut the enemy position in half. Our armour was defeated and the attempt failed. On July 26th another major attack was staged to the north from the Tel-el-Eisa salient. This again failed, in the face of heavy German counter-attacks, partly because the infantry failed to clear gaps through the enemy minefields so that the tanks could get forward, but mainly because there was a lack of enough fresh, well-trained troops to maintain the impetus of the assault.

On July 30th, General Auchinleck reluctantly concluded that, with the troops he had, no further offensive operations were feasible at the moment. He expected to be able to return to the attack about the middle of September. By then he would have at his disposal 44th Division, just arrived from England and now being trained in desert warfare, 8th Armoured Division, also newly arrived and being rearmed with American medium tanks, and 10th Armoured Division, retraining and re-equipping. For his reluctance he was relieved of his command by the Prime Minister. In the event, in spite of strong pressure from the Cabinet, General Alexander, in consultation with General Montgomery, put back his date more than a month.* By that time General Montgomery had

* Generals Alexander and Montgomery took over command on August 15th, 1942.

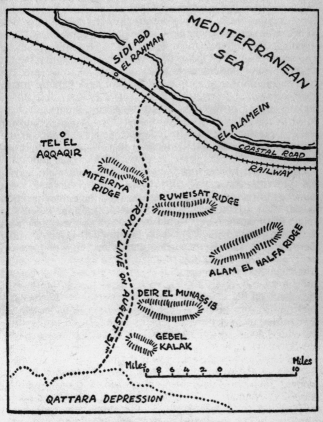

MEDITERRANEAN SEA

SIDI ABD EL RAHMAN

EL ALAMEIN

COASTAL ROAD

RAILWAY

TEL EL AQQAQIR

MITEIRIYA RIDGE

RUWEISAT RIDGE

FRONT LINE ON AUGUST 31

ALAM EL HALFA RIDGE

DEIR EL MUNASSIB

GEBEL KALAK

Miles 10 8 6 4 2 0

Miles 10

QATTARA DEPRESSION

The El Alamein Position

two extra British divisions and a mass of new tanks and guns such as the Eighth Army had never seen before. Since he made a complete job of it when he started, there is no doubt that the postponement was justified by the result. Nor is there any doubt that his supreme self-confidence and his gift of "the common touch" had an electric effect upon the troops. With the advantage of being a new broom, he inspired first curiosity, then interest, then admiration. The admiration was well-deserved. There is, however, no cause to magnify either his great victory or his great personal qualities by suggesting that the Eighth Army had ceased to exist as a fighting force when he took it over. It had, in fact, captured more than 7,000 prisoners during July. It had stopped Rommel's advance to the Delta. It had paved the way for a major offensive which it was then too weak to undertake.

There is a rather tragically ironical footnote to all this from the German side. "We were very much impressed and very much disturbed by the way you attacked us all through July," said General Bayerlein. "You very nearly succeeded in breaking through our position several times between the 10th and the 26th. If you could have continued to attack for only a couple of days more you would have done so. July 26th was the decisive day. We then had no ammunition at all for our heavy artillery and Rommel had determined to withdraw to the frontier if the attack was resumed."

Personal reputations apart, it was a very good thing for us and a very bad thing for Rommel that it was not resumed. Once back on the escarpment, with his communications short- ened and in a naturally strong defensive position, he would have needed a great deal of "winkling out." In all probability he would have escaped the overwhelming defeat which over- took him, since there would have been no political or psy- chological objection to withdrawing farther from the frontier, as there was to any withdrawal at all from El Alamein. In any case his fate must have been postponed, for our buildup, nearly three hundred miles to the westward, would have taken much longer to prepare. Indeed, it could hardly have been completed before the British and American landings in North Africa on November 8th. In that case Rommel must have seen the red light and retired to Tunisia in his own time.*

Why did he not withdraw as soon as he realised that he

* Rommel's own arguments against standing at Sollum will be found in the Appendix, Page 221. They appear conclusive.

could not break straight through to Cairo? The answer given by various critics both on the German and on our side is that he was ignorant of logistics. "His obvious weaknesses in the administrative field should deprive him of any lasting recognition as a great general," asserts Milton Shulman in *Defeat in the West*. Liddell Hart remarks, more mildly, that "a definite defect was his tendency to disregard the administrative side of strategy." These criticisms seem to stem directly from Rommel's reply to Halder's question regarding supplies: "That's your problem," rather than from any positive evidence of his failure to appreciate the importance of logistics. The supply problem was, in fact, the problem of the German and, primarily, of the Italian High Command. Isolated in his desert headquarters, Rommel could do no more than say what he needed and try to insist that he be given it. He could not fly over and ear-mark the shipping. He could not compel the Italians to surrender the petrol which was said to be lying about in profusion in Southern Italy but which in fact they could not spare even for their own fleet. He could not order away German divisions from France, though they were serving no useful purpose there, since it was obvious that an invasion could not be attempted in 1942. He could only argue, demand and protest. That he did unceasingly, to the annoyance of the Italians and of his own Army Command. He was not in the happy position of General Eisenhower when he wished to concentrate a corps east of Tebessa during the operations in North Africa the next year. "Logistics staffs opposed my purpose. . . . They wailed that our miserable communications could not maintain more than an armoured division and one additional regiment. . . . I nevertheless ordered the concentration of the corps of four divisions to begin and told the logistics people they would have to find a way to supply it." That was their problem and no one has argued that General Eisenhower was ignorant of logistics.

There is another passage from *Crusade in Europe* which is worth quoting in this context because it shows what can be done when there are quick brains and willing hands at the shore end:

As a result of splendid action in Washington an extra shipment of 5400 trucks had been brought into the theatre. The shipment immeasurably improved our transport and supply situation and had a profound effect in all later operations. It was accomplished under circumstances that should give pause to those people who picture the War and Navy departments as a mass of entangling red tape. The shipment demanded a special convoy at a time when both merchant shipping and escort vessels were at a premium. General Somervell happened to be visiting my headquarters and I explained to him our urgent need for this shipment. He said that he could be loading it out of American ports within three days, provided the Navy Department could furnish the escorts. I sent a query to Admiral King, then in Casablanca, and within a matter of hours had from him a simple "Yes." The trucks began arriving in Africa three weeks after I made my initial request.

At his home base, until September 1942, Rommel had General Halder "unable to restrain a slightly impolite smile" when he was asked for help.

Had Rommel's requests been entirely unreasonable or had he been told that, reasonable or not, they could not be complied with because of other commitments, there would have been no excuse for his persistence. In fact, he could easily have been given, early in 1942, the little extra he needed to take Cairo. All the troops and supplies would, at that time, have reached him in safety. In the late summer of 1942, when the British had recovered control of the Central Mediterranean and convoys could not pass Malta with impunity, he was still fobbed off by Kesselring and Cavallero with promises that his forces would be made up and his supply problems solved. On August 27th, just before the Alam-el-Halfa battle, there was a meeting at which they both guaranteed Rommel 6000 tons of petrol, 1000 tons of which were to be air-lifted. "That is my condition: the whole battle depends on it," said Rommel. "You can go on with the battle," replied Cavallero, "it is on its way." Such assurances should not have been given, least of all by Kesselring. Better than any one else, he knew the effect of the arrival of Spitfires in Malta.

Rommel's own staff suspected Kesselring of "double-crossing" him, of continually reporting against him and the Afrika Korps to Goering, while assuring the Army Command that all was going well in North Africa. I have been told that this is unfair to Kesselring, who could act only through the Italians. Nevertheless, Ciano, on September 9th, 1942, speaks of Kesselring "running to Berlin to complain of Rommel." Only a week earlier Cavallero was "repeating his optimistic declarations and saying that within a week the march (to the Delta) will be resumed." Probably Ciano's own shrewd comment sums it up best: "Victory always finds a hundred fathers but defeat is an orphan." The fact remains that Kesselring, as Commander-in-Chief South from April, 1942, was Rommel's immediate superior and could have ordered him not to advance to El Alamein, not to attack or to withdraw.

At the end of July, General Auchinleck had correctly judged that Rommel must attack before the end of August. He added, in his appreciation, that he would "hardly be strong enough to attempt the conquest of the Delta except as a gamble and under very strong air cover," since only in armour was he likely to have any superiority. In fact Rommel fought the battle of Alam-el-Halfa, which began on August 31st, under many disadvantages, besides that of having to attack an enemy in prepared defensive positions. Though he was slightly superior in numbers, six of his divisions were Italian. These had to be stiffened with his only German reinforcements, 164th Infantry Division and the Ramcke Parachute Brigade of four battalions. In guns and armour he had no superiority at all. The R.A.F. held complete command of the air. The nature of the Alamein position was such that it was almost impossible to achieve surprise or to profit by skill in manœuvre. Lastly, he was himself so ill with an infection of the nose and a swollen liver, probably the result of neglected jaundice, that he could not get out of his truck. For one who relied much more on his personal observation and judgment during the progress of a battle than on a preconceived plan, this was perhaps the greatest handicap of all.

Rommel attempted to achieve a decision in the only way in which it could have been achieved, by feinting in the north, making a holding attack in the centre and staging his main effort in the south. His intention was to penetrate above the Qattara Depression and then strike north to the sea. By this means he hoped to turn the whole position, just as he had turned the Gazala Line three months before. Had he succeeded the Eighth Army would have been trapped and its communications cut.

Unfortunately for Rommel, this was precisely what General Alexander and General Montgomery, and General Auchinleck and Major-General Dorman-Smith before them, had deduced that he would do. General Montgomery had also seen, immediately on his arrival in the desert, that the answer was to refuse his left flank, fortify the Alam-el-Halfa Ridge, which

Rommel dare not by-pass, and lead his armour on to its defences. He had, therefore, called up the whole of 44th Division, entrenched it on the ridge and dug in artillery and tanks to support it. He had also cunningly allowed a "going" map to be captured which showed good going south of Alam-el-Halfa where in fact there was very soft sand.

To do Rommel justice, his *Fingerspitzengefühl* came into play at once, even when he was lying helpless in his truck. "He wanted to break off the battle the first morning," said Bayerlein, "as soon as it was obvious that we had not achieved a surprise. It was I who persuaded him to let me continue." (Bayerlein was then temporarily commanding the Afrika Korps, General Nehring having been wounded on the night of August 31st in an air attack.) "The strength of the defences of the Alam-el-Halfa Ridge came as a complete surprise to me," added General Bayerlein. "I made sure I could take it and went on attacking it much too long."

When I showed him the passage in Alan Moorehead's biography in which he describes how General Montgomery put his finger on Alam-el-Halfa almost as soon as he looked at the map, Bayerlein shook his head ruefully. "Excellent, excellent," he murmured, with the respect of one professional for another. "That was very good generalship indeed."*

Bayerlein gave the rest of the credit to the R.A.F. "We were very heavily attacked every hour of the day and night," he said, "and had very heavy losses, more than from any other cause. Your air superiority was most important, perhaps decisive." He added a rude remark or two about Kesselring, whose promises had apparently included command of the air by the Luftwaffe.

His gamble having failed, on September 3rd Rommel began to withdraw. Wisely, General Montgomery did not attempt to follow him up. He could afford to wait.

Three weeks later, for the first time in his life except when he was wounded, Rommel was compelled to report sick and fly to Germany for treatment. Before going into hospital at Semmering, he had an interview with Hitler at his headquarters. He told the Führer that Panzer Group Afrika was standing in front of the door of Alexandria but that it was

---

* The story seems to have been somewhat over-dramatised. The Alam-el-Halfa position had already been mined and prepared, to some extent, for defence before General Montgomery arrived. He developed an existing plan.

impossible to push it open unless they were reinforced and the supply position improved. Above all, they could do nothing without petrol. (Ciano notes in his diary on September 2nd that "three of our oil-tankers have been sunk in two days," on September 3rd that "the sinking of our ships continues; to-night there have been two," and on September 4th that "two more ships have been sunk to-night.")

Rommel received another assurance, this time from the highest authority. "Don't worry," said Hitler, "I mean to give Africa all the support needed. Never fear, we are going to get Alexandria all right." He then volunteered a story that very small shallow-draught vessels, like landing-craft, were already in mass production, especially for Africa, and that some two hundred of them would be available almost immediately. They were to be armed with two 88 mm. guns each and would be much more difficult targets than tankers. They would be able to slip over at night and by means of them the petrol problem would be solved. No reference to these craft is to be found in the minutes of the Führer Conferences on Naval Affairs for 1942, but Hitler may have referred to light craft called, after their inventor, *Siebelfaehren*. These were quite unsuited for work in a seaway, such of them as existed were mostly in dock for repairs and there was no question of their being in mass production. Hitler, as usual, was letting his imagination run away with him.

This was not all. After the interview, he took Rommel out and showed him the prototype of the Tiger tank and of the *Nebel Werfer,* the formidable multiple mortar which we encountered later in Italy. These were also in mass production and Africa was first priority for deliveries. In fact, said Hitler, quantities of *Nebel Werfer* would be sent over at once by air, all available air-transport being used for the purpose. Incidentally, there was a new secret weapon of such appalling power that the blast "would throw a man off his horse at a distance of over two miles."

Rommel laughed about this last embellishment. Yet Hitler may not have been talking so wildly. In the first atomic bomb test in New Mexico a building four miles from the blast centre was moved two feet off its concrete foundation.

For the rest, Rommel, having seen the Tiger tank and the *Nebel Werfer,* took his Führer's promises seriously. The fact that he did so no doubt explains an optimistic speech which he made to foreign journalists in Berlin on October 3rd. In it he predicted that the Germans would soon be in Alexandria.

(General von Thoma, who saw him for a few days before he left North Africa, formed the impression that he was not really confident but spoke with confidence to impress the troops, particularly the Italians. That was, however, before his interview with Hitler.) It was not until about a fortnight later that Rommel began to have doubts. He confided them to his wife. "I wonder if he told me all that to keep me quiet," he said reflectively. For the first time he was vaguely suspicious of the Führer.

Meanwhile it had been decided at the same interview that Rommel should not go back to North Africa. When he came out of hospital, he was to be given an Army Group in the southern Ukraine. General Stumme would replace him in command of Panzer Group Afrika. Hitler was solicitous about his health; a change of climate would do him good, he said. It may well be that he did not want his own deceptions to be discovered.

Then, when Rommel was still in hospital at Semmering, Hitler telephoned to him personally at noon on October 24th. "Rommel, there is bad news from Africa," he said. "The situation looks very black. No one seems to know what has happened to Stumme. Do you feel well enough to go back and would you be willing to go?" Rommel had had only three weeks' treatment. He was still a very sick man and in no condition to return to the desert and fight a desperate battle. It never occurred to him to refuse: his heart was with the Afrika Korps. He left next morning at seven by air, stopped in Italy for a conference with von Rintelen about petrol supplies, landed in Crete and was in his headquarters in North Africa by 8 P.M.

When he arrived the battle was already lost. "Alamein was lost before it was fought," said General Cramer. "We had not the petrol." "Rommel could do nothing," said General Bayerlein, who had been on leave and followed two days afterwards. "He took over a battle in which all his reserves were already committed. No major decisions which could alter the course of events were possible."

Incredible though it seems, the German Intelligence Service was firmly of the belief that the British could not possibly attack during October. An officer from Army Command headquarters was especially sent over at the beginning of the month to say so. No wonder the unfortunate General Stumme died of heart failure twenty-four hours after General Montgomery's bombardment opened. (It appears that he fell or jumped out of his car during a British air attack without the driver noticing. The car returned without him and he was later found dead.)

In justice to Stumme it should be said that he had inherited the defence scheme from Rommel. Bayerlein assures me that the latter had arranged every detail of the dispositions before leaving Africa. That he took the very unusual course, for him, of splitting his armour, with 15th Panzer Division in the extreme north and 21st Panzer Division in the south, both too close behind the line and both sub-divided into battle groups, can only have been due to his distrust of the Italian divisions, which held the greater part of it.

His distrust was justified. Cowed by the fire of more than a thousand guns, attacked incessantly from the air, the Italians had little fight left in them when the attack was launched. But for the German infantry and paratroops interspersed amongst them, they would have broken more quickly than they did.

This time General Montgomery was greatly superior in numbers and immensely so in tanks, guns and ammunition. El Alamein was an old-fashioned battle of material. Yet it was far from mere "iron-mongering." It was preceded by a most elaborate cover plan. To suggest an attack in the south, while concealing the preparations for the real attack in the north, and at the same time to make it appear that arrangements in the south were still incomplete, the most elaborate and ingenious measures were taken. Hundreds of dummy vehicles were placed over tanks in the assembly areas; dummy lorries were parked in gun-positions so that the guns could be moved in at night and hidden under them; dummy tanks and dummy guns replaced the real articles in the staging areas as they went forward; mock dumps were started in the southern area and built up so slowly that they could not be ready until November; a fake wireless network was operated there with fake messages; a dummy pipeline, with dummy petrol stations and reservoirs, was built in the wrong direction and deliberately not completed; the movement of every vehicle was controlled to guard against tell-tale tracks in the sand. Aided by the fact that the R.A.F. allowed the Luftwaffe little chance of air reconnaissance and by the entirely wrong information supplied by the German Intelligence, the deception was so successful that the date of the attack, the direction of the main thrust and the location of the armour were completely hidden from the Germans. This involved the physical concealment in 13th Corps area to the north of two extra divisions,

240 guns, 150 extra tanks, to say nothing of such items as 7,500 tons of petrol.

"It was not until D plus 3 that the enemy finally concentrated all his resources against our real attack," writes Field-Marshal Alexander. D plus 3 (October 26th) was the day that Rommel took over and it is interesting to speculate whether he would have been so thoroughly deceived had he been in North Africa all through October. That he would have placed any reliance on German Intelligence reports is unlikely, for he had the lowest opinion of them.

To Bayerlein alone he admitted that the battle was lost. The admission did not deter him from making a desperate attempt to restore it. In the north, 15th Panzer Division had already been badly mauled by being thrown in piecemeal against the strong concentrations of 10th Armoured Corps. Gathering up the survivors, bringing up 21st Panzer Division by a forced march from the south, ordering forward 90th Light, Rommel was planning a counter-offensive within a few hours of his arrival—and against the right spot, the British salient in the north. Two days previously he had been in a hospital bed in Semmering; that afternoon, with the sun behind him, he was leading a mass tank attack of the two staunch divisions which had so often followed him. He knew the ground. He had had time for reflection in the aircraft flying south. Nevertheless it was a quick appreciation and a gallant effort.

The attack was broken up by artillery fire and air bombardment before it could get to grips. It was renewed the next day and beaten off by the 2nd Rifle Brigade and the Australians. Rommel had suffered losses in tanks which he had no hope of replacing. Determined and savage fighting followed when the 9th Australian Division thrust northwards again and took on successfully the pick of the German troops.

Then General Montgomery switched the direction of his attack. In the early hours of November 2nd he struck farther south, at the junction between the Germans and the Italians. The infantry broke through on a 4,000-yard front and opened the road for the armour. It was no easy passage. Ninth Armoured Brigade lost 87 tanks to Rommel's usual screen of anti-tank guns. First Armoured Division, coming through the gap, were set upon by 21st Panzer Division. "The enemy fought with the certain knowledge that all was at stake and with all the skill of his long experience in armoured fighting," wrote General Alexander in his despatch. At one moment he almost broke through our salient. "Operation Supercharge" was, however, the beginning of the end. That night Rommel decided to withdraw. He might still have got out most of the Germans with the transport he had. The Italians would have had to walk, but most of them would have preferred to surrender rather than suffer the attentions of the R.A.F. on the long road home. On November 3rd, when the withdrawal had already started, came an order from O.K.H., the German Army Command. "The position requires," it read, "that the El Alamein position be held to the last man. There is to be no retreat, not so much as one millimetre! Victory or death!" It was signed "Adolf Hitler."

For once Rommel was caught in two minds. He knew that the order was ridiculous and that to obey it must make greater disaster certain. Yet it was so explicit that he felt that it could not be disregarded. Against Bayerlein's advice he caused it to be circulated to the troops. General von Thoma, commanding the Afrika Korps, asked to be allowed to retire to Fuka and Daba. Rommel would not give him permission. Von Thoma nevertheless withdrew his troops during the night. "I cannot tolerate this order of Hitler," he said. Rommel turned a blind eye.

Next morning von Thoma went out to confirm a report, which Rommel refused to believe, that British columns had broken through in the south and were already west of the Germans. At noon, General Bayerlein, having had no word from von Thoma, drove out in his command car to look for him. As he approached the Tel-el-Mansr position, heavy fire forced him to leave his car and make for the ridge on foot. When he was within two hundred yards of it he saw the general standing beside his burning tank. British tanks (they were, in fact, the 10th Hussars) ringed him round. All the German tanks and anti-tank guns on the position had been destroyed. Bayerlein waited until he saw British carriers drive up to von Thoma and carry him off. Then he himself withdrew unobserved. When he arrived back at headquarters, south of Daba, he and Rommel heard the 10th Hussar troop leaders talking about having captured a German general. That night General von Thoma dined with General Montgomery in his headquarters mess and invited the Eighth Army Commander to stay with him in Germany after the war. These mutual courtesies were criticised in England. They were not regarded as out of place in Africa.

Next morning Bayerlein attained his ambition of commanding the Afrika Korps, just when it had virtually ceased to exist. "What can I do in face of this order of Hitler's?" he asked Rommel. "I cannot authorise you to disobey it," said Rommel with unusual diplomacy. But there could be no more question of obeying it if any one was to be saved.

For the moment, with the shock of defeat coming on top of his illness, Rommel was a broken man. Nevertheless, though his staff found him more than ordinarily difficult to deal with, he conducted the retreat with great skill. This time he had no hope of turning on his pursuers. His remaining force amounted to little more than a composite division: eighty German tanks were left against nearly six hundred British. He could only save what he might out of the wreck. He was lucky to save anything at all. Had not heavy rain come on the night of November 6th, turning the desert into a morass and preventing the movement of the troops sent to cut him off, he would have been encircled at Matruh. Had the R.A.F. had the technique of "ground strafing" which it later acquired, he would not have got that far. Had air transport been developed as General Slim developed it in the much more difficult conditions of Burma, completely-equipped forces would have been dropped well behind him and supplied by air. General Montgomery has also been criticised by both sides for being too cautious. "I do not think General Patton would have let us get away so easily," said Bayerlein, who, having fought in France afterwards, compared Patton with Guderian and Montgomery with von Rundstedt. He added, however, that "the best thing Rommel ever did in North Africa was this retreat." As the Eighth Army covered the seven hundred miles from El Alamein to Benghazi in fifteen days and as this time Rommel was not allowed to stand at El Agheila, there is perhaps, not much room for criticism of either commander.

On November 8th came the Allied landings in North Africa. Tripoli at once became of minor importance. Rommel received no reinforcements but they were poured into Tunisia by sea and air. Six months later they were all prisoners. Of the many bitter pills which Rommel had to swallow, before the last, one of the bitterest must have been to see what the German High Command could do in a lost cause and to compare it with what they had failed to do in support of a winning one. In November two regiments of airborne troops and an engineer battalion were flown in. They were followed by odd infantry units, tanks and artillery and formed into a scratch division. By the middle of December, 10th Panzer Division had arrived. Another infantry division, 334th, was brought over in the latter half of the month. A Grenadier regiment came from Crete. There appeared also a heavy tank battalion, the 501st, armed with the new Tiger tanks which Rommel had been promised. The redoubtable Herman Goering Panzer Division was on its way. Other German units, apart from various Italian formations, were added before the end to swell the Allied game-bag. What could not Rommel have done with half of this force five or six months earlier?

There is no profit in following Rommel's retreat or the advance of the Eighth Army through Tripolitania. With his 25,000 Italians, his 10,000 Germans and his sixty tanks, he was steadily and relentlessly pushed back. All the way he made the most skilful use of mines, road demolitions and booby-traps to slow up his enemy. Often his German rear guards had to fight desperately to extricate themselves, for this time he sent the Italians on ahead. Temptingly strong defensive positions had to be abandoned because he had not the troops to hold them. Ninetieth Light Division made a stand outside Tripoli itself, but Rommel's old victims at St. Valéry, 51st Highland Division, riding in on the back of tanks, turned them out in a moonlight attack. Tripoli was occupied without any further resistance. On January 23rd, the 11th Hussars, who had struck the first blow across the frontier wire when Italy came into the war, drove into the city at dawn.

There is no greater test of troops or a commander than a long retreat, nothing which so quickly breaks the spirit as the knowledge that one must fight only to be able to withdraw. Rommel was sick at heart as well as in body. It was during the retreat that he learnt how loyalty to his Führer was rewarded. At the end of November he was summoned home for an interview. Hitler treated him, for the first time, to one of his famous scenes. Rommel had told him that the position in North Africa was hopeless and that it would be better to sacrifice what was left of the material and get the Afrika Korps out to fight again in Italy. Hitler said that he was a defeatist and that he and his troops were cowards. Generals who had made the same sort of suggestion in Russia had been put up against the wall and shot. He would not yet do that to Rommel but Rommel had better be careful. As for Tripoli, it was to be held at all costs for otherwise the Italians would make a separate peace. Rommel asked him whether it was better to lose Tripoli or the Afrika Korps. Hitler shouted that the Afrika Korps did not matter. For the first time, Rommel told his family, he realised Hitler's contempt for the whole German people and the fact that he cared nothing for the men who fought for him. Nevertheless he answered back. Let Hitler come out to Africa and see for himself or let him send some of his entourage to show them how to do it. "Go!" screamed Hitler, "I have other things to do than talk to you." Rommel saluted and turned on his heel. After he had shut the door, Hitler came running after him and put his arm on his shoulder. "You must excuse me," he said, "I'm in a very nervous state. But everything is going to be all right. Come and see me to-morrow and we will talk about it calmly. It is impossible to think of the Afrika Korps being destroyed."

Rommel saw him next day, with Goering. "Do anything you like," said Hitler to Goering, "but see that the Afrika Korps is supplied with all that Rommel needs."

"You can build houses on me," said Goering in the German phrase. "I am going to attend to it myself."

The Reichsmarschall took Rommel with him in his special train to Rome and invited Frau Rommel to go with them. When they met at Munich station Goering was wearing a grey semi-civilian suit with grey silk lapels. His tie was secured by a large emerald clip. The case of his watch was studded with emeralds. On one of his fingers, to Rommel's horror, was a ring with an enormous diamond. More horrifying still, his nails were varnished. Goering displayed the ring to Frau Rommel at the first opportunity. "You will be interested in this," he said, "it is one of the most valuable stones in the world." This was the first time Frau Rommel had met the Reichsmarschall. She, too, was startled. In the train he spoke only of pictures. "They call me the Maecenas of the Third Reich," he said and described how Balbo had sent him a statue of Aphrodite from Cirene. North Africa was not otherwise mentioned during the journey, and Goering resisted all Rommel's attempts to turn the conversation from statues to supplies. However, he gave Rommel the *Flugzeugführerabzeichen,* the Air Force pilot's cross, in diamonds, and seemed to think that that should satisfy him.

In Rome, where they stopped at the Excelsior, it was the same story. "Goering did nothing but look for pictures and sculpture," said Rommel with profound contempt. "He was planning how to fill his train with them. He never tried to see any one on business or to do anything for me." To Frau Rommel, Goering remarked that her husband seemed very depressed. "He is not normally so," she replied. "As a rule he is very optimistic. But he takes a very realistic view." "Ah!" said Goering, "he does not comprehend the whole situation as I do. We are going to look after him, we are going to do everything for him." He then went off into a long and boastful monologue about his own achievements, past, present and future. He appeared to Frau Rommel to be on the verge of megalomania. Contrasting this extraordinary figure with the shrewd and capable Goering who appeared before the judges at Nuremberg one wonders whether, at this period, he had not gone back to morphia. Apart from art, his only interest seemed to be his model railway. He was photographed in a guard's uniform with a green flag. The story was all over Rome that he had gone to a party dressed in a toga. Rommel put up with it for three days. Then he said: "I'm doing no good over here—only losing my temper: I'd better get back to the Afrika Korps."

He flew off next day, convinced that Goering was mad and Hitler not much better. It was the second stage of his disillusionment.

Though Tripoli fell in defiance of the Führer's wishes, this was not the end of Rommel in North Africa. His title had changed three times during 1942. Up to January 21st he was still commander of the Panzer Group Africa. Then he became supreme commander of the Panzer Army in Africa and held this appointment until October 24th. On his return to El Alamein on Stumme's death he arrived with the title of supreme commander of the German-Italian Panzer Army. On February 22nd the Army Group Africa was formed and he was given command of it. It consisted of 5th Panzer Army, under General von Arnim, composed of the new forces which had been rushed to Tunisia, and of 1st (Italian) Army under General Messe, comprising the two Italian Corps, 20th and 21st, and the Afrika Korps, which had been driven out of Libya. The 1st Italian Army was, in fact, the German-Italian Panzer Army under a new name. Thus, instead of being "put up against a wall and shot," he was promoted to command all the Axis forces in Tunisia. The German High Command still believed that it would be possible to retain a bridgehead around Tunis and Bizerta and keep a large Allied army immobilised, as at Salonica in the first war. It is surprising that the command should have been given to Rommel, who believed nothing of the sort.

Nevertheless, even before being gazetted to his new appointment, he showed a real flash of his old form. From

Tripoli he had retired to the Mareth Line. This was an immensely strong position, another but more elaborately prepared El Alamein. The French, who had fortified it as an African Maginot Line against any Italian advance from Libya, considered it impregnable by frontal attack. It could not be turned, they said, because the going to the west was *"incroyable."* In any case, to outflank it meant a turning movement of 150 miles. Rommel rightly judged that General Montgomery would need time to think this over. Since he never lost the offensive spirit for long and did not propose to sit down and wait to be attacked, he looked round for something to undertake meanwhile. It need not necessarily be against the Eighth Army: there was also the Allied First Army, which would doubtless come in on his rear as soon as he was again at grips with General Montgomery.

He chose precisely the most vulnerable spot. In the southern sector of the First Army front, across the Faid plain between Gafsa and Fondouk, lay the American 2nd Corps. Behind it was the Kasserine Pass. Defensive positions had been only sketchily prepared. The U.S. 1st Armoured Division was dispersed behind the front, half of it north towards Fondouk, where Intelligence was convinced that any attack must fall. Though they lacked nothing in courage and were quick to learn, the troops at this time were green and untried, under commanders who had as yet had no experience of modern war.

This was Rommel's meat. He had already pulled out his faithful 21st Panzer Division and rearmed it with the tanks of an independent tank battalion sent to reinforce Tunisia. With about a hundred tanks, supported by Stukas, he fell upon the American Armoured Division on February 14th. The forward positions were quickly overrun and Rommel pushed on with his armour through the hastily-constructed defences of the Kasserine Pass. The mixture of American, British and French troops added to the confusion. There was "no co-ordinated plan of defence and definite uncertainty as to command." A big salient had been driven into the Allied lines. With his forces almost intact, Rommel had open country in front of him and few natural obstacles to an advance northwards. He might very well turn the whole front in Tunisia and bring on a general withdrawal, if not a disaster. It was the Gazala Line over again.

Such was the situation when General Alexander came up to

command. "It was clear to me," he writes, "that although Rommel's original intention had been merely to give such a blow to 2nd Corps as would leave his right rear secure while he prepared to meet Eighth Army, he now had much bigger ideas. From previous experience I knew him to be a man who would always exploit success by every possible means, to the limit of rashness, and there now glittered before him the prospect of a tactical victory."

On February 20th things looked so black that General Alexander had to wire to General Montgomery to do something to make a diversion. The latter at once agreed and said what he would do. "We will soon have Rommel running about between us like a wet hen," he added. Thanks largely to good generalship by General Alexander, who rightly predicted that Rommel would turn north, where the glittering prize lay, the German thrust was stopped two days later. Rommel withdrew in good order, leaving behind him only nine tanks, plenty of mines to discourage pursuit and some very shaken initiates to war in North Africa.

"The Battle of Kasserine had given me many anxious moments," says Field-Marshal Alexander in his dispatch. "As in his advance to El Alamein, Rommel had over-exploited a considerable initial success to leave himself in a worse position than before; he can hardly be blamed for his attempt to snatch a great victory, for on both occasions he came very near it, but the result was equally disastrous to him."

The commitment of substantial American forces to battle for the first time in this area was certainly "bad news" to Rommel. In his own papers he wrote:

> From the moment that the overwhelming industrial capacity of the United States could make itself felt in any theatre of war, there was no longer a chance of ultimate victory there. Even if we had overrun the whole African continent—as long as a small bridgehead remained offering good operational possibilities, and provided the Americans were able to bring in their material—we were bound to lose it in the end. Tactical skill could only postpone the collapse, it could not avert the ultimate fate of this theatre of war.

Speaking about the battles around Thala on February 22, 1943 and Rommel's controversy with Kesselring and Colonel-General von Arnim, Rommel wrote:

Irrespective of his actual merits, Field-Marshal Kessel-ring had not the slightest idea of the tactical and operational conditions in the African theatre. He saw it all through rose-coloured spectacles and created illusions for himself concerning the significance of our victory over the Americans. In particular, he thought that many more such opportunities would occur and that the fighting value of the Americans was low. Although they could not yet be compared with the core of the Eighth Army—veterans of many battles—yet this lack of experience was made up for by their far better and more plentiful equipment and by their tactically more flexible command.

And speaking of the African battles in retrospect:

What was really amazing was the speed with which the Americans adapted themselves to modern warfare. They were assisted in this by their tremendous practical and material sense and by their lack of all understanding for tradition and useless theories.

That the retreat had not broken Rommel's nerve nor changed his habits in battle is shown by an incident which occurred about this time. The authority for it is Dr. Loeffler, one of the German counsel at the Nuremberg Trials, who was serving in tanks in Tunisia and was an eye-witness. Under heavy fire, Rommel drove up in his staff car to the commander of a tank battalion who was sitting inside his tank with the lid closed, at the entrance to a village. Rommel rapped on it. "What are you doing?" he asked the battalion commander when he opened up. "It is impossible to get on," replied that officer. At the same moment a salvo from a British battery burst all round the tank. The lid was hastily closed and the battalion commander imagined that Rommel must be dead. Ten minutes later there was another rap on the lid. It was Rommel, who had driven forward into the village and now returned. "You are quite right," he said, "there are four anti-tank guns at the other end of the street. Another time you might go and get that sort of information for yourself."

This was Rommel's last battle but one in Africa. The last was Médenine, on March 5th. Rommel was too late by a few days to catch Montgomery off balance. When 15th and 21st Panzer Divisions went in to the attack, a strong force was waiting for them. The battle of Alam-el-Halfa was repeated. "The infantry held their positions against strong infantry and

146

tank attacks with no wire and few mines to protect them,"
says Major-General de Guingand, Chief of Staff of the Eighth
Army. "The anti-tank guns were sited to kill tanks and not to
protect the infantry. The effect of the concentrated use of our
artillery was devastating. . . . It was the perfectly fought defensive battle. . . . Rommel completely failed even to penetrate our positions." He left 52 of the 140 tanks with which
he started on the battlefield. The British casualties were 130
all ranks killed and wounded. No tanks were lost. General de
Guingand says that prisoners reported that Rommel had gone
round trying to whip up enthusiasm and to impress upon the
troops the importance of the battle but was obviously a very
sick man, with his throat bandaged and his face covered with
desert sores. An eye-witness quoted by General Alexander
relates that he told a party which stopped near him that unless
they won this battle the last hope in Africa was gone.

A week later he left for Germany. Various explanations have
been given for his abrupt departure before the battle of the
Mareth Line. For example, General Eisenhower writes:
"Rommel himself escaped before the final debacle, apparently
foreseeing the inevitable and earnestly desiring to save his
own skin." He did, indeed, foresee the inevitable. But no one
who has followed his career up to this point will believe that
consideration for his own skin ever influenced any action of
Rommel's from the day that he became a soldier. It has been
said that the Italians demanded his withdrawal, but I can find
no evidence of this. More plausibly, ill-health and the need for
further treatment have been given as the reasons for his return. It has been said that Hitler ordered him out because of
the effect upon German morale if he were captured. Since
Hitler had not yet begun to realise that all was lost in Tunisia
and was still contemplating an offensive against Casablanca,
this is improbable. It was not, indeed, until May 8th that the
High Command issued the order that Africa would now be
abandoned and that the German and Italian forces would be
withdrawn by sea. By that time, like so many of Hitler's
orders, it could no longer be obeyed. The capitulation followed four days afterwards.

The explanation given by Rommel's family, which came
first-hand from him, is that he flew out on his own initiative
and without orders, to beg Hitler again that he be allowed to
save the German troops at the sacrifice of the material. He
was again refused and again called a defeatist and a coward.
When he then proposed to go back and see it through with

them, permission was refused. I see no reason to doubt their story.

The Afrika Korps did not forget him. Until the end his old divisions fought as stubbornly as under his leadership. Nor did his memory fade at once from the minds of his opponents. In *Operation Victory* General de Guingand mentions that he left Africa before the battle of the Mareth Line. Nevertheless he continues to refer, perhaps subconsciously, to "Rommel's troops."

After the fall of Tunis, Rommel was summoned to *Wolfsschanze*, the "wolf's lair," the code name for Hitler's headquarters near Rastenburg in East Prussia. Hitler seemed desperate but was in a more reasonable mood. "I should have listened to you earlier," he said. "Africa is lost now." Rommel spoke of the general position of the German forces and suddenly asked the Führer: "Do you really think we can have the complete victory we aim at?" "No!" answered Hitler. Rommel pressed him. "Do you realise the consequences of defeat?" he asked. "Yes," Hitler replied, "I know it is necessary to make peace with one side or the other, but no one will make peace with me." In recounting this interview to Frau Rommel and Manfred, Rommel said that Hitler was a modern Louis XIV and quite unable to distinguish between his own interests and those of the German people. It never occurred to him that he might abdicate if he were the obstacle to peace. Rommel added that it was only when he was completely depressed that it was possible to reason with him. As soon as he was again surrounded by sycophants who assured him that he was on top of the world, he switched round immediately. Rommel had also realised, late in the day, that hatred was the mainspring of Hitler's character. When he hated, his hatred was passionate. He could not govern or control himself: he wished simply to kill. Manfred remembered this conversation later and still remembers it.

On April 6th, at Wadi Akarit, 15th Panzer and 90th Light Division, "fighting," said General Alexander, "perhaps the best battle of their distinguished careers," temporarily staved off disaster but could not prevent the junction of First and Eighth Armies. On April 29th they and 21st Panzer Division "continued to show an excellent spirit," in spite of heavy losses. On April 30th First Army was to be reinforced by the best formations of Eighth Army. General Montgomery selected 7th Armoured Division, 4th Indian Division and 201st

Guards Brigade. The two divisions were those which had won the first British victory in Africa under General Wavell. On May 7th the 11th Hussars of 7th Armoured Division, the original and authentic "desert rats," entered Tunis. On May 12th, after a last battle in the hills above Enfidaville, General Graf von Sponeck surrendered 90th Light Division to his old enemy, General Freyberg and his New Zealanders. The last of the Afrika Korps went into captivity—without its leader. The desert war was over.

It remained for Field-Marshal Keitel, in a fit of pre-death-bed repentance, to say the last word about it:

"One of the biggest occasions we passed by was at El Alamein. I would say that, at that climax of the war, we were nearer to victory than at any other time before or after. Very little was needed then to conquer Alexandria and to push forward to Suez and Palestine. . . ."

General Halder, however, remains unrepentant. In a turgid and ill-written book, *Hitler als Feldherr,* designed to put all the blame for Germany's defeat on the Führer, to exculpate the General Staff and to provide a new version of the "stab in the back," he still maintains that "to beat England decisively in North Africa was impossible." Control of the supply lines of the Mediterranean could not be wrested from her. German submarines arrived with a loss of fifty per cent. (In fact, two were lost out of sixty.) England could bring everything she wanted through the Red Sea. (He does not mention that it all had to come round the Cape of Good Hope.) "It was, from the beginning, only a question of time. . . ." Fortunately for the British, the German General Staff has always produced its Halders.

CHAPTER 10

The Atlantic Wall

In the late summer of 1943 Rommel was where many German generals on the Russian front would have been glad to change places with him—commanding Army Group B in Northern Italy, with headquarters near Lake Garda. On his return from North Africa he had first gone into hospital at Semmering for six or seven weeks and was then posted as a "military adviser" to Hitler's headquarters. A rumour that the

Allies, at Mr. Churchill's insistence, were about to stage an invasion of Europe through the Balkans caused Hitler to send him to Greece but he was in Athens only twenty-four hours when, on the news of the fall of Mussolini on July 25th, the Führer hurriedly recalled him by telephone. Army Group B was then being formed around Munich, for Hitler already suspected that the Italians were about to surrender or, possibly, to change sides.

His suspicions were strengthened when Rommel, with General Jodl, went to Badoglio's headquarters to discuss the question of sending more troops to Italy. General Roatta, Badoglio's Chief of Staff, did everything possible to prevent the move, which would, he said, be most unpopular with the Italians. He also objected to Jodl's placing an S.S. guard on his billet. What right had Jodl, he asked, to bring "Political troops" into Italy? What would Jodl have said if he had given him as a guard a company of Jews? Jodl, who had heard a report that he and Rommel were to be poisoned, said nothing but kept his S.S. Rommel decided that the sooner Army Group B moved into Italy the better. They were his Tiger tanks which I watched, on the morning of September 9th, as they moved along the Rivergaro road to occupy Piacenza.

When the armistice was announced in our prison-camp the evening before, I had hastily bought a well-worn alpaca suit and a large straw hat from the caretaker. Now, out on a "recce" and looking, as I fondly imagined, every inch an Italian peasant, I was leaning over a garden wall, enjoying the sunshine and my first taste of freedom for sixteen months. The sight of German tanks in that quiet countryside was unwelcome, as was the appearance of two S.S. men with tommy-guns in the garden a few minutes later. I had to slip away hurriedly into the vines and thence across the fields to the camp to report. I heard afterwards that everyone who saw me—except, fortunately, the S.S. men—recognised me for what I was and wondered what I was doing in Alfredo's second-best suit.

Even in a prison-camp we had known, what our Intelligence apparently did not know, that the Germans were ready to react vigorously to an Italian surrender. One of our tame guards had reported, at least a fortnight before, that German divisions were streaming over the Brenner. We had not expected that the reaction locally would be quite so quick. Some of us, indeed, hoped to take the train from Piacenza that afternoon, for Rome and the south. Having nearly all been captured in North Africa, we would have been less optimistic had we realised that Rommel was in command. (It was, we still feel, a strange oversight that 50,000 British prisoners-of-war in Italy received no orders or information of any kind at the time of the armistice. The result was that most of them, obeying a six-months-old order to "stay put," were carried off to Germany. Negotiations with Badoglio went on from the end of July until September: someone might have given us a thought.)

Apart from making occasional sweeps through the hills, Rommel's troops did not hunt us about unduly. In the desert his order of priority had been (1) petrol and oil, (2) water, (3) food, (4) prisoners. "We can pick them up later," he used to say. Apparently he still observed it. Once the Germans had a tight hold on Northern Italy, they seemed more interested in looting their former allies of food and machinery and sending the young men off to German labour-camps than in rounding up the odd prisoners who were still at large.

Rommel, characteristically, was bored with his comfortable appointment. Possibly he did not like serving again under Kesselring: certainly he had hoped for another fighting command. Summering in the Italian lakes was not his idea of war. Moreover, immediately after the armistice, he began to have trouble with the S.S. and with Sepp Dietrich, commanding the S.S. Corps. There were reports of widespread looting and of brutal behaviour in Milan and other northern cities. Rommel was indignant, both because of these incidents and because he was not allowed to interfere with the discipline of the S.S. He forwarded a long list of S.S. officers for punishment and, since he was at least free to control the location of his troops, ordered the S.S. units out of Milan. "How are things going now in Milan, Field-Marshal?" he was asked by Himmler, paying a visit of inspection to Italy. "Better, since we moved the S.S. out," replied Rommel. The S.S. were not, however, so easily defeated. When Rommel complained to an S.S. general about their looting, the general, knowing that Rommel collected stamps, sent him a magnificent (looted) collection.

It was thus with relief that, at the beginning of November, Rommel learnt that he had been given a special mission by the Führer. He was to inspect the coastal defences in the west, from the Skagerrak to the Spanish frontier, and report on their readiness to resist invasion. Some expert advice on the naval side would clearly be needed. Rommel's Chief of Staff, General Gausi, who had been with him in North Africa until he was wounded on May 31st, 1942, knew just the man. This was Vice-Admiral Ruge, then commanding the German naval forces in Italy and previously in charge of minesweepers. (After the first war, he was interned for his share in scuttling the German Fleet in Scapa Flow.) Gausi had met and liked Ruge, and Rommel applied for him on Gausi's recommendation. There could have been no better choice. Vice-Admiral Ruge, still living in Cuxhaven and teaching German to British naval officers, is the type of officer we like to think peculiar to the British Navy. In fact, all navies produce it for it is a product of early training, discipline and the sea. Since he was a man of intelligence, energy and integrity, Rommel took to him at once and Ruge became his close friend and confidant.

Why was it that Admiral Ruge, for his part, felt himself at ease with Rommel from their first meeting, even though the Field-Marshal, returning unexpectedly to his headquarters, caught him in an old bridge coat, with a muffler round his neck? It was his answer to that question which enabled me to place Rommel and will, perhaps, help to explain him to many English readers. "He was a type one meets more often in the Navy than in the other services," said Admiral Ruge. When, with that in mind, I looked again at Rommel's photograph, covering up the cap, and reflected on all the stories I had heard about him, the odd pieces of his personality seemed to slip into place. Perhaps because my own father was a sailor and I spent much of my early life at sea, I felt that I could now understand this very unusual German general. He had hardly seen salt water until his last assignment. But think of him in the line of Nelson's captains, an unromantic Hornblower, rough, tough and ruthless but not without chivalry, and he runs true to type.

The qualities which he showed in the desert and elsewhere are not peculiar to sailors. Soldiers, too, can be bold and determined and tireless and brave. They can have good, orderly minds without much book-learning and with no interest in the arts. They also can be brusque in manner, direct of speech, intolerant of inefficiency and anxious to get on with a job. But when one adds some of Rommel's other characteristics, his manual dexterity and skill in improvising mechanical devices; his extreme simplicity and contempt of "frills"; a mild streak of concealed and subconscious puritanism, so that no one felt inclined to tell a dirty story in his presence; above all, his intense devotion to home and family, then the combination recalls to me my father and his contemporaries as strongly as do the clear blue eyes with the network of fine lines round them. Admiral Sir Walter Cowan, whom he captured in the desert, serving at seventy-two with an Indian cavalry regiment, and with whom I was afterwards in a prison-camp, may not appreciate the comparison but I can picture the two of them barking away at each other, neither prepared to yield an inch, and yet understanding each other perfectly. They were, indeed, very much two of a kind and Admiral Ruge would have made a good, though less prickly, third.

Reporting for duty on November 10th, Ruge was sent to Berlin to collect all the maps and charts and information he could find. When he had got the papers together they were destroyed in an air-raid. It was not until the beginning of December that he and Rommel were able to start work in Denmark. The inspection of the Danish coast took ten days. Then Rommel moved the headquarters of Army Group B to Fontainebleau and began to study the French coast. (The German Bight of the North Sea was excluded from his task.) He had not been in France since 1940 and what he saw, or failed to see, appalled him. The great "Atlantic Wall," with which the German propaganda machine had succeeded in impressing its own people as well as the Allies, was a fake, a paper hoop for the Allies to jump through.

The German Navy had, indeed, erected batteries for the protection of the principal ports. These had been linked up, to some extent, by batteries of the Army Coastal Artillery. But whereas the naval guns were in steel cupolas, the army artillery was merely dug in and had no overhead cover against shells or bombs. (Admiral Ruge explained that the Army Command was unwilling to put its guns under concrete because of the consequent restriction of the field of fire. From 1942 onwards the scarcity of steel made it impossible to obtain the necessary turrets.) As for the string of strong-points, in many cases they had no concrete shelters at all. These were especially lacking along the coast between the Orne and the Vire. Where they existed, the head cover was only 60 cm. thick and useless, therefore, against the preliminary air bombardments which were to be expected.

Even the elementary precaution of surrounding the strong-points with minefields had been ignored. In three years, only 1,700,000 mines had been laid. The monthly rate of supply when Rommel arrived was 40,000—a fraction of what we laid in 1941 below the Sollum-Halfaya escarpment. There were no shallow-water mines below low-water level, nor were the minefields to seaward sufficient. Beach obstacles were of the most primitive sort, quite ineffective against tanks and not much use even against infantry. The fact was that no serious and concerted attempt had yet been made to put the French coast into a state of defence against invasion. Nothing was done outside the ports until after the St. Nazaire and Dieppe raids and then the effort was half-hearted.

Admiral Ruge blames the engineer-general in charge, who was not up to his job. He was bogged down in detail and never thought out a clear over-all plan. "He was not the man to reconcile the differing views of Army and Navy." The German High Command was equally to blame for not supervising him. In the absence of prodding from above, the local commanders took things easy and decided for themselves how much or how little to do. France had, indeed, become a home of rest for tired generals and tired divisions from Russia. The permanent garrison was composed of "category" troops of very poor quality, under the sort of officers whom such troops attract. The Todt organisation, which had built the Siegfried Line, was busy repairing bomb damage in Germany.

As may be imagined, Rommel set to with a will to put this right. Beginning just before Christmas, he spent his days making long trips by car with his staff to various sections of the coast and to all the headquarters, down to divisions. By daylight he inspected the defences; when the early darkness of the winter afternoons stopped outdoor work, he held conferences. "He got up early," says Admiral Ruge, "travelled fast, saw things very quickly and seemed to have an instinct for the places where something was wrong. On one typical winter inspection we arrived at Perpignan late one night. We left at 6 A.M. next morning, without breakfast. Driving through snow and rain, we reached Bayonne at 2 P.M. An hour later, having received the report of the local commanding general, we left, without luncheon, for St. Jean-de-Luz, on the Spanish frontier. There we inspected batteries. We arrived at Bordeaux at 7 P.M. and conferred with General von Blaskowitz. At 8 P.M. we had an hour off for supper, our first meal of the day. We settled down to work again at 9 P.M., but fortunately the engineer-general fell asleep over the table." To the snug staffs of the coastal sectors Rommel blew in like an icy and unwelcome wind off the North Sea.

Of his own headquarters, which he had moved to La Roche-Guyon, north-west of Paris, he saw little, except at night. The fact that they were in a fine old castle, full of historical associations, since it had belonged to La Rochefoucauld, Duc de Roche-Guyon, aroused no interest in him. Nor could he be persuaded for a long time to visit Mont St. Michel for pleasure. When at last Admiral Ruge succeeded in dragging him there, he remarked that it "would make a good dug-out," but, said Ruge, enjoyed pottering about in it. On the other hand, he needed no persuasion to go twice to Paris to inspect a revolving gun-turret in concrete which German technicians had constructed.

Unfortunately for Rommel, he was very far from having a free hand. He could give no direct orders to the troops but could only make suggestions to the Commander-in-Chief West (Field-Marshal von Rundstedt) or to the High Command. Since he was working under personal instructions from Hitler and at the same time was subordinate to von Rundstedt, efficiency was impossible and some friction inevitable. Actually von Rundstedt and Rommel got on better than might have been expected. Von Rundstedt was an aristocratic and dignified German officer of the old school, a very able if orthodox strategist. He might easily have resented the arrival in his area of a jumped-up Field-Marshal with no staff training and no recent experience of European war. The ill-defined set-up had in it all the makings of a bitter quarrel. Happily von Rundstedt was by no means as stiff as he appeared to be and had a sense of humour. Long after Rommel was dead he told Captain Liddell Hart that he had no complaint to make of him. "Whenever I gave him an order he obeyed. . . . I do not think he was really qualified for high command but he was a very brave man and a very capable commander."

That did not alter the fact that the Commander-in-Chief West, who, when he took over early in 1942, had seen as quickly as Rommel the weaknesses of the Atlantic Wall, did not believe that it could be so strengthened as to form a real obstacle to an invasion. Nothing, he felt, could prevent the Allies landing in force. As a result, he had failed to speed up the work on the defences. It was only at the beginning of 1944 that Rommel sought and obtained an independent command. At the end of January he was made Commander-in-Chief of the German Armies from the Netherlands to the Loire. These included the occupation troops in Holland, the 15th Army, holding from the Dutch frontier to the Seine, and the 7th Army, from the Seine to the Loire. General Blaskowitz's Army Group G controlled the 1st Army, covering the Bay of Biscay and the Pyrenees and the 19th Army, holding the Mediterranean coast. Field-Marshal von Rundstedt remained Supreme Commander over all.

This was a logical arrangement. According to his staff, it was suggested by von Rundstedt: according to Admiral Ruge, the proposal came from Rommel. Whoever was the author of it, one feels that von Rundstedt's attitude was: "I don't personally see any sense in trying to do anything with the Atlantic Wall but if Rommel feels that he can, better let him get on with it." The reaction of the staffs on both sides was one of profound relief.

Get on with it Rommel did and it was a very good thing for the Allies that he was not given six months longer. By then the physical difficulties of the landing would have been immensely greater.

He was still working under serious handicaps. "He had very little influence with the Navy," said Admiral Ruge, "and none at all with the Air Force." It was not until July 1st, more than three weeks after the invasion, that he was able to write to Commander-in-Chief West: "With a view to obtaining unified command of the Wehrmacht and concentration of all forces, I now propose to take over command of the headquarters and units of the other two services employed in the Army Group area or co-operating with it. . . . Close co-operation between the flying formations and the flak corps and the heavily engaged army can be guaranteed only by the strictest command from one headquarters. Duplication of orders leads to military half-measures. . . ." This was labouring the obvious. But the jealousy between the Services and the system of private armies owing allegiance to Goering, Himmler, etc., was one of the major causes of German defeat.

Moreover, the knowledge that von Rundstedt's disbelief in fixed defences was shared by the Army Command, always inclined to discount anything done by Rommel, did not fail to percolate down to subordinate commanders. As late as April 22nd Rommel was writing:

My inspection tour of the coastal sectors . . . shows that unusual progress has been made. . . . However, here and there I noticed units that do not seem to have recognized the graveness of the hour and some who do not even follow instructions. There are reports of cases in which my orders that all minefields on the beach should be alive at all times have not been obeyed. A commander of a lower unit gave an order to the contrary. In other cases my orders have been postponed to later dates or even changed. Reports from some sectors say that they intend to try to put one of my orders into effect and that they would start doing so the following day. Some units knew my orders but did not make any preparations to execute them. *I give orders only when they are necessary. I expect them to be executed at once and to the letter and that no unit under my command shall make changes, still less give orders to the contrary or delay execution through unnecessary red tape.*

Rommel must have missed the ready obedience of the Afrika Korps. In the desert he had not had to give orders twice.

Lack of backing from above and of enthusiasm below were no help in a race against time. Rommel was accustomed to the first. As for the second, no one was better than he at rousing the spirit of tired and apathetic troops. Like a mate of a sailing-ship, he could "put a jump into a wooden dog." "He had a knack of handling men and of talking to them," said Admiral Ruge. "Like many of us who had been young officers in 1918, he had done some deep thinking after the revolution about the relations between officers and men. That is one of the reasons, I think, why our Army and Navy kept their discipline so long under such very difficult circumstances. Wherever we went at this time in France he spoke freely to all ranks. He explained his ideas to them clearly and patiently and told them exactly what he wanted them to do. Naturally, they listened for, apart from his reputation, he had great commonsense, a gift of quiet humour and an instinct for the human side of a situation often lacking in trained staff officers. A new spirit was very soon evident in the troops and the work of preparing to resist the invasion began to go ahead."

On the other side of the Channel, General Montgomery was speaking in just the same simple, direct and effective fashion to the troops who were to carry it out and to the factory workers who were to keep them supplied.

In neither case were these "pep-talks" greatly appreciated by higher authority. Both commanders were suspected of aiming at a personal "build-up." The British newspapers, says Moorehead, were encouraged to "go slow" on Montgomery. As far back as the summer of 1941, the Army Propaganda Department had been instructed, apparently by General

Halder, not to make too much of Rommel. Baron von Esebeck had been refused permission to rejoin him in North Africa. Rommel's enemies in high places were now in a quandary. They had to make the most of the Atlantic Wall, if only to intimidate the Allies. They could not publicise it and the work being done on it without at the same time publicising the man in charge. They contented themselves, therefore, with describing him in private as a mountebank and a seeker after notoriety. They added that he had never been the same since his illness in North Africa. Rommel, meanwhile, like Montgomery, realised that propaganda and the exploitation of his own personality were merely another weapon. "You can do what you like with me," he said to his chief cameraman, "if it means the postponing of the invasion by even a week." In private, says Admiral Ruge, he remained modest and unassuming. "He was not a vain man and he had no wish to push himself forward."

Personal jealousies Rommel could ignore: scarcity of material was an obstacle that could not be overcome. At this period enormous quantities of steel and concrete were being used for submarine shelters and for the launching-sites of V1's and V2's. The new submarines and the secret weapons were Hitler's latest prescription for winning the war. Had they not been spotted in time, they might well have enabled him, if not to win it, at least to prolong it indefinitely. Perhaps rightly, they were still given priority over fixed defences. Rommel had, therefore, to make do with what he could lay his hands on. Hitler might agree, as he did, that all coastal defence batteries should be put into concrete emplacements, with at least six feet of concrete overhead. But even armed with this order Rommel could not get the concrete, simply because there was not enough to go round. When the invasion came, many batteries had no overhead cover at all and were quickly blotted out from the air.

Rommel nevertheless managed to get a prodigious amount of work done and, in this new field, showed his innate talent for improvisation. In a few months, though hampered by supply and transport difficulties and, towards the end, by continual air attacks, he succeeded in having four million mines laid, as against less than two million in the previous three years. Given time, he proposed to lay fifty to a hundred million and, after surrounding all strongholds with deep minefields, to fill up the country between them with mines, wherever it was "tankable." What would the answer have been if he had thus converted whole areas of France into vast mine swamps? The point was not raised at Field-Marshal Montgomery's post-war conference at Camberley in May, 1946, though it had occurred to one distinguished commander and student of war, Lieutenant-General Sir Francis Tuker. General Patton might have been puzzled.

Because mines, like everything else, were in short supply, they were not at all of conventional construction. Rommel raided depots and arsenals, where he discovered stocks of hundreds of thousands of old shells. These he made into mines, as did the Japanese, more primitively, in Burma. (Under the Japanese system, an unfortunate individual sat with his shell in a hole in the road and was supposed to touch it off when a tank ran over him.) Nor were the minefields laid in conventional pattern. Rommel's idea was to employ mines in as many different ways as possible. "Here he had to fight many a battle against the engineers," said Admiral Ruge. "They wanted to lay their mines by the book while he was always for variety." Rommel and Ruge were, in fact, still making a comparative study of mining tactics ashore and at sea when the invasion overtook them.

Rommel's open mind greatly impressed his naval adviser. "He was an unconventional soldier and, unlike many of the General Staff, he was very much interested in technical things. He saw the point of any new device of a technical kind very quickly. If one gave him an idea in the evening he would often telephone in the morning and suggest an improvement. He had a strong mechanical bent and his suggestions were always sound." In the many "gadgets" that were improvised to make a landing difficult, one can see the traces of the young officer who took his new motor-bicycle to pieces and put it together again, just as one can see, in the deceptions and ruses employed, the artful enemy we knew in North Africa.

Amongst the "gadgets" were, for example, the beams driven into the beaches below low-water mark, some with mines on the top, some with steel cutters to act as "tin-openers." There were homemade "nutcracker" mines in blocks of concrete. There were mined logs with a seaward slope. There were the obsolete tank obstacles, made out of three iron bars at right-angles, which were now useless against tanks but, as Rommel pointed out, could still impede infantry if set below high-water mark. There were naval mines sunk in shallow water with floating lines attached to the horns. Ashore there were poles driven in on open fields and wired together with mines on top to impede glider landings. Many of these and other such devices were, however, not ready by June 6th because of difficulties of supply, of transport and of labour.

Amongst the deceptions were, naturally, dummy minefields, though Rommel had to complain that they would hardly be convincing to air reconnaissance if cattle were allowed to graze over them. There were dummy batteries which, in fact, were later heavily bombed. There was the usual camouflage, though here again Rommel had to point out that it was not much use camouflaging a battery position in a green field with black nets. There were arrangements for make-shift smoke from straw and leaves, real smoke apparatus being in short supply. Infantry and artillery commanders were ordered to be ready to light fires on dummy batteries and on dummy emplacements and entrenchments behind the line, to distract enemy gunfire from the beaches. But, on April 22nd, "there are no reports from any place that these preparations have been made."

As a preliminary measure, when the invasion was imminent, Rommel was anxious that VI's should be used against the British concentration areas in the South of England. He was refused, though many of the installations were ready, because there were not yet enough VI's to allow of a continuous fire being kept up. It was, perhaps, too late. But it is interesting to note that General Eisenhower says that, had the Germans succeeded in perfecting these weapons six months earlier and had they been used principally against the Portsmouth-Southampton area, "the invasion of Europe would have proved exceedingly difficult and perhaps impossible."

Similarly, Rommel wanted the Navy to mine the navigation channels and the Luftwaffe to drop the new pressure-box mines all round the Isle of Wight. The Navy objected to laying mines too close to the shore and the Führer would not allow the pressure-box mine to be used because there was no known method of sweeping it and the Allies might lay similar mines and "block our harbours completely." (He was, presumably, still thinking of his new submarines.)

The real conflict of opinion was, however, on the whole broad question of how the invasion could best be resisted. Rommel apparently had no doubts. *"We must stop the enemy in the water,"* he said, *"and destroy his equipment while it is still afloat."* The first twenty-four hours, in his view, would be decisive. Once the Allies secured a bridgehead it would be impossible to drive them back into the sea or to prevent them breaking out. He based his belief entirely on the factor of air superiority. "He had never forgotten how the R.A.F. had kept him and his army of 80,000 men nailed to the ground for two or three days in North Africa." The air force that would accompany the invasion would be incomparably more powerful. As for the Luftwaffe, it would be shot out of the skies and the reinforcements promised by Goering, like the supplies for North Africa, would never appear. Road and rail traffic would be completely disrupted and movement in the back areas would become impossible. It was no use, therefore, thinking of conventional large-scale counter-offensives: the troops would never get up to make them or would arrive in disorder and too late. If this reasoning were correct, then the main line of resistance must be the beach. Every man in the forward divisions must be ready to fight at once if a landing were attempted on his part of the coast. Reserves, head-quarters and ancillary services must be right up behind the fighting troops. The armour must be in close support, so that the guns of the tanks could actually bear on the beaches. If this strong belt of resistance were eventually broken, at least it would hold up the invaders for some time and their breakout would be local.

The Army Command, the Commander-in-Chief West, his staff and the majority of the army, corps and divisional commanders took the more orthodox view. With 3,000 miles of coast line to defend; with only 59 divisions, most of them second-class and only ten of them armoured, with which to defend it; with no certainty where the main landing would be made, it was useless to think of preventing the Allies setting foot above high-water mark. The only correct course was to keep the reserves, including the armour, well in rear, to wait until the main effort was identified beyond doubt and then to launch a large-scale counter-offensive at the right moment. That might be when the invaders were ashore and still building-up. It might be when they had moved out of their bridgehead but were temporarily "off balance." Von Rundstedt justifiably considered himself a good enough general to select it according to circumstances.

For Rommel it may be said that his appreciation of the effects of Allied air power was proved accurate. It was only with the utmost difficulty that troops could move behind the front and then across country, by night and in small formations. One division from the south of France took twenty-two days to cover the four hundred miles to Normandy and had to do most of it on foot. General Bayerlein, now commanding the crack Panzer Lehr Division, ninety miles south of Caen, took more than three days to get up and lost five tanks, 130 trucks and many self-propelled guns before he came into action, though he was well provided with "flak" and had trained his division in the use of cover and camouflage. In the Falaise gap, roads, highways and fields were so choked with destroyed equipment and with dead men and animals, says General Eisenhower, "that it was literally possible to walk for hundreds of yards at a time stepping on nothing but dead and decaying flesh."

On the other hand, Rommel can be accused of grossly overestimating the chances of holding the Atlantic Wall. It was no good saying, at the end of April, that "we must, in the short time left, bring all defences up to such a standard that they will be proof against the strongest attack." For that he should have been in charge two years before, with unlimited material and the men to put it into place. Even so, there is no such thing as a defensive belt "proof against the strongest attack." That was a lesson that he and his "Ghost Division" had helped to teach in 1940. As it was, his defences were not even a quarter complete. Nor could he have had any confidence in the men who manned them. Dug-outs, convalescents from the Eastern Front, boys without battle experience, with a residue of renegade Poles, Rumanians, Jugoslavs and Russians, they were not likely to stand up to the sort of sea and air bombardment he had himself foretold. His reputation as a strategist would rank higher if he had backed von Rundstedt's proposal for evacuating, before the invasion, the whole of southern France up to the Loire. Had that been done, he might have fought his last battles in the moving warfare of which he was a master. But such a plan, as he knew, was foredoomed. Selling ideas of retreat to the Führer was a task more hopeless than that of defending the Atlantic Wall. However, as will be seen in the next chapter, he is not to be judged entirely on what he said and seemed to believe at this period.

General Montgomery had no doubt what Rommel would do. His analysis of his old opponent's plans and personality was a masterpiece. "Last February," he said, in May, "Rommel took command from Holland to the Loire. . . . It is now clear that his intention is to defeat us on the beaches. . . . He is an energetic and determined commander; he has made a world of difference since he took over. He is best at the spoiling attack; his forte is disruption; he is too impulsive for a set-piece battle. He will do his level best to 'Dunkirk' us—not to fight the armoured battle on ground of his choosing but to avoid it altogether and prevent our tanks landing by using his own tanks well forward. On D-day he will try (a) to force us from the beaches; (b) to secure Caen, Bayeux, Carentan. Thereafter he will continue his counter-attacks. . . . We must blast our way on shore and get a good lodgment before he can bring up sufficient reserves to turn us out. Armoured columns must penetrate deep inland and quickly. . . . We must gain space rapidly and peg out claims well inland. . . . While we are engaged in doing this, the air must hold the ring and must make very difficult the movement of enemy reserves by train or road towards the lodgment areas. The land battle will be a terrific party and we shall require the support of the air all the time—and laid on quickly."

It came about as both men predicted. Rommel did try to "Dunkirk" us. The air did hold the ring. The first twenty-four hours were decisive. Once the Allies secured their bridgeheads, only by some gross mistake on their part could they have been thrown back into the sea. Would von Rundstedt have had a better chance of defeating them in open warfare when they debouched from it? With the troops at his disposal and in face of Allied air supremacy, it seems unlikely. Nor was General Montgomery the man to give him the opportunity of catching him "off balance." Progress might have been slower but one feels that it would have been just as sure.

In fact, neither of the plans for resisting the invasion was put to the test for neither von Rundstedt nor Rommel was free to do as he wished. Because Hitler, if he did not inspire it, backed Rommel in his belief that the beaches must be the main line of resistance, von Rundstedt was unable to form his army of manœuvre. Because von Rundstedt, against Hitler's intuition and Rommel's judgment, took the orthodox staff view that the main landing would come in the Pas de Calais, the nearest point to England and the direct road to the Ruhr, Rommel was not able to concentrate a strong armoured force immediately behind the Normandy beaches, where he and Hitler expected it. Three weak armoured divisions only were placed at his disposal for the whole front from the Scheldt to the Loire. The rest were in reserve, nominally under the orders of Commander-in-Chief West. Even he could not move them without the permission of Keitel, Jodl and Hitler which, as usual, came too late. In the forward area in Normandy, Rommel had only his old 21st Panzer Division, now re-formed, with very few of the old personnel. According to von Esebeck, it was removed from his command while he was away seeing Hitler the day before the invasion and transferred to von Rundstedt's Panzer Group West. He retrieved it and used it to advantage, for it was this division which prevented the capture of Caen the first day. But, rightly or wrongly, Rommel did not feel that its commander, Major-General Feuchtinger, handled it with the boldness of von Ravenstein in the desert. When he reached the front he found it, says von Esebeck, held up by airborne troops. "How many gliders were there," asked Rommel. "Hundreds and hundreds," replied Feuchtinger. "How many did you shoot down?" "Three or four." "You have lost your chance," said Rommel. Feuch-tinger, for his part, complained that, until Rommel's return, he could get no orders from any one and that he had been forbidden to move without them.

As in Africa, "too little and too late" was the crime of the German High Command. For weeks before the invasion Rommel had begged to be allowed to move the 12th S.S. Panzer Division, the *Hitler Jugend,* to the mouth of the Vire, near Carentan. It was near Carentan that the Americans landed. Carentan was one of the three points which General Montgomery had predicted that Rommel would try to secure. When it was thrown in at Caen, the division fought desper-ately under its fanatical Nazi leader, Kurt Meyer. It might not have stopped the landing but that was the way Rommel had planned to stop it. Rommel was refused the division by von Rundstedt. Yet von Rundstedt was not to blame. He could not move it without permission from Jodl and Jodl could not move it without permission from Hitler! No general could control a battle under such conditions.

It was very shortly after the bridgehead had been secured that Rommel and von Rundstedt found themselves for the first time in complete and open agreement. Asked by Captain Liddell Hart long afterwards whether he had hopes of de-feating the invasion at any stage after the landing, von Rund-stedt replied: "Not after the first few days. The Allied Air Forces paralysed all movement by day and made it very difficult by night. They had smashed the bridges over the Loire as well as over the Seine, shutting off the whole area. These factors greatly delayed the concentration of reserves there—they took three or four times longer to reach the front than we had reckoned." The word "we" did not include Rommel, who was thus posthumously proved correct in his diagnosis, if not in his proposed treatment. The story was told by von Rundstedt's Chief of Staff, General Blumentritt, to the author of *Defeat in the West* how, towards the end of the month, Keitel called up von Rundstedt and asked desperately, "What shall we do?" To which von Rundstedt replied impassively: "Do? Make peace, you idiots! What else can you do?" and hung up. Admiral Ruge relates that, much earlier, Rommel told him that the war must be brought to an end at all costs. "Better end this at once, even if it means living as a British Dominion," he said, "rather than see Germany ruined by going on with this hopeless war." "On June 11th we talked for about two hours. I said that in my opinion Hitler ought to resign and open the road to peace. As an alternative I said that he ought to commit suicide. Rommel replied, 'I know that man. He will neither resign nor kill himself. He will fight, without the least regard for the German people, until there isn't a house left standing in Germany.' "

Rommel's reports were only slightly more discreet. On June 12th he sent forward an appreciation of the position on the previous day. After a conventional reference to the obstinate resistance of the German troops in the coastal sectors, which had delayed the Allied operations, he went on in a vein of almost unrelieved pessimism:

The strength of the enemy on land is increasing more quickly than our reserves can reach the front. . . . The Army Group must content itself for the present with forming a cohesive front between the Orne and the Vire and allowing the enemy to advance. . . . It is not possible to relieve troops still resisting in many coastal positions. . . . Our operations in Normandy will be rendered exceptionally difficult and even partially impossible by the extraordinarily strong and in some respects overwhelming superiority of the Allied Air Force and by the effects of heavy naval artillery. . . . As I personally and officers of my staff have repeatedly proved and as unit commanders, especially *Obergruppenführer* Sepp Dietrich, report, the enemy has complete control over the battle area and up to sixty miles behind the front. Almost all transport on roads and in open country is prevented by day by strong fighter-bomber and bomber formations. Movements of our troops in the battle area by day are also almost completely stopped, while the enemy can move freely. . . . It is difficult to bring up ammunition and food. . . . Artillery taking up positions, tanks deploying, etc. are immediately bombarded with annihilating effect. . . . Troops and staffs are forced to hide during the day. . . . Neither our flak nor the Luftwaffe seems to be in a position to check this crippling and destructive operation of the enemy Air Force. . . . The effect of heavy naval artillery is so strong that operation by infantry or panzer formations in the area commanded by it is impossible. . . . The material equipment of the Anglo-Americans, with numerous new weapons and war material, is far superior to the equipment of our divisions. As *Obergruppenführer* Sepp Dietrich informed me, enemy armoured divisions carry on the battle at a range of up to 3,500 yards with maximum expenditure of ammunition and splendidly supported by the enemy Air Force. . . . Parachute and airborne troops are used in such large numbers and so effectively that the troops attacked have a difficult task in defending themselves. . . . The Luftwaffe has unfortunately not been able to take action against these formations as was originally planned. Since the enemy can cripple our mobile formations with his Air Force by day while he operates with fast-moving forces and airborne troops, our position is becoming extraordinarily difficult.

I request that the Führer be informed of this.

ROMMEL

If Rommel imagined that the Führer could be induced to accept this "defeatist" view by references to his Nazi favourite, Sepp Dietrich, he was very much mistaken. On June 17th von Rundstedt managed to persuade Hitler to come to a conference at Margival, near Soissons. It was held at the headquarters, built in 1940, from which Hitler was to control the invasion of Britain. Von Rundstedt took Rommel with him. The two Field-Marshals both spoke out and left the Führer in no doubt what they thought about the prospect of throwing the invaders back into the sea. So far from that being possible, the only hope of preventing a break-out was to withdraw behind the Arne and continue the line to Granville, on the west side of the Cotentin peninsula. Such a line, running through the "*bocage*," close country with huge hedgerows, in the east, and thence over wooded hills, might perhaps be held with infantry. The remaining armour could then be reorganized and kept in reserve. Hitler's reply of "no retreat" was almost automatic. Rommel did not improve the atmosphere by protesting to Hitler against the "incident" of Oradour-sur-Glade, which had occurred a week before. Here the S.S. division, *Das Reich*, had, as a reprisal for the killing of a German officer, driven the women and children into the church and then set the village on fire. As the men and boys emerged from the flames, they mowed them down with machine guns. Afterwards they blew up the church and some six hundred women and children with it. It was unfortunate, they admitted, that there were two villages named Oradour and that they had inadvertently picked the wrong one. Still, reprisals had been carried out. Rommel demanded to be allowed to punish the Division. "Such things bring disgrace on the German uniform," he said. "How can you wonder at the strength of the French Resistance behind us when the S.S. drive every decent Frenchman into joining it?" "That has nothing to do with you," snapped Hitler. "It is outside your area. Your business is to resist the invasion."

When, greatly daring, von Rundstedt and Rommel tentatively broached the question of making overtures to the Western Powers, the conference quickly broke up. The farewells were not cordial on either side. Shortly afterwards a homing Vi hit the headquarters. There were, unfortunately, no casualties.

Rommel's reports for the next few weeks were strictly factual. No opinions about the future were expressed. "Army Group B will continue its attempt to prevent all efforts by the enemy to break through" was as far as they went. In reporting losses of 100,089 officers and men between June 6th and July 7th, as against 8,395 replacements brought to the front and 5,303 warned for transfer, Rommel merely commented: "The replacement situation gives grounds for some anxiety in view of increasing losses." He was, in fact, "browned-off." On June 29th he and Field-Marshal von Rundstedt had been summoned to Berchtesgaden. There the Führer had announced that mobile warfare must not be allowed to develop because of the enemy's air superiority and superabundance of motor vehicles and fuel. A front must be built to block him off in his bridgehead and he must be worn down by a war of attrition. Every method of guerrilla warfare must be employed. For Rommel's special benefit he added, in front of Keitel and Jodl, that "everything would be all right if you would only fight better." Rommel returned, furiously angry, to his headquarters at La Roche Guyon and handed on this bouquet to his Chief of Staff, Generalleutnant Dr. Hans Speidel, who had succeeded Gausi at the end of April.

Since General Speidel was to play and was, indeed, already secretly playing a much more important part in Rommel's life than that of a Chief of Staff, he requires special mention. In appearance astonishingly like the then British Secretary of State for War, Sir James Grigg, with the same somewhat owl-like expression and the same prehensile nose, he had (and has) an equally clear and exact brain and a somewhat more equable and philosophical temperament. This is not surprising since he is that very rare bird, a professional soldier who is also a professional philosopher. After joining the army in 1914, at the age of seventeen and serving throughout the war on the Western Front, part of the time in the same brigade as Rommel, he remained in it between the wars and started to study for the Staff College. At the same time he contrived to read philosophy and history at Tübingen University and became a Doctor of Philosophy *summa cum laude* in February, 1925. If this "double" is not a record, it must at least be rare.

As a staff-officer, Speidel, with his precise and analytical mind and his card-index memory, was marked for success, particularly as he combines with them warm, if well-concealed, human feelings and a mildly satirical sense of humour. Assistant Military Attaché in Paris in 1933 (he speaks impeccable French), he was made chief of the western section when he returned to Berlin. After seeing the French manœuvres in 1937 he wrote a pamphlet in which he said that the French army was not ready for a modern offensive war but that it and its leaders could be counted on for a desperate resistance if France were invaded. "Fortunately—or perhaps unfortunately—I was wrong," he remarked.

1A (G1) of the 9th Corps at Dunkirk, he confirms that it was Hitler's direct order which prevented von Rundstedt from using the two armoured corps of Guderian and von Kleist against the embarking British. "Had they been put in," he says, "not a British soldier could have left the coast of France." Shortly afterwards he was sitting in the Hotel Crillon in Paris drafting, with General Dentz, the terms of the French surrender. Since we always regarded General Dentz as a monster of duplicity for his behaviour in Syria and the French condemned him, first to death and then to life imprisonment, it is perhaps of interest that General Speidel thinks that he did the best he could in the circumstances and was "a patriot and a good soldier of France."

Speidel next became Chief of Staff to General von Stülpnagel, Military Governor of France, and held the appointment until the winter of 1941. Then, when he saw that all power was passing into the hands of the S.D., the security police of the S.S., he asked to be relieved of it, a fact which throws some light on his character and subsequent behaviour. So does his long friendship with Colonel-General Beck, the former Chief of the General Staff.

From France, he went to hold various high staff appointments in Russia. In front of Moscow with the 5th Army, he was later largely responsible for the planning of the southern offensive of the summer of 1942, which brought the Germans to the very verge of victory. As Chief of the General Staff of the 8th (Italian) Army throughout 1943 and the early months of 1944 he took part in all the great battles of that fateful year. Fatuously enough, I asked General Speidel about conditions in Russia. The cold must have been very severe? "Very severe, indeed," he agreed blandly, "the only thing to be said for it was that it made it almost impossible for staff officers to write." As for the causes of the ultimate failure: "Too many Russians and one German too many—Hitler."

Dr. Speidel, still only fifty-one, is now lecturing on philosophy at Tübingen University. As will be seen, he reached that peaceful haven after a somewhat stormy and adventurous voyage. Meanwhile, amid all the tumult of the Normandy fighting, he was the trusted adviser of the Commander-in-Chief of Army Group B on other than purely military matters.

On July 17th, the Allied Air Force at last overtook Rommel. There was nothing unusual in what happened to him. His staff-car was only one of thousands of German vehicles shot up on the roads of Normandy in July, 1944. Captain Helmuth Lang, who was in the car with him, gives the facts. From his statement it is clear that they were unlucky in picking a road along which our aircraft were operating.*

* In an article summarised in the *Reader's Digest,* the Countess Waldeck makes the suggestion that the aircraft may have been German with British markings, ordered by Hitler to eliminate Rommel because he had sent an "ultimatum" to the Führer on July 15th. There is no evidence to support this suggestion and so many improbabilities inherent in it that it need not be taken seriously. In any case, the "ultimatum" had not reached Hitler by July 17th. It was not forwarded until July 21st.

"As he did every day," writes Captain Lang, "Marshal Rommel on July 17th made a tour of the front. After visiting 277th and 276th Infantry Divisions, on whose sectors a heavy enemy attack had been repulsed the night before, he went to the headquarters of the 2nd S.S. Armoured Corps and had a conversation with Generals Bittrich and Sepp Dietrich. We had to be careful of enemy aircraft, which were flying over the battlefield continually and were quickly attracted by dust on the roads.

"About 4 P.M. Marshal Rommel started on the return journey from General Dietrich's headquarters. He was anxious to get back to Army Group B headquarters as quickly as possible because the enemy had broken through on another part of the front.

"All along the roads we could see transport in flames: from time to time the enemy bombers forced us to take to second-class roads. About 6 P.M. the Marshal's car was in the neighbourhood of Livarot. Transport which had just been attacked was piled up along the road and strong groups of enemy dive-bombers were still at work close by. That is why we turned off along a sheltered road, to join the main road again two and a half miles from Vimoutiers.

"When we reached it we saw above Livarot about eight enemy dive-bombers. We learnt later that they had been interfering with traffic on the road to Livarot for the past two hours. Since we thought that they had not seen us, we continued along the main road from Livarot to Vimoutiers. Suddenly Sergeant Holke, our spotter, warned us that two aircraft were flying along the road in our direction. The driver, Daniel, was told to put on speed and turn off on to a little side road to the right, about 300 yards ahead of us, which would give us some shelter.

"Before we could reach it, the enemy aircraft, flying at great speed only a few feet above the road, came up to within 500 yards of us and the first one opened fire. Marshal Rommel was looking back at this moment. The left-hand side of the car was hit by the first burst. A cannon-shell shattered Daniel's left shoulder and left arm. Marshal Rommel was wounded in the face by broken glass and received a blow on the left temple and cheek-bone* which caused a triple fracture of the skull and made him lose consciousness immediately. Major Neuhaus was struck on the holster of his revolver and the force of the blow broke his pelvis.

* Apparently from the pillar of the windscreen.

"As the result of his serious wounds, Daniel, the driver, lost control of the car. It struck the stump of a tree, skidded over to the left of the road and then turned over in a ditch on the right. Captain Lang and Sergeant Holke jumped out of the car and took shelter on the right of the road. Marshal Rommel, who, at the start of the attack, had hold of the handle of the door, was thrown out, unconscious, when the car turned over and lay stretched out on the road about twenty yards behind it. A second aircraft flew over and tried to drop bombs on those who were lying on the ground.

"Immediately afterwards, Marshal Rommel was carried into shelter by Captain Lang and Sergeant Holke. He lay on the ground unconscious and covered with blood, which flowed from the many wounds on his face, particularly from his left eye and mouth. It appeared that he had been struck on the left temple. Even when we had carried him to safety he did not recover consciousness.

"In order to get medical help for the wounded, Captain Lang tried to find a car. It took him about three-quarters of an hour to do so. Marshal Rommel had his wounds dressed by a French doctor in a religious hospital. They were very severe and the doctor said that there was little hope of saving his life. Later he was taken, still unconscious, with Daniel to an air-force hospital at Bernay, about 25 miles away. The doctors there diagnosed severe injuries to the skull—a fracture at the base, two fractures on the temple and the cheek-bone destroyed, a wound in the left eye, wounds from glass and concussion. Daniel died during the night, in spite of a blood transfusion.

"A few days later Marshal Rommel was taken to the hospital of Professor Esch at Vesinet, near St. Germain."

Early in July, no doubt as the result of his advice to Keitel to make peace, Field-Marshal von Rundstedt had been relieved of his command. He was replaced by Field-Marshal Günther von Kluge from the Russian front. Undeterred by this warning to defeatists, Rommel decided to make one more attempt to bring Hitler to reason. In consultation with General Speidel, who drafted it, he had sent a report to von Kluge two days before he was wounded and asked him to forward it personally to the Führer. It was along the same lines as his analysis of June 12th but even more pessimistic.

"The position on the Normandy front," he began, "is becoming daily increasingly difficult and is rapidly approaching its crisis." There followed references to the Allies' superiority in artillery and armour; to the heavy German losses and lack of reinforcements; to the inexperience of the divisions brought up; to their inadequate equipment; to the destruction of the railway network by air attack and the difficulty of using the roads; to lack of ammunition and the exhaustion of the troops. On the other hand, the enemy were daily providing new forces and masses of material, their supply lines were not challenged by the Luftwaffe and pressure was continually increasing. "In these circumstances," concluded Rommel, "it must be expected that the enemy will shortly be able to break through our thinly-held front, especially in the 7th Army Sector, and push far into France. . . . There are no mobile reserves at all at our disposal to counter a break-through. Our own air force has hardly entered the battle at all.

"Our troops are fighting heroically but even so the end of this unequal battle is in sight."

In his own handwriting Rommel added the words, "I must beg you to recognise at once the political significance of this situation. I feel it my duty, as Commander-in-Chief of the Army Group, to say this plainly."

Von Kluge's covering letter, dated July 21st, is of interest. It shows that, for all the high hopes with which he took over, it did not take him long to come to the same conclusion as von Rundstedt and Rommel. It also shows him to have exhibited, on this occasion at least, considerable moral courage, for he cannot have supposed that it would be popular at the Führer's headquarters.

My Führer [he wrote], I forward herewith a report from Field-Marshal Rommel, which he gave to me before his accident and which he had already discussed with me. I have now been here for about fourteen days and, after long discussions with the responsible commanders on the various fronts, especially the S.S. leaders, I have come to the conclusion that the Field-Marshal was, unfortunately, right. . . . There is absolutely no way in which we could do battle with the all-powerful enemy air force . . . without being forced to surrender territory. . . . The psychological effect on the fighting forces, especially the infantry, of such a mass of bombs raining down on them with all the force of elemental nature is a factor that must be seriously considered. It is not in the least important whether such a carpet of bombs is laid on good or bad troops. They are more or less annihilated by it and, above all, their equipment is destroyed. It only needs this to happen a few times . . . and the power of resistance is paralysed. . . .

I came here with the fixed intention of making effective your order to make a stand *at any price*. But when one sees that this price must be paid by the slow but sure destruction of our troops—I am thinking of the Hitler Youth division, which has earned the highest praise . . . then the anxiety about the immediate future on this front is only too well justified.

In spite of all our endeavours, the moment is fast approaching when this overtaxed front is bound to break up. . . . I consider it my duty as the responsible commander to bring these developments to your notice in good time, my Führer.

Five weeks later Field-Marshal von Kluge had been superseded and was dead. With death everywhere about for the asking and stray bullets making heroes of frightened men every moment of the day and night, he chose to die by his own hand. He felt, he said, that he failed his Führer in the control of the operations. This was not, however, his only reason for being unwilling to meet him.

CHAPTER 11

"A Pitiless Destiny"

When, after the explosion of the atomic bomb, American sailors went aboard the surviving target ships at Bikini, they gradually became gripped by a strange, obsessive fear. "Decks you can't stay on for more than a few minutes; air you can't breathe without a gas-mask but which smells like all other air; water you can't swim in; fish you can't eat: it's a fouled-up world," they said.* For fission products, having fallen like a coat of paint over these ships, could not be washed off by the Navy's old prescription of a good scrubdown fore and aft. The neutrons and gamma rays remained, detectible only by Geiger counters but threatening disease, disintegration and the novel horror of atomic death.

One need not be psychic or even unduly sensitive to atmos-

* *No Place to Hide* by David Bradley.

phere to feel that something evil, not to be registered by Geiger counters, still hangs in the air of Germany today. Miasmas no longer arise from the ruined cities; the countryside is clean and beautiful. Relieved from the worst of their material distress, the Germans go cheerfully enough about their work. In the village inns in the evenings they sing and dance and drink their beer more lightheartedly than most of us. Hatred of the occupying troops and their camp-followers is doubtless there but it is well concealed. Why, then, is one seldom quite at ease? Perhaps because one knows that so many of the Gestapo and S.S. are still at large, with false papers or free because those who might accuse them are buried; that the polite young man who waits on one so attentively in the hotel may have the blood of hundreds on his hands. (A Gestapo agent, wanted for sixty separate murders, was recently identified in the popular interpreter of a British camp.) Perhaps the reason is a little more remote—that the taint of the Nazi régime, which has not disappeared with the suicide or execution of its leaders, will not vanish with the death of the last of their accomplices. The acid of the unceasing spying and suspicion, of arrests at dawn, of torture and sadism and murder in cellars, above all, of the lying and hypocrisy which pervade a police state, has eaten in too deep. Like the fission products, it cannot be washed out. The shadow of Hitler still darkens the German scene. "It's a fouled-up world."

At least, so I felt as I listened to the story of the last days of Rommel and of the manner of his end. Not that there was anything at all sinister about the surroundings in which I heard it or anything at all morbid about those who told it to me. On the contrary, when I sat in General Speidel's house above the peaceful Black Forest town of Freudenstadt, I had a feeling almost of nostalgia for the Victorian and Edwardian interiors of my childhood. It was in just such houses as this, a little over-furnished to modern taste but so well-ordered, so solidly and smugly comfortable (though never, perhaps, quite so incredibly clean), that the middle-class English, too, used to live their comfortable and well-ordered lives, their money in sound investments, their trust in God and the Government, the servants in their place, the cat on the hearth, the policeman on his beat. One might have been in North Oxford, forty years ago.

Frau Rommel's little house, though it is filled with relics of Rommel, though paintings and photographs of him cover the

174

walls, though his death-mask is kept in a case in a corner, has the same atmosphere of tranquillity and security. So has Aldinger's. So has that in which I found Dr. Strölin, the last of my informants. In each the story had to be interrupted and papers removed so that an embroidered cloth could be laid for tea. In each the china was Meissen, cherished and unchipped and afterwards restored to its cabinet. In each were those once familiar four-decker cake-stands which might be the symbol of a vanished age.

As for General Speidel, he looks what in fact he is, a don. His wife, much too young, one would say, to be the mother of a seventeen-year-old daughter, might never have had a care in the world beyond minor domestic worries. The children are handsome, punctiliously well-mannered and brought up to speak when they are spoken to. Aldinger and his wife are typical pillars of small-town society. Dr. Strölin has the assured air of a man long accustomed to position and authority. Frau Lucie Maria Rommel, though her strong face is heavily lined, shows no other sign of an experience as harrowing as any woman has had to undergo. Much more Northern Italian than German in appearance, with her black hair and grey eyes, she has none of the sentimentality to be found in so many Germans. When she speaks of *"mein Mann,"* it is cheerfully and with pride. For nearly thirty years they had a good life together, in spite of two wars, and were happy. Of her husband's end she is willing to talk when one has her confidence. She does so without bitterness but with great disdain for those who were responsible. Only once did she show how deep her feelings still are after five years. When we drove up together to her former house on the hill above Herrlingen, now a school, she stayed in the car outside the gates. "I like to see the children in the garden," she said, "but I do not wish to go in there again."

Manfred, the son, now studying law at Tübingen University, is a pleasant and perfectly normal young man, devoted to his mother and to the memory of his father, and entirely free, so far as one can judge, of any "complexes." He is neither unbalanced nor embittered by what he saw at the impressionable age of fifteen.

Yet, against this background of almost Victorian normality, elsewhere now hard to find, these seemingly normal people had been involved, or had deliberately involved themselves, in a struggle with a régime so ruthless that death was far from the worst of its punishments for those who challenged it. It was this contrast which, to me, made the whole story more disquieting and macabre. Incidentally, they had all displayed a four-o'clock-in-the-morning courage which convinced me that their nerves were stronger than my own.

Rommel returned from North Africa in March, 1943, having, as they say, "had" Hitler. For a long time he had known that Keitel and Jodl were both professionally and privately his enemies. Goering he despised and distrusted, suspecting him of having been prejudiced by Kesselring against himself and the Afrika Korps. Recently he had been warned by General Schmundt that his stock had slumped with the Party bosses and particularly with the mysteriously influential Bormann. He had, in fact, no friend at court except Schmundt himself, who still spoke up for him. However, until after El Alamein he continued to believe that the trouble with the Führer was his entourage and that he would act fairly and see reason if only he would free himself from his sycophants.

Now he had no such illusions. He had come to realise that there was in Adolf Hitler neither fairness, generosity nor loyalty to those who served him. Nor was he open to reason. This was a distressing revelation to Rommel, a straightforward, simple man with little subtlety, except in battle. Since he had never been a political soldier and was completely out of touch with current politics, the shock was at first purely personal and professional. He had lost faith in a man who had been his friend and patron and was head of the armed forces. It was only gradually that he came to see that more than victory was being endangered, that, thanks to Hitler, Germany was on the way to degradation as well as to defeat.

His eyes were opened during the months he was in Germany before he took over command of Army Group B. He had long disapproved of the Nazi "scum." For the first time he now learnt at first hand from German officers what the Gestapo and the S.S. had done in Poland and Russia, what they were still doing there and in the occupied countries of Western Europe. For the first time he learnt of slave labour, of the mass extermination of Jews, of the battle of the Warsaw ghetto, of gas-chambers and the rest of it. In North Africa it had been assumed that Germany was fighting "a gentleman's war."

It was characteristic of Rommel that he went straight to Hitler himself with these discoveries. "If such things are allowed to go on," he said, "we shall lose the war." He then proposed the disbandment of the Gestapo and the splitting up of the S.S. among the regular forces. At the same time he begged Hitler to stop the enlistment of very young boys. "It is madness," he said, "to destroy the youth of the country." Such ingenuousness must have staggered Hitler. It may have amused Himmler, if Hitler communicated Rommel's proposals to him. Strangely enough, the Führer condescended to argue with Rommel at some length. But he left no doubt in the latter's mind that he had not the slightest intention of changing his methods. Rommel thus realised that his master's crimes were of commission also.

During the early part of the summer he brooded over these matters and, for the first time in his life, became politically conscious. His conclusions were those of many other German generals. Hitler would lead the country to ruin. He ought, therefore, to be curbed. So long as he had the Party, the S.S. and many young officers and soldiers of the Reichswehr behind him, there was no way of removing him short of civil war. It might be sufficient to remove his advisers and keep him as a figurehead, without any real authority. How could that be done? Before Rommel had followed out this line he was appointed to Army Group B and went off, first to Northern Italy and afterwards to France. He put the whole problem temporarily at the back of his mind and, as was usual with him, applied himself to the work in hand.

There were others, however, whose plans were more advanced and who for some time had had their eyes on Rommel. Dr. Goerdeler, Mayor of Leipzig, and Colonel-General Beck, former Chief of the General Staff, were the key men in the conspiracy against Hitler. They realised that, if it were to have any chance of success, they must find a popular figure, a modern Hindenburg, to put at the head of it when the time came. He must be one who already had the public confidence and who could not be suspected of acting from self-interest. He must be a soldier whom the Army would follow. General Beck, though his character and ability were of the highest, would not do. The majority of Germans had hardly heard of him and he had been dismissed by Hitler as far back as 1938. Among the serving generals there was none with a reputation, in the eyes of the public, which approached that of Rommel. After Hitler himself, he was probably the most popular man in Germany. Politically there was nothing against him. He had, indeed, to his own annoyance, been built up by the propagandists as a good Nazi. At the same time he was known to be respected by the British, with whom, at the crucial moment, he would have to treat. Outside a small circle, no one knew that he was at cross-purposes with the Führer. He was, therefore, the obvious choice, indeed the only one.

Fortunately the conspirators had just the right contact in Dr. Karl Strölin, *Oberbürgermeister* or Mayor of Stuttgart from 1933 and well-known abroad as chairman of the last meeting before the war of the International Federation for Housing and Town Planning. Immensely popular in Stuttgart and a man of great energy and ability, Dr. Strölin was one of those who had originally been a strong supporter of Hitler and the Party. That it was possible to be a Nazi, at least at first, without being a gangster is shown by a tribute paid to Strölin by the Consul-General of the United States in Stuttgart, who knew him there for seven years, from 1934 to 1941. "He is a man of the highest humane principles," he wrote in 1948 in a letter which I myself have seen, "as is confirmed by what I heard of him from Americans and Germans alike and especially from members of the Jewish faith, many of whom spoke of him with great appreciation and reverence. His nobility of character and untiring efforts on behalf of those in distress should entitle him to the greatest respect of the German people, as well as of those he served so unselfishly."

It was the rape of Czechoslovakia which turned Dr. Strölin against Hitler; it was his friendship with Dr. Goerdeler which made him a conspirator. Though he contrived, astonishingly, to remain Mayor of Stuttgart until the end of the war, he worked actively against the Nazis from 1939 onwards. The story of how he saved twenty-one members of the French Resistance, condemned to death in Alsace, has been told by one of them. It does the greatest credit to his intelligence and courage.

As an infantry captain in the first war, he served with Rommel in 1918, after being twice wounded, on the staff of the 64th Corps. Because they were both front-line soldiers and unhappy on the staff, they became friends. Though Strölin's interests were much wider than Rommel's, the friendship had been maintained between the wars. Recently Strölin had helped Rommel to move his family from Wiener Neustadt to Württemberg.

It was through Frau Rommel that Strölin started to work. In August, 1943, he had the courage to put his name to a document, which he and Goerdeler had drafted, demanding that the persecution of Jews and of the churches be abandoned, that civil rights be restored and that the administration of justice be taken out of the hands of the Party. This heretical paper was sent to the Secretary of the Ministry of the Interior. Strölin was promptly warned that he would be put on trial for "crimes against the Fatherland" if he did not keep quiet. "At least I was now satisfied," he said, "that nothing could be done by legal methods."

Strölin gave a copy of the paper to Frau Rommel. Towards the end of November or when he was home on short leave for Christmas, she cannot remember which, she in turn handed it to her husband. It made a profound impression on him, since his own mind had been working in the same direction. In December, Strölin also managed to visit Frau Rommel at Herrlingen when he knew that General Gausi, Rommel's Chief of Staff, would be there. His intention was merely to ask for an interview with Rommel but he found that Gausi was also against Hitler, having recently had to deal with some of his Gauleiters.

The fateful interview took place in Rommel's house in Herrlingen towards the end of February, 1944. Strölin had to make his way there secretly. He had been warned by the ex-Commissioner of Police at Stuttgart, the same Hahn whom Rommel had known in 1919, that he was on the list of those for immediate liquidation should a resistance movement develop in Germany. He also knew that his telephone was tapped and his conversations recorded.

The interview lasted between five and six hours and Strölin still has a vivid recollection of it. "I began," he said, "by discussing the political and military situation of Germany. We found ourselves in complete agreement. I then said to Rommel, 'If you agree about the situation you must see what it is necessary to do.' I told him that certain senior officers of the Army in the East proposed to make Hitler a prisoner and to force him to announce over the radio that he had abdicated. Rommel approved of the idea. *Neither then nor at any time afterwards was he aware of the plan to kill Hitler.*

"I went on to say to him," continued Strölin, "that he was our greatest and most popular general and more respected abroad than any other. 'You are the only one,' I said, 'who can prevent civil war in Germany. You must lend your name to the movement.' I did not tell him that it was proposed to make him President of the Reich: the idea was not, in fact, suggested until I returned and had a talk with Goerdeler, and I don't think he ever heard of it until the last day of his life.

"Rommel hesitated. I asked him again whether he saw any chance of winning the war, perhaps by means of the secret weapons. Rommel said that he knew nothing about secret weapons except what he had read in the propaganda reports, but that he personally saw no chance. Militarily, it was already lost. Did he think that Hitler realised how bad things were? 'I doubt it,' said Rommel, 'in any case he lives on illusions.' Could he not ask for an interview and try to open his eyes? 'I have tried several times,' said Rommel, 'but I have never succeeded. I don't mind trying again, but they are suspicious of me at headquarters and certainly won't leave me alone with him. That fellow Bormann is always there.'

"We left it that Rommel should try, at some suitable moment, to see Hitler and bring him to reason. If that failed, he should write him a letter setting out the whole situation, explaining to him the impossibility of winning the war and asking him to accept the political consequences. Finally, as a last resort, he should himself take direct action. He thought it over for some time and said at length: 'I believe it is my duty to come to the rescue of Germany.' With that I had no more doubts. He was not a highly intellectual man; he understood no more of politics than he did of the arts. But he was the soul of honour and would never go back on his word. Moreover, unlike most of the generals, he was a man with the courage to act."

In April, Strölin found a new ally when General Speidel was appointed Rommel's Chief of Staff. He was already in touch with the conspirators. Thereafter Strölin was in almost daily contact with him by courier and, through him, with Rommel. Speidel had discussions with his former chief, General Heinrich von Stülpnagel, Military Governor of France, and with General von Falkenhausen, Military Governor of Belgium. In some Rommel took part; about all he was kept informed. Stülpnagel was on the inner ring of the conspiracy. Together he and Speidel worked out the heads of an armistice agreement which they hoped to negotiate with Generals Eisenhower and Montgomery. If Hitler had not already been removed, it was to be made independently of him. It provided for the evacuation of the occupied territories in the west. In the east a shortened front would be maintained.

In fact, the western Allies could not have agreed to such

conditions. They were pledged not to make a separate peace without Russia. Moreover they had round their necks the "putrefying albatross" of unconditional surrender. Clamped on by their own choice at Casablanca, it "whipped the Germans together under the swastika," strengthened Hitler, prolonged the war and cost many thousands of British and American lives. Speidel and Stülpnagel, however, supposed that Mr. Churchill and President Roosevelt would welcome the chance of keeping the Red Armies out of Western Europe, provided they did not have to make terms with Hitler or the Nazis.

On May 27th another important meeting was held in Speidel's house at Freudenstadt. It was called at Rommel's request. There were present Speidel himself, representing Rommel, Strölin and von Neurath, former Foreign Minister of Germany and later Gauleiter of Czechoslovakia. Von Neurath was afterwards sentenced to fifteen years' imprisonment at Nuremberg. He must have thought it somewhat ironical that he had already run the risk of punishment far more severe at the hands of Hitler. I sat up with a slight start when General Speidel said casually: "We met around this table; von Neurath had the chair in which you are sitting."

With the German passion for documentation, Strölin had written a special memorandum. It gave, he said, a complete exposé of the present position and was intended for Rommel's guidance. "And do you mean to say," I asked him, "that you put all that on paper?" "Yes," he replied, "I had it copied in longhand in my office by one of my employees. He was very frightened and burnt the blotting paper afterwards. I don't think General Speidel much liked carrying it either. However, he went off with his copy in his pocket and I brought mine back with me to Stuttgart." It was like carrying a Mills bomb with the pin out.

Rommel himself was not as "security-minded" as he should have been. He spoke very freely in the mess about the war and about the Führer. Since he could trust his personal staff, this would not have mattered had one of them not been more conscientious than discriminating. —— kept the war diary, written in the first person as though personally by Rommel, and it was his duty, he felt, to record not merely the happenings of the day but the *obiter dicta* of the Field-Marshal. He was scrupulous in doing so. Rommel was amused when he saw an entry: "0700 hrs.—had breakfast (omelette), 0730 hrs.—battle of Caen begins." He was also amused when he read: "Went for a walk with Captain —— and Field-Marshal

von Kluge" and "discussed military situation with Captain
——: he agrees with my views." He was not, however, so
much amused when, idly turning over the pages, he came
across: "Hitler's orders are nonsense; the man must be mad,"
and "Every day is costing lives unnecessarily; it is essential
to make peace at once." "Good God, man," he said, "you are
going to bring me to the scaffold!" Aldinger was instructed to
prepare a revised and expurgated version at once. Later
Manfred and he burnt the original, which Aldinger had apparently intended to keep in his file. This typically German
practice of reducing everything to writing and of preserving
the most incriminating documents hanged many of the conspirators.

At the May 27th meeting, General Speidel drew the military picture. When he had finished, von Neurath said: "With
Hitler we can never have peace: you must tell Rommel that
he must be prepared to act on his own responsibility." That
was the feeling of the others also and that was the message
which General Speidel took back to the headquarters at La
Roche Guyon.

Meanwhile Rommel's will to act had been fortified from a
very strange quarter. Ernest Jünger, author of *Storm of Steel*,
the frontline soldier who believed, even after 1914-18, that
war was the noblest occupation of man, was one of the first to
write against the Nazis in an allegorical novel, the *Marble
Cliffs*, which was suppressed. He had now secretly prepared a
draft peace treaty, founded on the idea of a Europe united on
the basis of Christianity—the abolition of frontiers and the
return of the masses to the Christian faith. Only thus could
the threat of Bolshevism be defeated. Rommel found it moving
and convincing and was anxious that it should be published
when the opportunity came. It was now for him to create that
opportunity.

From February onwards Rommel was in perhaps the most
extraordinary position in which any general ever found himself. On the one hand he was the chosen defender of the
Atlantic Wall, entrusted by Hitler with the task of defeating
the invasion on the beaches. As such he was again being
publicised in the German Press: as such he was regarded, not
only by the Allies but by the German Army. On the other
hand he was convinced that the invasion could not, in fact, be
defeated and was secretly committed to proposing an armistice to Generals Eisenhower and Montgomery when it succeeded—unless he could first bring Hitler to reason.

This dilemma he discussed in many long talks with Admiral Ruge. "To continue the war is crazy," he said. "Every day costs us one of our towns—to what purpose? Merely to make it more certain that Communism will sweep over Europe and bring all the Western Powers down together." At the same time he recognised that it was no use thinking of trying to make peace independently of Hitler unless and until the invasion succeeded. "In Africa I was my own master," he said, "and the troops looked to me for decisions. Here I am only Hitler's deputy." Subjected daily to intensive propaganda and believing implicitly in the mysterious secret weapons, the rank-and-file would have regarded any one who spoke of surrender as a traitor and, with most of the junior officers, would have refused to follow him. Thus an attempt had to be made to defeat the invasion and at the same time preparations had to be made for an approach to the Allies.

By a remarkable feat of mental balance Rommel contrived to ride these two horses together. As a soldier he did his utmost to arouse the sleeping army of the west and to inspire the troops with the determination to prevent a landing. He also worked night and day to improve the neglected defences of the Atlantic Wall. In his orders he declared that it was, or soon would be, impregnable. The Allied commanders themselves were given an exaggerated idea of its actual strength. When the landing was successfully made, he battled desperately to throw the invaders off the beaches. Had he been completely single-minded, had he believed implicitly in his own predictions, he could not have done more. Nor could any general have more persistently risked his own life. He thus kept faith, professionally, with the Führer. He also kept faith with the Army. There was not a hint of irresolution in his leadership. Though he had always hated sacrificing troops unnecessarily, he flung them in in counter-attacks, with what feelings may be imagined. "I have never before sent men to certain death," he said to Ruge. His strategy and tactics may be criticised: no one on our side has ever suggested that he "pulled his punches."

At the same time he fulfilled to the letter the conditions he had made at his meeting with Dr. Strölin in February. His situation report of June 12th gave Hitler fair warning that things were "extraordinarily difficult" and that Allied superiority, particularly in the air, left little hope of preventing a break-out. On June 17th at Soissons he had the personal interview which it was agreed that he should seek. He then gave

Hitler a military alternative to asking for peace—that of taking up a defensive line behind the Orne. When permission could not be obtained, both he and von Rundstedt broached the question of coming to terms with the Western Powers. Finally, on July 15th, he sent his last message to Hitler. Before he received a reply and thus before he could take the final step of an approach to the Allied commanders, he was wounded. Only in this one particular did the agreed programme remain unfulfilled.

As things turned out, it would have been better had Rommel died of his wounds. Most men would have done so. He showed once again his extraordinary resilience and vitality. Baron von Esebeck, who himself had a narrow escape, since he usually travelled with Rommel and only stayed at headquarters on July 17th to write a "piece" about him, saw him in the hospital at Vesinet about July 23rd. He was sitting on the side of his bed. "I'm glad it's you," said Rommel: "I was afraid it was the doctor. He won't allow me to sit up. I'm sure he thinks I am going to die," he added, "but I haven't any intention of dying. You'd better take a picture of me." With this, he stood up, put on his uniform jacket over his pyjamas and made von Esebeck take a photograph in profile, showing the right, or undamaged, side of his face. "The British will be able to see that they haven't managed to kill me yet," he said. He then went on to speak quite normally to von Esebeck and repeated what he had already told him on June 12th, after he had written his report to Hitler, that the war was lost. "He was especially bitter," said von Esebeck, "about the complete failure of the Luftwaffe. He said nothing about the attempt on Hitler's life."

Speidel and Ruge also visited Rommel a few days after he was wounded. They found that he had succeeded in shaving himself! An unfortunate Surgeon-Major-General who told him that he must really keep quiet was severely "bitten." "Don't tell me what I must do or mustn't do," said Rommel, "I know what I can do." Thereafter Ruge visited him nearly every day to read to him. "I read a book called *The Tunnel* by Kellermann," he said. "It was about building a tunnel from Europe to the United States, exactly the sort of thing he liked. We used to talk about 'after the war.' He had been very much impressed by the enormous rise and fall of tide on the coast of Brittany and said that he would like to be actively interested in a project for drawing power from the tides. Anyway, he wanted to do something technical and practical."

With Admiral Ruge, Rommel spoke freely about the plot. "That was altogether the wrong way to go about it," he said. "The man is a devil incarnate but why try to make a hero and a martyr of him? He should have been arrested by the Army and brought to trial. The Hitler legend will never be destroyed until the German people know the whole truth."

"I was in fear for Rommel," said Ruge, "and hoped that it might be possible to get him into the hands of the British. But, good friends as we were, I never plucked up courage to suggest it to him. In any case he was bent on going home."

On August 8th, in spite of the objections of Professor Esch, chief medical officer at Vesinet, and of Dr. Schennig, of Army Group B, Rommel insisted on being removed to his house at Herrlingen. "He was determined," said Frau Rommel, "not to fall, seriously wounded, into enemy hands." Both doctors accompanied him. They put him in charge of Professors Albrecht and Stock, of the clinic of Tübingen University. Professor Albrecht specialised in brain surgery. When he examined Rommel's injuries he said, "I shall have to revise my lectures to my pupils. No man can be alive with wounds like that." He added that he would have preferred to have Rommel in his nursing-home at Tübingen "for his own protection."

Contrary to all expectation, the wounds mended quickly. Rommel became visibly stronger every day. Meanwhile Frau Rommel found it strange that, of all the high dignitaries of the Reich and of the Army Command, no one took the trouble to telephone to inquire about his condition.

Had she but known it, the hand of Hitler was already closing over her husband. He would have been suspect, in any case, for the "defeatist" views which he had expressed. But there was a track which led straight to him. On the evening of July 20th, when it was already known that the attempt had failed and that Hitler was alive and giving orders, General Heinrich von Stülpnagel was summoned by Field-Marshal von Kluge to La Roche Guyon. Von Kluge was privy to the plot but not actively concerned in it. Had it succeeded, he would have gone over openly to the conspirators and himself approached the Allies for an armistice. As things were, he was of opinion that there was now nothing to be done. He said as much to von Stülpnagel. Then, to his horror, he learnt that, before leaving Paris, von Stülpnagel had already ordered the arrest of the Gestapo and the S.D., the S.S. security police. Moreover, he expected von Kluge to proceed with the original plan. Von Kluge at once made it clear that he had no intention of doing anything of the sort. After a very strained discussion he told von Stülpnagel to go back to Paris and release the S.D. immediately.

The commander of the S.S., General Oberg, was prepared to try to hush things up and pretend that von Stülpnagel's orders for arrest had been merely an exercise. Next day, however, there came a message for General von Stülpnagel to report to Army Headquarters in Berlin. He set off by car. At what moment in that long drive he determined to take his life, no one can tell. Perhaps it was as he neared Verdun, where he had fought with distinction in the bloody battles of the first war. That, at any rate, was the spot he chose. He made his driver take the car to the banks of the Meuse canal and leave him. Wading in, he drew his pistol and shot himself through the head. He succeeded only in destroying his eyes. The driver heard the shot, found him and pulled him out of the water. He drove him, unconscious, to the hospital in Verdun. An operation was performed and an eye removed. As he began to recover consciousness, von Stülpnagel called out repeatedly, "Rommel!" According to Colonel Wolfgang Müller, it was the surgeon who communicated with the Gestapo in Paris. According to General Speidel, the S.S. and Gestapo were already standing around his bed. The discrepancy may be merely one of time. The Gestapo heard, at first or second hand. It was in the company of the Gestapo that General von Stülpnagel completed his journey to Berlin. There he was tortured. No one knows what he said, if, indeed, he said anything more. In his delirium he had already said enough. Having been tortured, he was tried and hanged. Speidel says that he was a brave and honourable man, *"chevalier sans peur et sans reproche."* It is a pity that he was not more accurate with his pistol.* When, on August 18th, Field-Marshal von Kluge, also summoned to Berlin, decided to follow the same path, he took poison and made no mistake.

At Herrlingen the weeks passed quietly, the only events the visits of Professor Albrecht. He was delighted with his patient's progress. Rommel was able to get up and to sit in the

---

* He is not to be confused with Otto von Stülpnagel, who committed suicide in a French prison while awaiting trial for crimes against hostages. I have not heard of any such charge against Heinrich.

garden in the sunshine and soon to go for walks. There was only one rather strange incident during his early convalescence. In the middle of August, not long after his return home, a man tried to get into the house by a subterranean passage which led to the air-raid shelter. When challenged and fired on by the guard, he fled. No great attention was paid to this affair. There were many queer characters, deserters, escaped prisoners-of-war and foreign labourers, on the run in Germany during the summer of 1944.

On September 6th, Rommel had another unexpected visitor. General Speidel came to the house to tell him that he had been suspended the day before from duty as Chief of Staff to Army Group B. To-morrow he was to report to Berlin to General Guderian, now Chief of Staff to the Army Command. "He told us," said Frau Rommel, "that Keitel and Jodl had been talking of my husband as a 'defeatist' and warned him to beware of them. Because of his state of health he told him no more. My husband imagined that they were looking for someone to blame for the military situation in the west. He thought that this explained why the German press and radio had spoken of his 'accident' and not of an enemy attack and why they had been so slow in publishing the news that foreign papers came out with it several days before."

General Speidel was not given the chance to report to Berlin. Perhaps it was feared, from a misreading of his character, that, like Field-Marshal von Kluge, Generals Beck, von Stülpnagel and others, he would try to take the easier way out. At 6 A.M. there was a heavy knock at the door of his house in Freudenstadt. It was an S.S. officer with an armed guard. General Speidel was to accompany him immediately. In such haste was he that he did not stop to search the house. Frau Speidel was able to remove a photograph of General Beck which hung (and still hangs) in a place of honour in the sitting-room. She was also able to hide certain papers. Her husband was carried off by car to Stuttgart and thence by train, closely guarded, to Berlin and the Gestapo prison on the Prinz Albrechtstrasse. His personal assistant telephoned later in the morning to Herrlingen and informed Rommel of the arrest. It was never officially communicated, though Rommel was still nominally in command of Army Group B. Rommel wrote a letter of protest to Hitler personally, which he sent to Sepp Dietrich, asking him to forward it to the Führer. If it was forwarded, Hitler sent no reply.

That afternoon friends in Herrlingen warned Frau Rommel

by telephone that two suspicious-looking men had been seen near their house, apparently trying to get into the grounds. When approached, they had moved off. Aldinger was able to establish that, about 3:30 P.M., the two men, one of whom wore dark glasses, had taken post in the woods, on the high ground behind the house. He also learnt that they had new passports which described them as engineers from Regensburg. They said that they were employed on war work and had been evacuated to the Herrlingen area. The proprietor of a local inn also reported to Rommel's secretary, Adjutant Böttcher, who had been with him for some years, that the men had cars parked near his premises.

In the evening, having learned of Spiedel's arrest, Strölin took the risk of coming over from Stuttgart to Herrlingen. He found the house guarded and Rommel, distressed and in some degree alarmed, made a sign to him to speak in whispers. An overhearing set might somehow have been slipped into the house, he said. On his desk was a pistol. Strölin asked him why he wanted it. "I'm not afraid of the English or the Americans," said Rommel, "only of the Russians—and the Germans." He then showed Strölin a copy of the message he had sent to Hitler and they discussed whether there was any possibility of helping Speidel. Rommel explained that he had already telephoned to Army Command but could get no satisfaction. Nor would they even tell him why his Chief of Staff had been arrested. It was the last time Strölin saw Rommel alive. Frau Rommel telephoned soon afterwards to ask him not to come to the house again. She already feared the Gestapo.

There was another visitor a few days later. This was one Maier, the local Party boss from Ulm. He came ostensibly as a friend and asked Rommel, while they were having tea, whether he could trust his servants. The head of the S.S. in Ulm had told him, he said, that Rommel no longer believed in the possibility of victory and was in the habit of criticising Hitler and the High Command. Even Manfred felt that his father spoke too freely to Maier. "Victory!" he exclaimed, "why don't you look at the map? The British are here, the Americans are here, the Russians are here: what is the use of talking about victory?" When Maier said something about Hitler, Rommel replied, "That damned fool!" Maier begged him to be more careful. "You should not say things like that, Field-Marshal," he warned him; "you will have the Gestapo after you—if they are not after you already."

An Italian journalist has recently produced a story to the effect that Maier went home and wrote a thirty-page report of this conversation, which he took next day to Berlin and handed personally to Bormann. The Rommels do not believe it. Maier, who came from Heidenheim, spent some months with Manfred Rommel in a French prisoner-of-war camp at Lindau and assured him that he had never had any suspicion that his father had been murdered. He later died in an American concentration camp and cannot be questioned. The story may very well be true. The employment of a stool-pigeon was an old Nazi trick.

A month passed before the next move was made. Rommel was now able to go by car to Tübingen for treatment. He was due to do so on October 10th. On the 7th a telephone message came from Field-Marshal Keitel. Rommel was to be in Berlin on the 10th for an important interview. A special train would be provided for him on the evening of the 9th. Rommel telephoned to Professor Albrecht to put off his treatment, explaining that he had been summoned to Berlin. Both Albrecht and Stock advised him strongly against undertaking so long a journey. Rommel told Aldinger to get on to Keitel personally. The telephone was answered by General Burgdorf, head of the Army Personnel branch. "My husband spoke to him himself," said Frau Rommel. "Captain Aldinger and I were in the room. He asked him to tell Field-Marshal Keitel that the doctors would not allow him to travel in his present state of health. Then he went on to ask what it was all about and whether it would not be possible to send an officer to see him. General Burgdorf replied that the Führer had given orders that Field-Marshal Keitel should see him to discuss his future employment." Rommel had not expected to be employed again, after what had passed between him and the Führer. In any case he could not be fit for an active command for some months. Aldinger formed the impression that he was uneasy, but for once Rommel did not confide in him. Nor did he say anything to his wife, though she had been in fear for him ever since the arrest of General Speidel. Manfred had returned that morning to his A.A. battery.

Five days passed and there was no further word from Berlin. On October 11th, Admiral Ruge came to the house to dinner and stayed the night. They talked until after midnight. Rommel told Ruge about the order to go to Berlin and said that he had refused because he did not feel well enough. He added, "I shall not go to Berlin: I would never get there alive." "I pooh-poohed this at first," said Admiral Ruge, "but he went on to say, 'I know they would kill me on the way and stage an accident.' I think it was this belief that influenced him two days later."

On October 13th came a telephone call from headquarters of War District 5 at Stuttgart. Rommel and Aldinger were out and a soldier servant took the call. He was told to inform the Field-Marshal that General Burgdorf would arrive at Herrlingen next day at noon. He would be accompanied by General Maisel. General Maisel also belonged to the Personnel branch. Since July 20th he had been engaged in investigating the cases of officers suspected of complicity in the plot against Hitler. When Rommel received the message he said very little. To Aldinger he remarked that the two generals were doubtless coming to talk to him about the invasion or about a new job. For the rest of the day he was unusually silent.

Next morning Manfred arrived on leave by the 6 A.M. train. He found his father already up. They breakfasted together and then went for a long walk. Rommel told his son of the expected visit. "What are they coming for?" asked Manfred. "Is it about a new appointment for you?" "That's what they say," replied Rommel. Manfred thought that his father seemed worried. However, he pulled himself together and talked to the boy about his own affairs and his future. Rommel wanted him to be a doctor, not a soldier. It was 11 A.M. when they returned to the house.

At noon precisely General Burgdorf arrived with General Maisel and a Major Ehrenberger, another *Ordonnanzoffizier*. They came in a small green car. The driver wore the black uniform of the S.S. The two generals shook hands with Rommel. Frau Rommel, Manfred and Captain Aldinger were introduced. After a moment General Burgdorf said that he wished to speak to the Field-Marshal alone. Frau Rommel went upstairs to her room. Rommel led Burgdorf into a downstairs room and Maisel followed. As they moved away, Rommel turned to Aldinger and told him to have the papers ready. He had already warned Aldinger to prepare a file of his orders and situation reports issued during the Normandy fighting, for he suspected that he was to be interrogated about the invasion. Aldinger's file was, of course, in order and he remained talking to Major Ehrenberger outside the front door while Manfred went upstairs to continue colouring some maps for his father. It was nearly an hour later that General Maisel came out. He was followed after a minute or two by General

Burgdorf. Rommel was not with them. He had gone upstairs to his wife.

"As he entered the room," said Frau Rommel, "there was so strange and terrible an expression on his face that I exclaimed at once, 'What is the matter with you? What has happened? Are you ill?' He looked at me and replied: 'I have come to say good-bye. In a quarter of an hour I shall be dead. . . . They suspect me of having taken part in the attempt to kill Hitler. It seems my name was on Goerdeler's list to be President of the Reich. . . . I have never seen Goerdeler in my life. . . . They say that von Stülpnagel, General Speidel and Colonel von Hofacker have denounced me. . . . It is the usual trick. . . . I have told them that I do not believe it and that it cannot be true. . . . The Führer has given me the choice of taking poison or being dragged before the People's Court. They have brought the poison. They say it will take only three seconds to act.' " Frau Rommel begged her husband to go before the Court. He had never been a party to the killing of Hitler, nor would he ever have agreed to it. "No," said Rommel, "I would not be afraid to be tried in public, for I can defend everything I have done. But I know that I should never reach Berlin alive."

As he was taking leave of his wife, Manfred entered the room cheerfully, to see what had become of his father. The generals were waiting for him. Rommel said good-bye to his son also. Then he turned and went into the room next door. Manfred followed at his heels. Rommel called for his soldier servant and sent him to find Aldinger. To Aldinger he explained what was in store for him. He was now quite calm but Aldinger could hear Frau Rommel sobbing in her room. Aldinger was not disposed to take it like this. "I told him," he said, "that he must at least make an attempt to escape. Why could we not try to shoot our way out together? We had been in as bad places before and got away. 'It's no good, my friend,' he said, 'this is it. All the streets are blocked with S.S. cars and the Gestapo are all around the house. We could never get back to the troops. They've taken over the telephone. I cannot even ring up my headquarters.' I said we could at least shoot Burgdorf and Maisel. 'No,' said Rommel, 'they have their orders. Besides, I have my wife and Manfred to think of.' Then he told me that he had been promised that no harm should come to them if he took the first choice. A pension would be paid. He was to be given a state funeral. He would be buried at home in Herrlingen. All the details of the funeral had been worked out and explained to him. . . . But if he were brought before the People's Court and condemned, as of course he would be, then it would be quite another matter. . . . 'I have spoken to my wife and made up my mind,' he said. 'I will never allow myself to be hanged by that man Hitler. I planned no murder. I only tried to serve my country, as I have done all my life, but now this is what I must do. In about half an hour there will come a telephone call from Ulm to say that I have had an accident and am dead.' When he had made up his mind, it was of no use to argue with him. . . ."

Some of the few surviving conspirators feel that Rommel should have insisted on being taken before the People's Court and should there have struck a last blow for Germany by denouncing Hitler. His appearance in the dock, they say, would have shaken confidence in the régime. Had Rommel been more of a fanatic; had he been prepared to sacrifice his wife and child; had he been in better health; had he been sure of reaching Berlin; had he been willing to be branded as a felon and to die on a hook, perhaps without a chance of speaking, he might have chosen differently. His proper course is endlessly debatable: the choice, heroic or not, had to be made within an hour.

Having taken his decision, Rommel went downstairs with Manfred and Aldinger. The generals were looking at the garden. They came over to the car and Rommel got in first into the back seat. Burgdorf and Maisel followed him. Major Ehrenberger had already left to make the arrangements. The car drove off.

Twenty-five minutes later the telephone rang. Aldinger answered it. It was Major Ehrenberger, speaking from Ulm. "Aldinger," he said, "a terrible thing has happened. The Field-Marshal has had a hæmorrhage, a brain-storm, in the car. He is dead." Aldinger did not reply. "Did you hear what I said?" asked Ehrenberger. "Yes," said Aldinger, "I heard." "Then please tell Frau Rommel that I am coming back to the house at once." Aldinger walked slowly upstairs to Rommel's widow. He had no need to speak. Half an hour afterwards a car was heard on the drive. Aldinger went to the door. Ehrenberger said that he wished to see Frau Rommel. Aldinger answered that she was unable to receive him. Ehrenberger did not insist. Together he and Aldinger drove, in silence, to the hospital at Ulm. Aldinger was taken to a small room where

Rommel's body was lying. "I would have liked to be alone with him," said Aldinger, "but Ehrenberger would not leave me."

Tears ran down his cheeks as he told me the story. For thirty years Rommel had been his friend as well as his hero. It needed an effort to remember that this precise little man, who might have spent his life in some Government office, had been through so many battles in two great wars. Back from the table his plump, pretty young wife wept quietly over her sewing. In this house Rommel would not be forgotten.

While Aldinger was away, Colonel Kuzmany, commander of the troops in Ulm, came to the house at Herrlingen. Frau Rommel saw him. He was deeply moved, though he did not suspect the truth. Immediately after Rommel had been taken to the hospital, he said, Generals Burgdorf and Maisel had come to his headquarters to announce the sudden death of the Field-Marshal. Then they ordered him to make preparations for a state funeral.

Later in the afternoon, Aldinger drove Frau Rommel and Manfred to the hospital. The chief medical officer told them that the two generals had brought in Rommel, dead, at 1:25 P.M. On their orders he had given him an injection to stimulate the heart. "There was no reaction," said the doctor, in a flat voice. Aldinger felt that he was on the point of saying something more but did not dare. He did add, however, that there was to be no post-mortem—on orders from above. Then he led them to the room. "When I saw my husband," said Frau Rommel, "I noticed at once an expression of deep contempt on his face. It was an expression we had never seen on it in life." It may still be seen on his death-mask.

Next evening, the 15th, they went to the station to meet Rommel's sister, whom they had summoned from Stuttgart. Aldinger had been ordered to report to Military Headquarters in Ulm and they took him there on the way. "While we were waiting outside," said Frau Rommel, "General Maisel suddenly appeared. He came over to the car and began to offer me his sympathy. I turned away from him without speaking and pretended not to see his outstretched hand." Aldinger said that Maisel had asked him where Frau Rommel was and "how she was taking it." "In the car outside," said Aldinger, "and how do you suppose?" When Rommel's sister saw her brother's body she, too, remarked at once on that look of contempt which the others had noticed the evening before. They had not yet told her how he died.

Rommel's body was taken back to the house, where it lay beneath a swastika flag, the face uncovered, in the room in which the interview with the generals had taken place. Under orders from Ulm, two officers mounted guard over it with drawn swords.

Generals Burgdorf and Maisel went off to Berlin. After they had left, Aldinger discovered that Rommel's cap and Field-Marshal's baton were missing. Characteristically, he telephoned to General Burgdorf and demanded that they be returned, together with any papers taken from the body. The cap and baton were recovered. Rommel's message of July 15th, a copy of which Aldinger knew had been in his breast pocket, was not returned. Burgdorf was killed in the last days' fighting in Berlin. Maisel is still alive in the American zone. To a German denazification court before which he appeared in Frankfurt two years ago Maisel said that the car had been stopped a few hundred yards away from the house on the Blauberen road. He and the driver were ordered by General Burgdorf to get out as he wished to be alone with Rommel. "Approximately five minutes later we noticed that General Burgdorf had left the car and was walking up and down in the road alongside it. After another five minutes he waved to us. When we approached we saw the Field-Marshal leaning lifelessly against the back seat." The S.S. driver, Dose, said that Rommel was doubled up and sobbing but practically unconscious and obviously in his death throes. The S.S. were good judges of such matters. Dose sat him up and put on his cap, which had fallen on the floor. Maisel also told the Court that he had not wanted to believe that Rommel, a special favourite of Hitler, had had anything to do with the attempt on his life. But when General Burgdorf read his statement from two typewritten sheets, Rommel's demeanour was such that "I got the impression that the accusing statements were absolutely correct." His story was not challenged. Frau Rommel had been invited to give evidence but refused, not wishing to see General Maisel again, even in the dock. The case was adjourned for further evidence. In the summer of 1949 General Maisel was pronounced an offender in Category II of the denazification law. The conviction carried with it a sentence of two years' imprisonment. Since Maisel had already been in custody for more than two years while his case was being investigated, this sentence will not be served. Burgdorf was described to me as "a drunken, foul-mouthed butcher who should never have been a general." Of Maisel, a general of his acquaintance said: "If there was any dirty, underhand work going on, you could be sure that Maisel was somewhere at the bottom of it."

"I would like to get my hands on General Maisel," said General Johann Cramer of the Afrika Korps.

With the public announcement of Rommel's death began the flood of telegrams and letters of condolence. Hitler sent a not very effusive telegram on October 17th:

"Please accept my deepest sympathy on the loss of your husband," it read. "The name of Marshal Rommel will always be linked with the heroic fighting in North Africa." It will be observed that neither Normandy nor wounds were mentioned.

Dr. Goebbels and his wife also expressed their deepest sympathy. Joachim von Ribbentrop said that he had been very much moved to hear that Rommel had died "as the result of his serious wounds in France." He assured Frau Rommel that "his successes belong to the history of this great period." Kesselring wrote later that "there were times when I did not always agree with him, just as he did not always understand me. . . . [But] I was very glad when he was appointed to an important command in the West because I knew that his experience of fighting against the British and Americans would be of the greatest value. . . . His energy, his inspiring personality and his intuition would have prevented many things that might have been prevented." General Gambara, one of the best of the Italian generals, wrote that "he will always live in the hearts and minds of those who had the honour to see him, as I did, always calm and fearless under fire." Field-Marshal Model, von Kluge's successor as Commander-in-Chief West, published an Order of the Day in which he referred to him as "one of the greatest of German commanders . . . with a lightning power of decision, a soldier of the greatest bravery and of unequalled dash. . . . Always in the front line, he inspired his men to new deeds of heroism by his example. . . ."

There were one or two omissions. Neither then nor later was there any message from Keitel or Jodl. Heinrich Borgmann, Hitler's adjutant, omitted to add the conventional "Heil Hitler" to his letter. A few days later he resigned his appointment.

Himmler's condolences came in unusual form. The content was also unusual. Three days after Rommel's death he sent his personal assistant, Berndt, mentioned earlier in this book as joining the Afrika Korps from the Propaganda Ministry, to deliver a personal message to Frau Rommel. The message was that he, Himmler, knew the whole story, that he was horrified and that he would never have had a hand in such a thing. Berndt was now serving with the S.S. He had gone back to the Propaganda Ministry and been thrown out by Goebbels for repeating Rommel's remark that the war was lost. To Himmler's message he added a gloss of his own. Hitler, he declared, was equally innocent. It was the work of Keitel and Jodl. Later he wrote a strange, ecstatic letter from the front before he, too, was killed. There had, he said, been some "higher purpose" in Rommel's death but Hitler was not guilty of it. That is doubtless what he believed, for he was one of those who never lost faith in their Führer. But Himmler, if, indeed, he had no hand in it, at least knew that Keitel and Jodl would never have dared to make away with Rommel without their master's orders. Nor were there many important killings about which he himself was not consulted. The responsibility for the arrangements may never be exactly fixed. Even in systematic Nazi Germany, orders for murder at the Field-Marshal level would hardly be put on paper. Rommel's family and friends have no doubt who spoke the operative word.

The funeral took place on October 18th. It was an elaborate affair. Like the gangsters of Chicago, the Nazis had a mortuary sense. They, too, did not stint the trappings of death and were greater masters of ceremonial. Hitler had ordered national mourning and Rommel was buried with full military honours. All the troops in the neighbourhood were turned out. The coffin was carried from the house, covered with a huge swastika flag, while a guard in steel helmets and white gloves presented arms. Thence it was taken to the town hall of Ulm. Here, in a great vaulted chamber used for entertainments and civic functions, Rommel lay in state. The outside of the building had been hung with banners: the pillars inside were crowned with eagles, flags and laurels. On the bier were placed his marshal's baton, his helmet and his sword. The jewels of his decorations, earned in two wars, glittered on a velvet cushion. Four officers, wearing the brassard of the Afrika Korps, mounted guard. They were relieved, as the time for the ceremony approached, by four generals of the Reichswehr. In the square outside were paraded two companies of infantry with a company of the Air Force and, a delicate touch, one of the Waffen S.S. There was a military band. Thousands of people thronged the square, amongst them many boys and girls, to whom Rommel was always a hero. They watched the arrival of high officers of all the services, of representatives of the Party, of the Reich and of Germany's allies. Last came Field-Marshal von Rundstedt, the senior serving officer of the German Army. As he entered the hall with Rommel's family, the band played the funeral march from the *Götterdämmerung*. Field-Marshal von Rundstedt then delivered an oration in the name of the Führer who "as head of the Army, has called us here to say farewell to his Field-Marshal, fallen on the field of honour."

Von Rundstedt, greatly aged, it was observed, described how Rommel had received his wounds by enemy action in Normandy. "A pitiless destiny," he continued, "has snatched him from us, just at the moment when the fighting has come to its crisis." He then recited Rommel's services in the two world wars, dwelling at length upon his campaigns in Africa and upon the esteem in which he was held even by the enemy. Normandy was passed over more lightly, with the comment that he had "worked indefatigably to prepare against the invasion" and, when the battle began, had joined in it without any thought of his own safety.

The peaks of oratory and of irony were scaled by the Field-Marshal, or the anonymous author of his speech, when he declared that "this tireless fighter in the cause of the Führer and the Reich" had been "imbued with the National-Socialist spirit" and that it was this which had given him his force and had been the mainspring of all his actions. He ended the passage with the immortal words: "His heart belonged to the Führer."

"In the name of Adolf Hitler" he then placed a magnificent wreath at Rommel's feet, while the band played *"Ich hatt' einen Kameraden,"* perhaps the most moving of all tributes from one soldier to another. Hitler was ever a sentimentalist.

From the town hall the coffin was taken on a gun-carriage, dragged by one of those huge infantry half-tracks, to the crematorium. In this case no evidence was to be left which an exhumation might reveal. In the seats of the half-track, young soldiers sat bolt upright, their hands folded. The guard presented arms again, the band played, the generals and the Party leaders stood stiffly to attention, there were more speeches, Rommel's decorations were carried before him on their velvet cushion, the Führer's wreath was to the fore.

Admiral Ruge, brought down by special train from Berlin, represented the German Navy. He did not know the truth but he suspected something from von Rundstedt's manner in the town hall and from the fact that the Field-Marshal did not come to the crematorium. Amongst the mourners were also Frau Speidel, Strölin and von Neurath. It needed courage on their part to attend that ceremony. Frau Speidel could hardly expect to see her husband alive again for the doors of the prison in the Albrechtstrasse seldom opened outwards. She and her children were in deadly danger. Strölin had guessed the truth as soon as Frau Rommel had telephoned to him on the evening of the 14th that her husband was dead. Each morning since he had waited at dawn for that heavy knocking that had aroused the Speidels. Was it not he who had set Rommel's feet on this path? Von Neurath, too, was deeply involved. The Gestapo were certain to be present. There they were, indeed, a little withdrawn, suave young men in civilian clothes, watching from behind the wall. It is no wonder that Frau Speidel seemed afraid to reply to Strölin's greeting.

Arrests at this moment would, however, have been out of place. The producer had decided that this last act must be played on a note of dignity and sorrow. "Deep respect for the dead Field-Marshal" was the stage direction.

Next day Rommel's ashes were brought home to Herrlingen. Lying in a narrow valley with wooded hills rising steeply on either side, Herrlingen is a pretty village of white houses with red-tiled roofs and window-boxes. A clear, fast-running stream flows through it. It looks at its best in the spring, when the gardens are full of blossom, or, as then, in the autumn, when the leaves have turned to golden-brown. The white church, too, has charm, with its steep, barn-like roof of weathered slate and its square tower, surmounted by a faded green cupola. Restored by the first King of Württemberg in 1816, it contains monuments dating back to the fourteenth century. Cottages cluster round it. The churchyard, shared by Catholics and Protestants alike, though the church is Catholic, slopes in terraces to the road, beyond which runs the river. In the spring the graves are a mass of pansies and wallflowers. In front of the tombstones of their parents are small wooden crosses, miniature replicas of those one sees in military cemeteries, commemorating the young men of Herrlingen who fell in Africa, at Cassino, at Riga, at Bjelgorod or, more often, simply *"in dem Osten."* The churchyard is enclosed by a white wall, against which have been planted flowering shrubs. Here, in an angle of the wall, was the plot reserved for Rommel. From it only the church behind, the tops of the trees beyond the road and, to the left, the grassy slopes of a bare hill, as steep as Monte Matajur, are visible. It is a peaceful spot. Here, in the presence of his friends and family, all that could die of Rommel was lowered into the grave.

Though it is not an easy thing to question a woman about her feelings as she stands by the graveside of her murdered husband, I came to know Frau Rommel well enough to ask her whether she had not been tempted to make a scene and publicly to denounce his murderers. "It was hard not to," she said. "In the town hall, when Field-Marshal von Rundstedt was speaking, I longed to call out that they were all acting a lie. But what would have been the use? They would have hushed it up somehow or else my husband would have been publicly disgraced. In any case he was dead. . . . And I had to think of Manfred. I did not care any more for myself but you must know what they did even to distant cousins of those who were executed after July 20th . . . Manfred would have been killed. They counted on all that: they were very clever. No, it was my husband's decision and I could not change it after he was gone."

Thus all passed off according to plan. Only a hypercritical observer would have asked why Marshal von Rundstedt stumbled in reading his speech, as though it had been given to him only a few minutes before. Why did he make no attempt to speak to Frau Rommel? Why, on passing Strölin and von Neurath, did he raise his eyes and give them so queer a look? "He knew or guessed," said Strölin, "and hated the part they had made him play." He must also have disliked his lines. For von Rundstedt was a soldier and a gentleman, with a long-standing contempt for Hitler and the Party.* There was a soldier of another sort who also had his doubts. "What was the matter with that funeral?" asked an S.S. officer of Strölin's acquaintance. "Somehow I had a feeling that there was something not quite right about it."

Such doubts were not general. Outside the inner circles of the Party and of the High Command the great mass of Germans believed that Rommel had died of his wounds and mourned him sincerely, even in the midst of their own trou-

---

* F. M. von Rundstedt has since assured me that he had no such suspicions and that, had he had, he would have refused to take part in the ceremony. I accept his word unhesitatingly, but I have let the passage stand because it reflects the feelings of Strölin and others and the under-currents of the day.

bles. I asked Captain Hartmann from Heidenheim whether he had had any suspicion. "None, at first," he said. "Then, a few days after the funeral, I was out for a walk with a friend. Suddenly he turned to me and asked if I knew anything, as it all seemed rather queer. I began to think. I had seen Rommel after his death and he looked perfectly peaceful. There were no signs of violence, no trace of gunshot wounds or anything of that sort. But I had also spent a whole day with him at Herrlingen three weeks before. He had then almost completely recovered from his wounds and was mentally absolutely fit. We talked about the first war and he could remember every name and date. He did not seem to expect to be employed again, because Goering and the OKH were against him. He was also convinced that the war was lost. But he never said anything to suggest that he had any fears for his own safety." Hartmann continued to wonder whether, perhaps, there was not indeed something rather queer. But it was not until April, 1945, when Frau Rommel told him, that he knew the facts.

Meanwhile life was resumed in the lonely house on the hill with such courage as might be. There was one change in the establishment. Frau Rommel had been given an old soldier servant to help with the housework. He was almost completely crippled, for most of one foot had been shot away. He had also been severely wounded in the chest by a shell splinter. Amongst his light duties he often answered the telephone. He did so on October 13th, when the message came that Generals Burgdorf and Maisel were arriving. Shortly after the funeral, Frau Rommel was ordered to send him back to duty. In spite of her protest that he could hardly hobble, he was sent off and into the line near Prague. By telephoning to an influential friend at Army Headquarters she managed to get him back again. He had only been in Herrlingen a short time when he was again ordered to report for duty with his regiment. Soon afterwards he was reported killed. It may all have been due to the man-power shortage or to the fact that Frau Rommel, now only the widow of a Field-Marshal, was no longer entitled to a soldier-servant. She still feels, however, that higher authority was strangely interested in the fate of a crippled private soldier.

Otherwise she was unmolested. The two S.S. men whom she discovered one night in her garden may have been there with no sinister intent. At any rate they went away when she challenged them and demanded to know what they were doing. "I was not nervous," she said, "though I quite expected that they would come for me, particularly towards the end when they were killing off so many people who knew too much. I was always nervous for Manfred. It would have been so easy to report him killed in action."

Manfred put his hand on her shoulder. "I was nervous for you and for myself as well," he said. "I also knew too much, and they might have thought that because I was young I was likely to talk. The C.O. of the battalion to which I had been transferred from my flak battery was a keen Nazi and I used to think he had his eye on me. That may have been my imagination. Anyway, I made up my mind in April to get myself taken prisoner as soon as the Americans were in Ulm and I knew that my mother was safe."

He was lucky not to be killed in the process. While making his way towards the French at Riedlingen on the Danube he ran into an S.S. patrol. The S.S. were then engaged on almost their last assignment. It was their duty and, no doubt, their pleasure to apprehend any German soldiers whom they found out of the line with no valid excuse and summarily to hang them from the nearest tree. The uniformed corpses dangling from the trees in the Black Forest and else-where must have puzzled our troops. They were, in fact, amongst the last emblems of the Nazi régime. Manfred was stopped and questioned. He had, however, prepared his story. He had almost fallen into the hands of the French a few minutes before but had escaped. He was now hastening to find his company commander. The French were in that village over there. The S.S. let him pass. Soon afterwards Manfred was indeed a prisoner. He was well treated. When General Ide Lattre de Tassigny learnt that he was his father's son he gave him a job as orderly-interpreter and took pains to get news of his mother.

Aldinger, who knew as much as any one, was, strangely enough, not interfered with, though he, too, spent some anx-ious hours before the surrender. Strölin also escaped arrest. In his case the explanation seems to be that the Gestapo Intelli-gence work was inefficient and that the trail never led directly to him. He was also so greatly respected by the people of Stuttgart and so well-known abroad that it may have seemed wiser to leave him alone. Perhaps also his friend the ex-Com-missioner of Police may have had something to do with it. To Strölin himself it remains a mystery.

General Speidel's escape was as nearly miraculous as anything can be which is the result of keen intelligence and iron self-control. It shows how well-armed is the philosopher against a brutish and irrational world. When the Gestapo questioned him in their prison on the Albrechtstrasse they were convinced that he was guilty. He must certainly have been on Dr. Goerdeler's list. Moreover, Goerdeler gave way under torture and it is known that he mentioned many names. Why, then, was General Speidel not hanged out of hand? "I think it was," he told me, "because I remained perfectly calm and argued everything out with them on a completely logical and unemotional basis. I made them feel that I was concerned, not with my own fate but with the facts. It was a bad moment when they confronted me with Colonel von Hofacker of General von Stülpnagel's staff, for I had heard that he had been drugged or tortured into talking. But I managed to catch his eye for a second and he pulled himself together and said that they could not have taken down his evidence correctly."

General Speidel survived two major "interrogations" in the Albrechtstrasse and many minor questionings. He was never for a second caught off his guard. He cannot possibly have persuaded the Gestapo that he was innocent but he was so greatly their intellectual superior that he inspired a doubt. He even made them feel slightly silly. He thus saved his life—for the moment. What is more, he very nearly succeeded in convincing them that, in his own words, "It was absolutely impossible that Rommel should have had anything to do with the events of July 20th, 1944." It was an exercise in dialectics, conducted without passion and apparently without anxiety. He could not save Rommel because Hitler's own passion and resentment were aroused. He wanted to kill Rommel, it would seem, not so much for being a traitor as for being right when he and Keitel and Jodl were wrong, over Africa and again over Normandy. For that he had come to hate him and hatred in his case had only one form of expression. Speidel had not attracted his hatred. It is possible that Hitler may also have felt that the execution of Rommel's Chief of Staff would arouse suspicions about the elaborate farce which he had staged to cover the removal of Rommel himself.

For seven months, then, General Speidel, or Dr. Speidel the philosopher, defeated the ends of Nazi justice. He was not, of course, set free. The Gestapo did not surrender their victims so easily and may still have hoped that the incontrovertible evidence would turn up. In the last weeks of the war Speidel was still in custody with other suspects at Urna, near Lake

Constance. There was a special guard under an S.S. officer and Speidel had little doubt that his orders were to see that they did not fall into the hands of the Allies alive. The military side of his brain now came into action. With the connivance of the commandant of the prison, who was friendly, he forged a telegram purporting to come from Himmler himself. It instructed the S.S. officer to be ready to move the prisoners to a safer place. He was to telephone to Himmler's headquarters for further instructions. The telephone in the prison was out of order. The S.S. officer had, therefore, to go elsewhere to telephone. While he was away, the commandant of the prison permitted the prisoners, General Speidel and more than twenty others, to escape. They took refuge with a Roman Catholic priest, who concealed them. Before they could be found, the Allied troops had overrun the area.

This is almost the end of the Rommel story. I must, however, go back a few weeks to what still seems to me the strangest chapter in it. Early in March 1945, when Hitler's world was visibly falling about his ears, Frau Rommel received a letter dated March 7. It was from *Der Generalbaurat für die Gestaltung der Deutschen Kriegerfriedhöfe* or, as we should say, the War Graves Commission.

> The Führer has given me an order [it ran] to erect a monument to the late Field-Marshal Rommel, and I have asked a number of sculptors to submit designs. I enclose some of them. At this moment it would not be possible to erect this monument or to transport it. One can only make a model. . . . I think that the Field-Marshal should be represented by a lion. One artist has depicted a dying lion, another a lion weeping, the third a lion about to spring. . . . I prefer the last myself but if you prefer a dying lion, that, too, could be arranged.
>
> The slab can be made immediately, as I have special permission from Reichsminister Speer. Generally monuments cannot now be made in stone. But in this special case it can be made and quickly shipped. . . .

To this letter Frau Rommel sent no reply.

ROMMEL'S RECORD OF SERVICE

WEHRPASS

19- 7-10— 3-10-15	Inf. Reg. 124
1- 3-14—31- 7-14	Z. Feld Art. Reg. 49
4-10-15—10- 1-18	Württemberg Geb. Batt.
11- 1-18—20-12-18	Gen. Kdo. 64
29- 7-18—19- 8-18	Z. 4/Landw. Fulda Reg. 6 d. Bayr. L. Division
20- 8-18— 8- 9-18	Z. 1 Landst. Fussart. Batt. *XX* A.K.
21-12-18—24- 6-19	Inf. Reg. 124
25- 6-19—31-12-20	R.W. Sch. Reg. 25 (Schwab. Gemund)
1- 1-21—30- 9-29	Inf. Reg. 13 (Stuttgart)
1-10-29—30- 9-33	Inf. Schule Dresden
1-10-33—14- 1-35	*III*/Inf. Reg. 17 (Jaeger Goslar)
15- 1-35—21- 1-35	R.W. Ministerium
25- 1-35—14-10-35	*III*/Batt. J.R.Go.
15-10-35— 9-11-38	Kriegsschule Potsdam
10-11-38—	Kommandeur der Kriegsschule W. Neustadt
23- 8-39—14- 2-40	Führerhauptq. Unterstab.
15- 2-40—14- 2-41	Stab. 7 Panzer Div.
15- 2-41—14- 8-41	Befehlshaber der Deutschen Truppen in Libyen
15- 8-41—21- 1-42	Kommando der Panzergruppe Afrika
22- 1-42—24-10-42	Oberkommando d. Pz. Armee Afrika
25-10-42—22- 2-43	Oberkommando d. Deutsch. Ital. Panzerarmee
23- 2-43—13- 5-43	Oberkommando d. Heeresgruppe Afrika
14- 5-43—14- 7-43	Arbeitsstab Gen. Feldmarschall Rommel
15- 7-43— 3- 9-44	Oberkommando d. Heeresgruppe B.
4- 9-44—14-10-44	Führer Res OKH (*V*)

THE ROMMEL PAPERS

When this book was already printed and about to be bound, I heard from Manfred Rommel that he had succeeded in recovering some of his father's papers which, because of their outspoken criticisms of Hitler and the German High Command, had been hidden before Field-Marshal Rommel's death lest they should fall into the hands of the Gestapo. I flew to Germany next day and at Herrlingen was able to examine part of a mass of diaries, narratives of battles and military appreciations, written or dictated at odd moments of leisure during the war, when Rommel was in hospital at Semmering in the summer of 1942 and in the interval between his relinquishing command in Tunis and taking over Army Group B. The extracts, which, thanks to the courtesy of the Rommel family and the eleventh-hour efforts of my publishers, I have been able to include here represent only a very small portion of what I have seen and a still smaller portion of the whole. Apart from their intrinsic interest, they serve to show that Rommel had a gift of direct, clear and forceful expression well in keeping with his character as a commander in war. The papers are obviously of great importance to all students of the North African campaign and it is hoped that an English translation of them may before long be published. I shall be happy if my own book, with these additional pages, helps to call attention to it.

D. Y.

THE RULES OF DESERT WARFARE

A paper prepared by Rommel as an introduction to his account of the war in Africa

Of all the theatres of operations, North Africa was probably the one where the war took on its most modern shape. Here were opposed fully motorised formations for whose employment the flat desert, free of obstructions, offered hitherto unforeseen possibilities. Here only could the principles of motorised and tank warfare, as they had been taught before 1939, be fully applied and, what was more important, further developed. Here only did the pure tank battle between large armoured formations actually occur. Even though the struggle may have occasionally hardened into static warfare, in its more important stages, in 1941-42 during the Cunningham-Ritchie offensive and in the summer of 1942 up to the capture of Tobruk, it remained based on the principle of complete mobility.

Militarily, this was entirely new ground, for our offensive in Poland and the West had been against opponents who, in their operations, had constantly to consider their non-motorised infantry divisions and whose freedom of decision was thus disastrously limited, particularly in retreat. They were, indeed, often obliged by this preoccupation to adopt measures which were quite unsuitable for holding up our advance. After our break-through in France, the enemy infantry divisions were overrun and outflanked by our motorised forces. When this happened, the enemy operational reserves had to allow themselves to be ground to pieces by our attacking forces, often in tactically unfavourable positions, in an endeavour to gain time for the retreat of the infantry.

Against a motorised and armoured enemy, non-motorised infantry divisions are of value only in prepared positions. Once such positions have been pierced or outflanked and they are forced to retreat from them they become helpless victims of the motorised enemy. In extreme cases they can do no more than hold on in their positions to the last round. In retreat they cause tremendous embarrassment since, as mentioned above, motorised formations have to be employed to gain time [to extricate them]. I myself had to submit to this experience during the retreat of the Axis forces from Cyrenaica in the winter of 1941-42 because the whole of the Italian and a large part of the German infantry, including the majority of what was to become the 90th Light Division, had no vehicles. Part of them had to be carried by a shuttle service of supply columns, part had to march. It was only thanks to the prowess of my armoured formations that the retreat of the Italo-German infantry could be covered, for the fully motorised British were in hot pursuit. Similarly, Graziani's failure can be attributed mainly to the fact that the Italian army, the greater part of it not motorised, was helpless in the open desert against the weak but nevertheless fully motorised British forces, while the Italian armour, though too weak to oppose the British with any hope of success, was compelled to accept battle and allow itself to be destroyed in defence of the infantry. Out of the purely motorised form of warfare which developed in Libya and Egypt there arose certain laws, fundamentally different from those [applicable] in other theatres. They will be the standard for the future, which will belong to fully motorised formations.

In the flat desert country, so well suited to motor transport, the encirclement of a fully motorised enemy produces the following results:

(a) The enemy is placed in the worst tactical situation imaginable, since fire can be brought to bear on him from all sides. Even when he is enveloped only on three sides his position is tactically untenable.

(b) When the envelopment is completed, he is tactically compelled to evacuate the area which he occupies.

The encirclement of the enemy and his subsequent destruction in the pocket, can, however, seldom be the primary aim of an operation but is usually only an indirect object, for a fully motorised force whose organisational structure is intact will normally and in suitable country be able to break out at any time through an improved defensive ring. Thanks to motorisation, the commander of the encircled force will be in a position to concentrate his main effort unexpectedly against a favourable point and force his way through. Time and again this was demonstrated in the desert.

It follows, then, that encircled enemy forces can only be destroyed:

(a) When they are not motorised or have been rendered immobile by lack of petrol or when they include non-mobile elements which have to be considered.

(*b*) When they are badly led or are deliberately sacrificed to save other formations.

(*c*) When their fighting strength is already broken and signs of disintegration are evident.

With the exception of cases (*a*) and (*b*), which occurred very frequently in other theatres of war, the encirclement of the enemy and his subsequent destruction in the pocket can be attempted only if he has first been so heavily engaged in open battle that the organic cohesion of the forces has been lost. Battles which aim at the destruction of the enemy power of resistance should be conceived as battles of attrition. In motorised warfare, material attrition and the disruption of the organic cohesion of the opposing army must be the direct aim of the planning.

Tactically, the battle of attrition is fought with the highest possible measure of mobility. The following points require particular attention:

(*a*) One should endeavour to concentrate one's own forces both in space and time, while at the same time seeking to split the opposing forces and to destroy them at different times.

(*b*) Supply lines are particularly vulnerable as all petrol and ammunition, essential requirements for the battle, must pass along them. Hence, one should protect one's own by all possible means and seek to confuse, or better still, to cut the enemy's. Operations in the opposing supply area will cause the enemy immediately to break off the battle elsewhere, since, as already shown, supplies are the basis of the battle and thus must be given priority of protection.

(*c*) The tank force is the backbone of the motorised army. Everything turns on the tanks; the other formations are mere ancillaries. War of attrition against the enemy tank units must, therefore, be carried on as far as possible by one's own tank destruction units. One's own tank forces must deal the last blow.

(*d*) Results of reconnaissance must reach the commander in the shortest possible time and he must then take immediate decisions and put them into effect as quickly as possible. Speed of reaction in Command decisions decides the battle. It is, therefore, essential that commanders of motorised forces should be as near as possible to their troops and in the closest signal communication with them.

(*e*) Speed of one's own movement and organisational cohesion of the force are decisive factors and require particular attention. Any sign of confusion must be dealt with as quickly as possible by reorganisation.

(*f*) Concealment of one's own intentions is of the greatest importance, in order to provide conditions of surprise for one's own operations and thus enable one to exploit the time required by the enemy command to react. Deception measures of all kinds should be encouraged, not least to make the enemy commander uncertain and compel him to move with hesitation and caution.

(g) Not until the enemy has been thoroughly beaten should one attempt to exploit success by overrunning and destroying large parts of his disorganised forces. Here again speed is everything. The enemy must never be allowed time to reorganise. The fastest possible regrouping for the pursuit, the fastest possible organisation of supply is essential for the attacking forces.

In the technical and organisational fields the following points must be given particular consideration in desert warfare:

(a) From the tank one must demand, above all, manœuvrability, speed and a long-range gun, for the side which has the more powerful gun has the longer arm and can the earlier engage the enemy. Weight of armour cannot make up for lack of gun-power, since it can only be provided at the expense of manœuvrability and speed, both of which are indispensable tactical requirements.

(b) The artillery, too, must have great range and, above all, be mobile in the highest degree, including its ammunition in large quantities.

(c) The infantry serves only to occupy and hold positions designed to prevent the enemy from particular operations or to force him into them. Once this object is attained it must be possible to move the infantry quickly and employ them elsewhere. They must, therefore, be mobile and be provided with equipment which enables them to take up defensive positions as quickly as possible at tactically important points of the battlefield.

It is my experience that bold decisions give the best promise of success. One must differentiate between operational and tactical boldness and a military gamble. A bold operation is one which has no more than a chance of success but which, in case of failure, leaves one with sufficient forces in hand to be able to cope with any situation. A gamble, on the other hand, is an operation which can lead either to victory or to the destruction of one's own forces. Situations can arise where even a gamble may be justified, as when, in the normal course of events, defeat would be merely a question of time, when the gaining of time is pointless and the only chance lies in an operation of great risk. The only time that a commander can calculate the course of a battle in advance is when his forces are so superior to the enemy's that his victory is self-evident from the start. Then the problem is no longer one of "what with" but only of "how." But even in such situations I think it is better to operate on the grand scale rather than to creep about the battlefield anxiously taking all conceivable security measures against possible and impossible enemy reactions.

Normally there is no ideal solution but each possible course has its advantages and disadvantages. One must select that which seems the best from the widest point of view and then pursue it and accept the consequences. Any compromise is bad.

One of the first lessons which I drew from my experience of motorised warfare was that speed of operation and quick reaction of the Command were the decisive factors. The troops must be able to operate at the highest speed and in complete co-ordination. One must not be satisfied here with any normal average but must always endeavour to obtain the maximum performance, for the side which makes the greater effort is the faster and the faster side wins the battle. Officers and N.C.O.'s must, therefore, constantly train their troops with this in view.

In my opinion the duties of a Commander-in-Chief are not limited to his staff work. He must also take an interest in the details of Command and frequently busy himself in the front line, for the following reasons:

(*a*) Exact execution of the plans of the Commander-in-Chief and his staff is of the greatest importance. It is a mistake to assume that every local commander will make as much of a situation as there is to be made out of it. Most of them soon succumb to a certain need for rest. Then it is simply reported that this or that can't be done for some reason or another—such reasons are always easy enough to think up. People of this kind must be made to feel the authority of the Commander-in-Chief and be shaken out of their apathy by him. The Commander-in-Chief must be the driving motor of the battle. One must always have to reckon with his appearance in personal control.

(*b*) The Commander-in-Chief must continually endeavour to keep his troops acquainted with the latest tactical knowledge and experience and ensure that they are acted upon. He must see to it that his subordinates are trained according to the most modern developments. The best form of "welfare" for the troops is a superlative state of training, for this saves unnecessary casualties.

(*c*) For the Commander-in-Chief, too, it is a great advantage to know the front and to have a detailed knowledge of the problems of his subordinates. Only in this way can he keep his ideas continually up-to-date and adapt them to the conditions of the moment. If, on the other hand, he conducts the battle as though he were playing chess, he will inevitably become inflexible in his theories. The best results are obtained by the commander whose ideas develop freely from the conditions around him and have not previously been channelled into any fixed pattern.

(d) The Commander-in-Chief must have contact with his troops. He must be able to feel and think with them. The soldier must have confidence in him. In this connection there is one cardinal principle to remember: one must never simulate a feeling for the troops which in fact one does not have. The ordinary soldier has a surprisingly good nose for what is genuine and what is fake.

ALLIED AIR SUPREMACY

Writing after the battle of Alam-el-Halfa, Rommel stresses the threat to the Axis forces of the growing Allied air superiority

The enemy will conduct the war of attrition from the air. His bombs will be particularly effective against the motorised forces, standing without cover in the open desert. Their vehicles, tanks and guns will offer a magnificent target for bombers and low-flying aircraft, whether on the march, in the attack assembly area or in the attack itself. In due course the enemy will be able to give our forces such a pounding that they will be virtually rendered unfit for action—and that without his having made any appreciable expenditure of the strength of his own troops. From the Command point of view he will gain the following advantages:

(a) He will be able to secure complete aerial reconnaissance reports.

(b) He will be able to operate much more freely and boldly since, in an emergency, his Air Force will be able to break up the approach march and assembly and, indeed, any operation of his opponents or to delay them until he has taken effective counter-measures.

(c) The slowing down of his opponent's movements will be accompanied by the speeding up of his own. Since speed is one of the most important factors in desert warfare, the effect of this development is easy to foresee.

Moreover, whoever has command of the air is in a position to inflict such damage on his opponent's supply columns that serious shortages will soon make themselves felt. By maintaining a continuous watch over the roads leading to the front he can stop completely all supply traffic in daylight and restrict it to the hours of darkness, thus occasioning an irretrievable loss of time.

For us, therefore, it was fundamentally necessary to dispose of such stronger air forces as would give us, if not equality in the air, at least something approaching equality. . . . Any one who has to fight, even with the most modern weapons, against an enemy with complete air superiority, fights like a savage against modern European troops, under the same operational and tactical handicaps and with the same chances of success.

We had now to try to put our defence against the expected British attack [the El Alamein offensive] into such a form that the British air superiority would have the least possible effect. For the first and most serious danger was that which threatened us from the air. As the result, we could no longer put the main burden of the defensive battle on to the motorised formations since these, as has been shown, were too vulnerable to attack from the air. Instead, we had to try to resist the enemy in fixed positions constructed for defence against the most modern weapons of war. We had to accept the fact that in future the enemy would be able to delay our operations at will by strong air attacks by day and similar attacks at night with the aid of parachute flares. Experience had taught us that no man could be expected to stay in his vehicle and drive on when attacked by enemy bombers and that it was useless to try to work to a time-table. Our positions had to be constructed so strongly that they could be held by their local garrisons independently and over a long period, without support of operational reserves, until, in spite of the delays caused by the R.A.F., reinforcements could arrive.

British air superiority threw to the winds all our operational and tactical rules, which hitherto had been followed with such success, simply because they could no longer be applied. Without strong air forces of our own, there was no answer to the problem of dealing with the enemy air superiority. The strength of the Anglo-American Air Force was, in all the battles to come, the deciding factor.

THE BATTLES OF 1942

Rommel's account of the battles of the spring and summer of 1942 runs to such length that it is impossible to give it here, in the limited space available, as a connected narrative. I

*have, therefore, selected passages which throw light on his
military thinking, on his relation with the German High Command, on his judgment of his opponents and on his plans,
vetoed by Hitler, for escaping complete disaster in North
Africa. Such passages have not been summarised but are given
in his own words with occasional interpolations in square
brackets. It will be seen that the views attributed to Rommel
in the book itself are confirmed by his own writings. The
words "operational" and "operations," which occur frequently
in the text, have a special significance in German military
phraseology, not easy to express exactly in English. The field
of "operations" lies between strategy and tactics. Rommel
himself, until the final stages, was an "operational" commander in North Africa, as was General Montgomery,
whereas Generals Wavell, Auchinleck and Alexander had
responsibilities in the sphere of strategy. "Operational reserves" are the reserves available to the commander in the
field. "Operation" is used by Rommel to describe a dynamic
movement of the bulk of his motorised forces*

After the end of our counter-offensive, which had led, at the beginning of 1942, to the reconquest of Cyrenaica, serious difficulties arose over supplies.

The reason, apart from the scant attention given to the African
theatre of war by the German High Command, who failed to
recognise its immense importance, was the half-hearted conduct
of the war at sea by the Italians, whereas the British Navy was
very active and the R.A.F. caused us tremendous trouble.

The German High Command, to which I was subordinate, continued to ignore the importance of the African theatre. They did
not realise that in the Near East we were able, with relatively
small means, to achieve successes which, in their strategic and
economic value, would have far surpassed the conquest of the Don
Bend. Ahead of us were territories containing an enormous wealth
of raw materials, Africa, for example, and the Middle East, which
could have freed us from all our anxieties about oil. The reinforcement of my army by a few German motorised divisions
would have been sufficient to bring about the complete defeat of
the entire British forces in the Near East.

It was not to be. Our demands for reinforcement by additional
formations were not granted. The decision was explained by the
statement that the Eastern Front required such vast quantities of
transport that the creation of further motorised units for Africa was
quite out of the question in view of Germany's limited productive
capacity. Quite clearly some people in the High Command believed all along that Africa was in any case a "lost cause," as had
been unequivocally stated as far back as 1941. It was apparently

their opinion that the investment of large quantities of material i
Africa would pay no dividends. A regrettably short-sighted an
misguided view!

For the supply difficulties which they were anxious to describ
as "insuperable" were far from being so. All that was wanted wa
a man with real personlity to deal with these questions in Rom
someone with the authority and drive to tackle the problems i
volved. This would undoubtedly have led to friction in certai
Italian circles but this could have been overcome by a missio
which was not encumbered with political functions. Our Govern
ment's weak policy towards the Italian State seriously damage
the German-Italian cause in North Africa.

The heavy burden placed upon German material resources b
the Eastern Front was certainly not to be underestimated, pai
ticularly after we had lost the greater part of our equipment ther
in the winter of 1941-42. But in spite of all this I am firmly con
vinced that, considering the tremendous possibilities offered b
the North African theatre, there were undoubtedly less importan
sectors of the front which could have spared some mechanise
divisions. It can truthfully be said that there was a lack of under
standing of the situation and hence of goodwill.

The consequences were serious. For a year and a half, up t
the moment when our strength failed in front of El Alamein, w
had, with only three German divisions, whose fighting strengt
was often ridiculously small, kept the British in Africa busy an
inflicted on them many a heavy defeat. After the loss of Afric
an increasingly large number of German divisions had to face th
British and Americans, until finally some 70 divisions had to b
thrown into the battle in Italy and France. Given six or seve
German motorised divisions we could, in the summer of 1942
have so thoroughly mauled the British that the threat from th
south would have been eliminated for a long time. With a certai
amount of goodwill, supplies for these formations could have bee
organised in sufficient quantities. Later on, in Tunis, when it wa
of course, already too late, it proved perfectly possible suddenl
to double the amount of our supplies. But at that time it had a
last come to be realised that we were up to our necks in troubl
in the Mediterranean theatre.

Earlier, after a period during which, out of total supply require
ments of 60,000 tons only 18,000 tons reached the German arm
on African soil, the situation temporarily changed, thanks to th
initiative of Field-Marshal Kesselring, whose air forces were able
during the spring of 1942, to gain superiority in the Central Medi
terranean. In particular, the heavy Axis air raids against Malt
contributed greatly to the fact that, for some time, the threa
to the sea routes was as good as eliminated. It was only becaus

of this that it was possible to increase the flow of material to Tripoli, Benghazi and Derna.

Nevertheless it was obvious that the British Eighth Army would be reinforced more rapidly than ourselves. The greatest efforts had been made by the British Government to provide the Eighth Army with all the material they could lay their hands on. Large convoys arrived one after the other in the Egyptian ports, bringing war material from England or America round the Cape. Naturally this 12,000 mile voyage, which the British transports could make at the most only a couple of times a year, involved tremendous problems for the enemy staff, already struggling with the serious problem created by the activity of our U-boats. But in spite of all this, the British Navy and Merchant Marine were able to maintain over this huge distance supplies to the British forces in the Near East on a scale far superior to our own. Petrol, moreover, could be obtained in abundance from the refineries of the Near East. Only rarely did the British supply ports become the target of serious German bombing attacks. From these ports the British could bring up their supplies to the front by three routes:

1. A well-constructed railway ran from the Suez area to the outer perimeter of Tobruk.

2. The British Navy had organised coastal shipping in an admirable manner and in Tobruk had one of the best ports in North Africa.

3. A well-built road sufficiently wide for supply columns to pass was available.

Above all, there were people on the British side with great influence who were doing everything they could to organise the supply service in the most efficient manner possible. Our enemy benefited by the fact that North Africa was the principal theatre of war for the British Empire and was therefore regarded as the most important by the British Government as well as from the fact that Britain had a first-class, powerful navy of her own while we had to deal with unreliable Italian naval staffs.

It was obvious to us that the British would try, with all the means at their disposal, to destroy my army as soon as they felt themselves strong enough to attempt it. Our southern flank lay wide open. Ritchie would have a great number of operational choices. Our supply lines would be constantly threatened. If we were compelled to withdraw owing to the danger of being outflanked we would be in very serious difficulties, for most of my Italian divisions were not motorised. But Ritchie was not to have the chance to exploit his many opportunities, for I had decided to anticipate his attack.

British Positions in the Marmarica

The basic British plan for the defence of the Marmarica was characterised by their efforts to impose upon the attacker a form of warfare which was better suited to the British Command than manœuvring in the open desert. Technically the execution of this plan was excellent, but the British approached the solution of the problem from false premises. In North Africa, a rigid system of defence in any position with an open southern flank was bound to lead to disaster. In these circumstances a defensive battle could only be successful if it were conducted as an operation. Naturally fortified positions might also be of great value—if they deprived the enemy of the chance of any particular operational action. But it was essential that they should not be occupied by the force destined for the operational defence.

The plan which my staff and I worked out gave the possibility of a decision in the most favourable circumstances. But the fate of my army did not by any means depend on the success of this conception alone. Following my usual practice, I calculated from the beginning on the basis that things might not go according to plan. As far as could humanly be foreseen the situation at the start of the battle would be far from unfavourable. With full confidence in our troops, their excellent tactical training and experience in improvisation, we approached the battle full of optimism.

Plan of Attack

The opening move of the offensive was to be made by a frontal attack of the Italian infantry divisions occupying the Gazala positions against the 50th British Division and the South Africans. A powerful force of artillery was earmarked to support this attack. The impression was to be created both by day and by night that tank assembly positions existed behind the front. For this purpose tanks and lorries were to be driven round in circles in this area. The British Command was to be made to expect our main attack in the northern and central part of the Gazala position. What we wanted to achieve was for the British tank formations to deploy behind the infantry on this sector of the front. To the British Command, the idea of a German frontal attack against the Gazala position could not have appeared too far-fetched as it was by no means impossible that we should prefer such an attack to the risky right hook round Bir Hacheim. If our attempt to mislead the British into concentrating their entire tank forces there should fail, then we hoped that they would send at least part of their tank brigades into that sector, and thereby split their striking force.

During daylight hours all movement of my motorised forces was to be directed towards the point of attack of the Italian infantry. But after nightfall the motorised group was to drive into its assembly area. This group consisted of the German Afrika Korps with the 15th and 21st Panzer Divisions, the 20th Italian Motorised Corps and the 90th Light Division with the three reconnaissance units. The beginning of the advance, which was to take the form of an enveloping attack on Bir Hacheim, was fixed for 2200 hours. From there the German Afrika Korps and 20th Italian Corps with the Ariete Tank Division and Trieste Motorised Division were to push on to the coast via Acroma, in order to cut the supply line and smash the British divisions in the Gazala position, together with the tank forces which were there assembled.

The 90th Light Division was ordered to push into the El Adem-El Hamed area together with the three reconnaissance units in order to prevent the withdrawal of the Tobruk garrison and the bringing up of reinforcements into the Acroma area. In addition the British were to be cut off from the extensive supply depots which they had established in the area east of Tobruk. In order to simulate the existence of massed tank forces in that area the 90th Light Division had been equipped with lorries on which were mounted aero-engines fitted with propellers, which were intended, by stirring up large quantities of dust, to suggest the approach of strong tank forces. We wanted to keep the British forces in that area from intervening in the Acroma battle, so long as our tank units were trying to achieve a decision there.

Following upon the destruction of the British forces in the Marmarica we had planned for a rapid conquest of the fortress of Tobruk. My freedom of operation had been limited by the Duce to the area bounded by the Egyptian frontier.

It had actually been intended that Malta should be taken by Italian and German parachute and landing forces before the offensive started but for some unaccountable reason our High Command abandoned this scheme. Unfortunately, my request to have this attractive little job entrusted to my own army had been turned down back in the spring. Consequently, in view of the steady increase in British war potential, we fixed the date of the attack for May 26th, 1942.

BATTLES FOR GAZALA POSITION

This covers the period from May 26th to June 15th. During these three weeks the battle of attrition was waged in the Western Desert in its most ruthless form. The battle opened very badly for us but in the fluctuating fighting which ensued, we succeeded, partly by means of attacks with limited objectives, partly by means of our defence, in defeating the superior British formations, in spite of the courage which their troops displayed.

In view of the superior strength of the British forces this victory of my German-Italian troops came as a complete surprise to world opinion. The dispositions of my adversary, Lieutenant-General Ritchie, were severely criticised. Was their defeat in fact caused by the mistakes of the British commander? After the battle I came across an article by the British military critic, Liddell Hart, which ascribed the shortcomings of the British Command during the African campaign to the fact that the British generals stuck too closely to infantry warfare. I had the same impression. The British Command had not drawn the inferences which it should have drawn from the defeat of 1941-42. Prejudice against innovations is a typical characteristic of an Officer Corps which has grown up in a well-tried and proved system. That was the reason why the Prussian Army was defeated by Napoleon. The same phenomenon demonstrated itself during the war amongst both British and German officers, who, in their preoccupation with complicated theories, had lost the ability to adapt themselves to the realities of the situation. A military doctrine had been worked out down to the last detail, and it was now regarded as the sum of military wisdom. In their opinion, only that military thinking which followed their standardised rules was acceptable. Everything outside these rules they regarded as a gamble and, if it succeeded, the result of luck and accident. This attitude of mind created prejudice, the consequences of which were quite incalculable.

For even military rules are affected by technical development. What was valid in 1914 is valid to-day only where the greater part of the formations engaged on both sides, or at least on the side which is attacked, consists of non-motorised infantry units. In this situation the armoured troops still play the part of the cavalry whose task it is to outrun and cut off the infantry. Quite different rules apply in a battle which is being fought by fully motorised adversaries on both sides, as I have already explained. However valuable it may be to base one's actions upon tradition in the field of soldierly ethics, this attitude must be condemned in the field of military science. For in these days it is not left to the military leaders alone to think up new methods, thereby rendering others valueless; to-day the possibilities of warfare are constantly being changed by technical progress. Hence, the modern army commander must be free of all excessive attachment to routine methods and must have an extensive understanding of technical matters. He must be ready to adapt his ideas to the situation at any given moment and to turn the whole structure of his thinking inside out, if conditions should make this necessary. I think that my adversary, General Ritchie, like many generals of the older school, had not completely realised the consequences which followed from the fully motorised conduct of operations and from the open terrain of the desert. In spite of the excellent and detailed way in which his plans had been worked out, they were bound to fail, for they were in effect a compromise.

In spite of the dangerous situation which existed on the evening of May 27th, which set us serious problems, I was full of hope about the further course of the battle. For Ritchie had thrown his armoured formations into the battle separately and at different times, thereby giving us the chance of engaging them each time with just about enough of our own tanks. This splitting up of the British armoured brigades was incomprehensible. In my opinion the sacrifice of the 7th British Armoured Division south and southeast of Bir-el-Harmat served no operational purpose whatever for it made no difference whether my Panzer divisions were engaged there or at the Trigh-el-Abd, where the remainder of the British armoured forces did eventually enter the battle. The principal aim of the British should have been to bring all their available armoured formations into action at one and the same time. They should never have let themselves be misled into splitting up their forces before the battle or during our feint against the Gazala position. The fact that their units were fully motorised would have enabled them to cross the battlefield at great speed, if and wherever danger had threatened. Mobile warfare in the desert has often and rightly been compared to a battle at sea where, in the same way, it is wrong to attack piecemeal, leaving part of the ships in port during the battle.

[*Here follows a detailed account of events up to the evening of May 29th.*]

BREAKING THROUGH THE MINEFIELDS

At first light on May 30th each of the divisions moved into the area assigned to it and took up a defensive position. During these movements we noticed the presence of strong British forces with tanks in the Ualeb area. This was the strengthened 150th British Brigade from the 50th Division. In the meantime part of the 10th Italian Corps had succeeded in crossing the British minefields and establishing a bridgehead on the eastern side of them, although the lanes the Italians cleared through the minebelts were subjected to heavy British artillery fire, which had a most upsetting effect on our moving columns. All the same, by noon contact had been established between the striking force and the 10th Italian Corps and thus a direct route opened to the west for supplies and reinforcements. During the day the British brigade was encircled in Got-el-Ualeb.

In the afternoon I drove through the minefield to the 10th Corps headquarters for a meeting with Field-Marshal Kesselring, the Italian Corps Commander and Major von Bülow, the Führer's adjutant, and told them my plans. The British minefield was to be shielded by the Afrika Korps from all attacks by British formations from the north-east. Meanwhile I intended to smash the whole of the southern part of the Gazala position and subsequently to resume the offensive. The operation would include the destruction of, first, the 150th British Brigade at Ualeb, and then the 1st Free French Brigade in Bir Hacheim.

The enemy had only hesitatingly followed up our withdrawal. The falling back of the German-Italian formations had evidently come as a surprise to him and besides this the British Command never reacted very quickly. Already on the morning of May 30th we had noticed the British taking up positions with 280 tanks on the east and 150 infantry tanks on the north of our front. We kept waiting for the British to strike a heavy blow. But in the morning only a few British attacks were launched on the Ariete and beaten off by the Italians and there were some slight British advances on the rest of the front. Fifty-seven British tanks were shot up that day.

In the afternoon I myself reconnoitred the possibilities of an attack against the forces occupying Got-el-Ualeb and I detailed part of the Afrika Korps, part of the 90th Light Division and the Italian "Trieste" Division for an attack on the following morning against the British positions there.

The attacking formations advanced against the British 150th Brigade on the morning of May 31st. Yard by yard the German-Italian units fought their way forward against the toughest British resistance imaginable. The British defense was conducted with considerable skill. As usual the British fought to the last round of ammunition. They used a new anti-tank gun of 57 mm. calibre. Nevertheless by the evening of the 31st we had penetrated a considerable distance into the British positions. On the next day the British occupying forces were to receive their final knockout. Again our infantry, after heavy Stuka attacks, burst against the British positions. On this day I accompanied the attacking troops with Colonel Westphal. He was unfortunately severely wounded the same day in a surprise British mortar attack and had to be taken back to Europe, so that I had to do without him in the days that followed. This was a bitter loss. For me his assistance had always been of outstanding value, because of his extraordinary knowledge and experience and readiness to make decisions.

The attack continued. One after another the sections of the elaborately constructed British defence system were taken by my troops, and by early afternoon the position was in our hands. The last British resistance was at an end. We took 3,000 prisoners, and destroyed or captured 101 tanks and scout-cars as well as 124 guns of every kind.

[*In describing the operations of the next few days, Rommel touches on the merits and demerits of his opponents.*]

That day the Guards Brigade had evacuated Knightsbridge, after the area had been subjected all morning to the combined fire of every piece of artillery we could bring to bear. This brigade was practically a living embodiment of the positive and negative qualities of the British soldier. An extraordinary bravery and toughness was combined with a rigid inability to move quickly.

[*After describing the capture of Tobruk, Rommel touches on his decision to advance into Egypt, contrary to the Duce's original orders.*]

This was a plan which might perhaps succeed. It was an experiment. The operation would not entail any risk to my army's safety. As things were we could have defended ourselves with success in every possible situation during our advance.

Later this advance came in for some criticism. It was said that the supply columns available in North Africa would not in the long run have been able to manage the long supply-route from Benghazi to El Alamein and that the British would have greatly benefited from the shorter supply route to their front from Port Said. To this there are the following counter-arguments:

(a) British superiority at Sollum would have had an even greater effect than at El Alamein. The enemy could have out-flanked our forces by deep detours and destroyed our motorised divisions with their armoured formations which, at the time of El Alamein, were heavily superior not only in numbers, as before, but also in quality. The prospect of withdrawing our non-motorised infantry from the Sollum front would have been even worse than from El Alamein. During the El Alamein battle they represented the bulk of the army, but they would have had no chance of effective action at Sollum, where the positions they occupied demanded no break-through attempts from the enemy but only an easy outflanking movement. They would have proved either an easy prey for the British motorised units or a burden in a withdrawal. Of course our supply columns had to cope with serious difficulties during the advance into Egypt. But it was essential to demand the same efforts from the supply staffs in Rome as from the tank crews and infantry, overtired after three weeks of fighting. Thus, supply by sea to the harbours in the forward area should have been improvised as it had always been promised would be done in these circumstances. When I gave the order for the thrust into Egypt, I assumed that the fact that final success in Egypt had been brought so close would have spurred the Italian High Command on to making some sort of increase in their effort, and I had, therefore, several times clearly and plainly asked for the exploitation of the captured harbours.

(b) There would have been no considerable improvement in our supply position at Sollum either, because then Benghazi and Tobruk, instead of Tobruk and Mersa Matruh, would have been within effective range of the British bombers. Benghazi would have been ruled out, for all practical purposes, for vessels of large tonnage, and this would have meant extending the transport route as far as Tripoli, which would have been beyond the capabilities of our supply-columns. For the British, on the other hand, to operate on the frontier would have scarcely made any difference to their supply position. At their disposal were railways, enough vehicles for road-supplies, and well-organised coastal shipping.

[The advance into Egypt was marked by heavy and confused fighting.]

The New Zealand Division under Freyberg, an old acquaintance of mine from previous campaigns, concentrated in the night and broke out to the south. The wild flare-up that ensued involved my own battle headquarters, which lay to the south. The Kiel battle-group and parts of the Littorio went into action. The exchanges of fire between my forces and the New Zealanders reached an extraordinary pitch of intensity. Soon my headquarters were surrounded by burning vehicles, making them the target for continuous enemy fire at close range. I had enough of this after a while and ordered the troops, with the staff, to move back southeastward. The confusion reigning on that night can scarcely be imagined. It was impossible to see one's hand before one's eyes. The R.A.F. bombed their own troops, German units were firing on each other, the tracer was flying in all directions.

BEFORE EL ALAMEIN

With amazing swiftness the British organised fresh reinforcements for Alamein. Their High Command had recognized that the next battle there would be largely decisive and they had considered the situation with sober care. The danger of the hour drove the British to extraordinary efforts. In times of extreme peril it is always possible to achieve objects until then considered impossible, for there is nothing like danger for sweeping aside preconceived ideas.

By July 13th the front was stabilised. From the point of view of command the British were here in their element, for their strong quality was a form of tactics which expressed itself in the modern kind of infantry fighting and static warfare. Their specialty lay in local attacks, carried out under the protection of infantry tanks and artillery. The Alamein position adjoined the sea to the north, and to the south it sank away into the Qattara Depression, a level area of moving sand with many salt-marshes, and therefore impassable for heavy vehicles. As the Alamein position could not, therefore, be outflanked, the war became one in which both sides disposed of great experience and knowledge, but neither could make use of revolutionary methods which would come as a complete surprise to the other. The outcome of this static war depended on who had more ammunition.

I had, therefore, wanted to escape in the last few days from this static warfare, in which the British were masters and for which their infantry had been trained, and to reach the open desert before Alexandria, where I could exploit the absolute operational superiority we enjoyed in open desert battles. But in this I did not succeed; the British knew quite well how to break up the thrusts of my severely weakened forces.

RETROSPECT

With these actions the great battle of the early summer came to an end. It had begun with a fantastic victory. After Tobruk had been captured, the extraordinary strength of the British Empire began to show itself again. For only a few days could we hope to go on past El Alamein and occupy the Suez Canal area. While we must fight every battle with the same forces, the British were able to throw fresh troops, fully armed and up to strength, into the fight and withdraw from the Alamein front for recuperation those divisions which had been badly hammered in Marmarica and Western Egypt. My troops stayed in the fight. My numbers grew always less, while at the same time the losses from dead, wounded and sick kept rising. Always it was the same battalions which advanced, largely in captured lorries, on the British positions, and then, springing from their vehicles, charged over the sand at the enemy. Always it was the same tank forces which drove into the battle, and the same gunners who fired the shells. The deeds performed in those weeks by officers and men reached the limits of human efficiency.

I had made extraordinary demands on my forces and spared neither the rank and file, nor their leaders, nor myself. It was obvious to me that the fall of Tobruk and the collapse of the Eighth Army was the one moment in the African war when the road lay open to Alexandria with only a few British troops to defend it. I and my colleagues would have been fools if we had not done everything to exploit this one and only chance. If success had depended, as it did in olden days, on the stronger will of the soldiers and their leader, then we would have overrun Alamein. But our sources of supply dried up, thanks to the inactivity and disorganisation of the supply depots in Europe.

Then the powers of resistance of many of the Italian formations collapsed. The duty of comradeship obliges me to make clear, particularly as I was supreme commander also of the Italians, that the defeats the Italian forces suffered in early July before El Alamein were in no way the fault of the Italian soldiers. The Italian soldier was willing, unselfish and a good comrade and, considering his circumstances, his achievement was far above the average. The performance of all the Italian units, more especially of the motorised forces, far surpassed anything the Italian Army had done for a hundred years. There were many Italian officers and generals whom we admired as men and as soldiers.

The cause of the Italian defeat sprang from the entire Italian military and state system, from the poor Italian equipment, and from the small interest shown in this war by many high Italian leaders and statesmen. This failure often prevented me from carrying out my plans.

THE BATTLE OF ALAM-EL-HALFA

By the end of August the urgently needed supplies of ammunition and petrol, promised by the Supreme Command, had still not arrived. The full moon, absolutely vital to our operation, was already on the wane. Further delay would have meant finally giving up our offensive. Marshal Cavallero, however, informed me that the petrol ships, heavily escorted, would arrive in a matter of hours, or the next day at the latest. Hoping for the fulfilment of this promise; trusting to the assurance of Marshal Kesselring that he would fly up to 500 tons over to North Africa in case of need; but above all certain that if we let the full moon go by we were losing our last chance of taking the offensive, I gave the order for the attack to be carried out on the night of August 30th-31st as planned.

Everything had been in readiness several days before; for we had reckoned with the arrival of the petrol at any minute. But in fact we did not want to start moving until after the arrival of the petrol, in view of the unreliability of Cavallero.

In the early stages of the battle, the British defended their strong positions with extraordinary toughness and so hindered our advance. As a result they were able to send warnings and situation reports back to headquarters and give the British Command time to put the necessary counter-measures into operation. Such a breathing space was of tremendous importance to the British. They needed to hold their front only until their striking forces had grouped themselves for the necessary action against the German-Italian forces which had broken through.

My plan, to go forward with the motorised forces another fifty kilometres by moonlight, and from there to proceed to a further attack northwards in the early morning light, did not succeed. The tanks were held up by unsuspected ground obstacles and we lost the element of surprise, on which the whole plan finally rested. In view of this we now considered whether we should break off the battle.

Had there been a quick break-through in the south by the motorised forces, the British would have needed time for reconnaissance, for making decisions and putting them into effect. During this time our movements need not have met with any serious counter-measures. But we had now lost the advantage of this breathing-space. The British knew where we were. I resolved that my decision, whether or not to break off the battle, should depend on how things stood with the Afrika Korps.

I learned soon afterwards that the Afrika Korps, under the outstanding leadership of the Chief of the General Staff, General Bayerlein, had in the meantime overcome the British mines and was about to push farther eastwards. I discussed the situation with Bayerlein and we decided to carry on with the attack.

Owing to the fact that the British tank forces were again assembled ready for immediate action, a wide outflanking drive to the east could not be carried out, in view of the constant menace to our own flank which would be presented by the 7th Armoured Division to the south and by the 10th and 1st Armoured Divisions in the north. We had to decide on an earlier turn northwards. In the event, the offensive failed because:

(a) The British positions in the south, contrary to what our reconnaissance had led us to believe, had been completed in great strength.

(b) The continuous and very heavy attacks of the R.A.F., who were practically masters of the air, absolutely pinned my troops to the ground and made impossible any safe deployment or any advance according to schedule.

(c) The petrol, which was a necessary condition of the carrying out of our plans, did not arrive. The ships which Cavallero had promised us were some of them sunk, some of them delayed and some of them not even dispatched. Kesselring had unfortunately not been able to fulfil his promise to fly over 500 tons a day to the vicinity of the front in case of need.

BRIGADIER CLIFTON

A night attack on the 10th Italian Corps cost the British particularly heavy losses, including many dead. There were also two hundred prisoners, among them Brigadier Clifton, commanding the 6th New Zealand Brigade. I had a conversation with him on the following morning. He had just been busy convincing the Italians that they must surrender, in view of the strong British tank forces facing their position, and the Italians had already taken the bolts out of their rifles, when, to his annoyance, a German officer had arrived and his plan came to nothing.

He seemed extremely depressed as a result. I tackled him about various acts, contrary to international law, committed by New Zealand troops. Clifton showed the most absolute certainty of victory, which was understandable now that our attack had been beaten back. He was an old Africa veteran, for he had led British troops against us since 1940, had been in Greece, and was also in the winter fighting of 1941-42.

He impressed us as a very brave man and very likeable. He insisted on becoming a prisoner of the Germans and not being sent to Italy. I tried to carry out his wish, and, evading general instructions, handed him over to a German depot in Mersa Matruh. However the O.K.H. later ordered that he should be handed over to the Italians.

But on the evening before he was due to be handed to the Italians, Clifton asked to go to the lavatory, where he got out of the window and vanished without trace. All troops were at once warned by wireless. A few days later some of my staff officers were hunting gazelle when they suddenly saw a weary foot-traveller coming across the desert, carrying what seemed to be a water-bottle in his hand. Closer observation revealed him as the much sought-after Clifton. He was at once arrested and brought in to us again. I expressed to him my recognition of his courage; for not every man would contemplate such a trek through the desert. He looked very exhausted, which was not surprising. To stop any more attempts at escape, I had him sent at once to Italy. Later I heard that he disappeared from the Italian prison camp in the disguise of a Hitler Jugend leader, with shorts and badge of rank, and in this uniform crossed over the frontier into Switzerland.

[*Rommel's information was incorrect.*]

EL ALAMEIN

[*Before going sick to Germany, Rommel made his plans to resist the expected British attack at El Alamein.*]

In attacking, the British were forced to aim at a penetration of our positions. It was clear to us that the British military machine was well-suited for this purpose. The whole of British training was based on the lessons drawn from battles in the First World War, in which everything revolved around material. The technical lessons had been learned but had not brought about any revolutionary change. Although the tactical deductions about mechanisation and armour had been outstandingly made by British military critics,* the responsible British leaders had not ventured to apply them since they had not yet been tried in practice—as the foundation of their training in peacetime, ready to be brought into play in case of war. The British had been suffering under this shortcoming for a long time and it put them at a great disadvantage. But it did not affect the coming battles for penetration of our position as, owing to the extensive minefields, the armoured units were deprived of their freedom of movement and were compelled to operate as infantry-supporting tanks.

In training and command we were, as all previous battles had shown, considerably superior to the British troops in the open desert. Though it could be assumed that, as far as tactics were concerned, the British had learnt a good deal from the many battles and skirmishes which we had with them, they could not possibly have profited fully from them as their shortcomings were not primarily due to their command but to the ultra-conservative structure of their army, which was in no way suitable for war in the open desert, though excellent for fighting on fixed fronts.

In spite of all this, we could not take the risk of shifting the main weight of the defensive action on to operations in the open desert for the following reasons:

(a) The proportionate strengths of the motorised divisions had become too unequal. While our adversary was constantly being reinforced by motorised units, we received only non-motorised forces, which, in the open desert, were as good as useless. We were forced, therefore, to choose a form of warfare in which they too could play their part.

(b) The British air superiority, the new air tactics of the R.A.F., and the resultant tactical limitations on the use of motorised forces, to which reference has already been made.

(c) Our permanent shortage of petrol. I did not want to get myself again into the awkward situation of having to break off a battle because we were immobilised by a shortage of petrol. In a mobile defensive action shortage of petrol means disaster.

* General Bayerlein says that Rommel was here referring to General Fuller and Captain Liddell Hart. Speaking of the latter, Bayerlein states that his theories of armoured warfare "made the greatest impression on Field-Marshal Rommel, and highly influenced his tactical and strategical conceptions . . . not only General Guderian but Rommel, too, could be called Liddell Hart's 'pupils' in many respects."

The Führer's call came through. The situation at El Alamein had developed in such a way that he must ask me to fly to Africa to take over command. I set off the next morning. I knew that there were no more laurels to be earned in Africa, for I had learnt from reports of my officers that supplies there had fallen far short of the minimum demands which I had made. It very soon became clear, however, that I had not had any idea of just how bad the supply situation really was.

When I arrived in Rome towards 11 A.M., I was met at the airport by General von Rintelen, Military Attaché and German General attached to the Italian forces. He informed me of the latest events in the African theatre. After powerful artillery preparation, the enemy had occupied parts of the positions to the south of Hill 31; several battalions of 164th Division and of the Italians had been completely wiped out. The British attack was still in progress and General Stumme was still missing. General von Rintelen further reported to me that only three issues of petrol remained for the Army in the African theatre, for it had not been possible in recent weeks to send more across, partly on account of the sinkings by the British, partly because the Italian Navy did not provide the transport. This situation was disastrous, since petrol for only 300 km. per vehicle between Tripoli and the front was so little that a prolonged resistance on our part was not to be expected. Shortage of petrol would completely prevent our taking the correct tactical decisions and would impose tremendous limitations upon our planning. I was extremely angry, for at my departure there had been at least 8 issues left for the Army in Egypt and Lybia and, in comparison with the minimum essential 30 issues, even that had been ridiculously little. Experience had shown that one needed one issue of petrol for each day of battle.* Without it one was crippled and the enemy could operate without one being able to take practical counter-measures. General von Rintelen regretted this situation and said that he had unfortunately been on leave and had thus been unable to give sufficient attention to the supply question!

Feeling that we would fight this battle with but small hope of even a defensive success, I flew across the Mediterranean in my Storch and reached my battle headquarters at dusk. In the meantime the body of General Stumme had been found at about midday and taken to Derna. The circumstances of his death had been roughly these: General Stumme had driven along the track to the battlefield and had been fired upon in the region of Hill 21 by British infantry with anti-tank and machine-guns. Colonel Büch-

* An issue in Africa appears to have been petrol for 100 km.

ting who accompanied him received a mortal wound in the head. The driver, Corporal Wolf, immediately turned the car. General Stumme leapt out and hung on to the outside of the car while the driver drove furiously out of the enemy fire. General Stumme must have suddenly had a heart attack and fallen off the car. The driver noticed nothing. On Sunday morning the General was found beside the track, dead, but without any injury.

General Stumme had always had far too high a blood pressure for Africa and was not therefore really fit for tropical service. We all deeply regretted his sudden death. He had spared no pains to command the army well and had been day and night at the front. Just before setting off for his last journey on October 24th he had said to his deputy that he felt it would be wise to ask for my return as, with his own short experience of the African theatre and in view of the tremendous British strength and the disastrous supply situation, he did not feel wholly certain of being able to bring the battle to a successful conclusion. I, for myself, was no more optimistic.

[*After a detailed description of the battle, too long to include here, Rommel gives a text of a telegram which reached him on the evening of November 1st and shows, as he says, how the situation was misunderstood in Rome.*]

"For Field Marshal Rommel

The Duce has authorised me to convey to you his fullest appreciation of the successful counter-attack led personally by you. The Duce conveys to you further his complete confidence that the battle now in progress will, under your command, be brought to a successful conclusion."

It soon became obvious that the Führer's Headquarters had no better knowledge of the African situation. It is sometimes a misfortune to enjoy a certain military reputation. One knows one's own limits but others expect miracles and set down a defeat to deliberate ill will.

[*After describing the concluding days of the battle, Rommel sums up.*]

EL ALAMEIN IN RETROSPECT

We had lost the decisive battle of the African campaign. It was decisive because the defeat resulted in the loss of the major part of our infantry and of our motorised forces. The consequences defied estimation. The amazing thing was that official quarters, both on the German and Italian side, attributed the trouble, not to the failure of supplies, not to our Air inferiority, not to the order to conquer or die at El Alamein, but to the troops and the

229

Command. The military career of most of these people who made such accusations against us was characterised by a continual absence from the front on the principle "weit vom Schuss gibt alte Krieger"—"far from the battle makes old soldiers."

It was even said that we had thrown away our weapons, that I was a defeatist, a pessimist in defeat or in critical situations and therefore largely responsible. The fact was that I did not sit down under the constant reproaches which were levelled at the gallant troops and this gave rise in the future to many a quarrel and bitter argument. These people, in particular, who had formerly been envious of me, now, after the defeat, suddenly had the courage to spread slander about us, where previously they had had to keep silent. The victim of this slander was the army, which after my departure, fell into British hands in its entirety, while highly-qualified armchair strategists were still thinking about operations against Casablanca.

It is no good denying that there were men in high places who were by no means lacking in the intelligence required to understand what was happening, but who lacked the courage to face soberly the unalterable conditions and to draw the necessary conclusions from them. They preferred to put their heads in the sand, live in a sort of military pipe-dream and look for scapegoats whom they usually found in the troops or in the field commanders.

With all my experience, I can confess to only one mistake—that I did not circumvent the "Victory or Death" order 24 hours earlier or did not disregard it altogether. Then the army, together with all its infantry, would in all probability have been saved in a more or less battleworthy condition.

In order to leave no doubt for future historians about the conditions and circumstances under which the Command and troops were labouring at the battle of El Alamein, I include the following summary:

An adequate supply system and stocks of weapons, petrol and ammunition are essential conditions for any army to be able successfully to stand the strain of battle. Before the fighting proper, the battle is fought and decided by the Quartermasters. The bravest man can do nothing without guns, the guns nothing without plenty of ammunition and guns and ammunition are of little use in mobile warfare unless they can be transported by vehicles supplied with sufficient petrol. Supply must approximate in quantity to that which is available to the enemy and not only in quantity but also in quality.

In future the battle on the ground will be preceded by the battle in the air. This will decide who will have to suffer under the operational and tactical disadvantages detailed above and

230

who will, therefore, from the start be forced into tactical compromise.

None of the conditions to which I have referred were in any way fulfilled and we had to suffer the consequences.

As a result of the British command of the air and hence of the seas in the Central Mediterranean, and of other reasons detailed elsewhere, the army's supplies were hardly sufficient to enable it to eke out a bare existence even on quiet days. It was out of the question to think of building up stocks for a defensive battle. The quantities of material which were available to the British far exceeded our worst fears. Never before in any theatre of war had such a concentration of heavy tanks, bombers and artillery with inexhaustible supplies of ammunition been engaged on so short a front as at El Alamein.

The British command of the air was complete. There were days when the British flew 800 bomber sorties and 2,500 sorties of fighters, fighter-bombers and low-flying aircraft. We, on the other hand, could at the most fly 60 dive-bomber and 100 fighter sorties. This number moreover became continually smaller.

Generally speaking, the principles of the British Command had not altered. Now as ever their tactics were methodical and cast to a pattern. On this occasion the British principles did in fact help the Eighth Army to success, for the following reasons:

(a) It did not come to a battle in the open desert, since our motorised forces were forced to form a front for the sake of the frontally engaged infantry divisions, who were without transport. The war took on the form of a battle of material.

(b) The British had such superiority in weapons, both qualitative and quantitative, that they were able to force through any kind of operation. The methods used by the British Command for the destruction of my forces were a result of their overwhelming superiority. They consisted of the following:

(a) Highly concentrated artillery fire.

(b) Continuous bombing attacks by powerful bomber forces.

(c) Locally limited attacks, which were carried through with lavish use of material and which revealed an extremely high state of training, entirely suited to the conditions.

Apart from this, the planning of the British Command was based on the principle of exact calculation, a principle which can only be followed where there is complete material superiority. In actual fact the British did not attempt anything which could be called an "operation" but relied solely on the effect of their artillery and air force. As always, the British Command showed a marked slowness in reaction. When, on the night of November

2nd-3rd, we started on the retreat, it was a long time before the enemy were ready to follow up for the pursuit. But for the intervention of Hitler's unfortunate order, it is highly probable that we would have escaped to Fuka with the bulk of our infantry. As always the British High Command showed its customary caution and little forceful decision. For instance, they attacked time and again with separate tank formations and did not, as might have been expected, throw into battle the 900 tanks which they could, without risk to themselves, have employed in the northern front, thereby using their vast superiority to gain a rapid decision with the minimum of effort and casualties. Actually, under cover of their artillery and air force, only half of that number would have been sufficient to wipe out my forces, which were frequently standing immobilised on the battlefield. Moreover, the British themselves suffered tremendous losses for this reason. Probably their Command wanted to hold its tanks in the second line so as to use them for the pursuit, as apparently their assault forces could not be re-formed fast enough for the follow-up.

In the training of their tanks and infantry formations, the British Command had put to excellent use the experience which they had gained from their previous battles with the Axis troops, but it is true to say the new methods which were now being applied were only made possible by the vast quantity of their ammunition and new war material.

In Germany, thanks largely to the efforts of General Guderian, the first traces of modern leadership in tank warfare began to crystallise in theory before the war. This resulted in the training and organisation of tank units on modern lines. The British Army, however, remained conservative and its responsible authorities rejected the principles of mechanised warfare which had been so eminently developed and taught by Englishmen in particular (Fuller & Liddell Hart).

The British artillery demonstrated once again its well-known excellence. Especially noteworthy was its great mobility and speed of reaction to the requirements of the assault troops. Apparently the British tank forces carried artillery observers who could report the requirements of the front in the shortest possible time to the artillery groups. In addition to their abundant supplies of ammunition, the great range of the British guns was of tremendous advantage to them. Thus they were able to bombard the Italian artillery positions while the Italian guns, whose range was often no more than 5-6 km., were quite unable to hit back. As by far the greater part of our artillery consisted of obsolete Italian guns, this was a particularly unpleasant state of affairs.

The courage of the German troops and of many of the Italians in this battle, even in the hour of disaster, was particularly worthy of admiration. The force could look back on a glorious record of one and a half years, such as is seldom achieved by any army. Every one of my soldiers was defending not only his homeland but also the tradition of the Panzer Army, Afrika. The struggle of my army will, in spite of its defeat, be a glorious page in the history of the German and Italian peoples.

BACK TO TUNISIA

During the retreat from El Alamein in November, 1942, Rommel prepared a plan for future operations in North Africa and this formed the basis of his discussions with Bastico, Cavallero, Kesselring, Goering and Hitler. There follows an outline of it in his own words

(a) In the existing conditions of supply, which permitted us neither the months-overdue replacements of tanks, vehicles and weapons nor a stock of petrol such as was necessary to carry through a mobile battle, we could not hope to be able to hold out against a powerful British attack in any position in Tripolitania. For all positions which were at all possible could be outflanked in the south and consequently it would be necessary to put the main burden of the defence on motorised forces. From the beginning, therefore, it was necessary to be prepared to evacuate Tripolitania in order to occupy the Gabes position, which, in the south-west, leant on the Schott Dscherid, and there finally come to a halt. In carrying out this withdrawal from Mersa-el-Brega to Tunisia there were two important considerations, on the one hand to gain as much time as possible and on the other to carry out the operation with the minimum losses of men and material.

Our problem in this retreat was the non-motorised force of Italians. The slowest formation, assuming that one does not want to abandon it, always determines the speed of retreat of the whole army. This is a disastrous disadvantage in the face of a fully motorised and superior attacker. It was necessary, for these reasons, to move the Italian divisions to the west into new positions, before the beginning of the British attack, to keep the motorised troops at Mersa-el-Brega so as to tie down the British, to mine the roads and to take advantage of every opportunity of inflicting damage on the enemy advanced guard. The British Commander had revealed himself as over-cautious. He risked nothing which was the least doubtful and any bold action was completely foreign to him. It was, therefore, the task of our motorised forces to give an impression of constant activity so as to make the British even more cautious and slow down their speed. It was clear to me that Montgomery would never take the risk of striking boldly after us and overrunning us, as he could have done perfectly safely. Indeed, looking at the operations as a whole, such a course would have cost him far smaller casualties than his methodical insistence on overwhelming superiority in each tactical action, at the sacrifice of speed.

In any case the retreat to Tunisia was to be carried out in several stages, the British to be forced into deploying as often as possible. This was a gamble on the caution of the British Commander which proved to be very well justified. The Buerat line was earmarked as the first position, the line Tarhuna-Homs as the second. Even there we did not intend to accept battle; instead the infantry was to move off beforehand, while the mechanised formations lightly engaged the enemy and delayed their advance. At Gabes, which, like El Alamein, could not be outflanked from the south, the stand was finally to be made.

(b) In the Gabes position the infantry could bear the main weight of the battle. The position did not lend itself to an attack by motorised forces and could only be broken through by the concentration of a tremendous quantity of material. Montgomery would take no risk and would need several months to bring up enough material from Libya so as to be able to attack the Wadi Akarit with good prospects of success. In the meantime the motorised forces were to be reinforced and refitted with the equipment which would be brought into Tunis while the retreat was going on. The 5th Panzer Army would have landed and we should have a chance of building up another striking force.

The great danger for us was the wide-open front in the west of Tunisia which offered the British and Americans in that area good opportunities of launching an offensive. We must, therefore, first strike there, stage a surprise attack with the whole of our motorised forces, destroy a part of the Anglo-American formations and drive the rest back into Algeria. Meanwhile Montgomery could not hope to do anything against the Gabes position until he had built up large stocks of ammunition for his artillery.

After the British and Americans had been beaten in western Tunisia and deprived of the power of staging an offensive, the quickest possible reorganisation would have to be made for an attack on Montgomery, to throw him back to the east and delay his deployment. Such an operation would obviously be one of considerable difficulty owing to the unfavourable nature of the ground.

(c) In the long run neither Libya nor Tunisia could have been held, for the African war was decided by the battle of the Atlantic. From the moment that the overwhelming industrial capacity of the United States could make itself felt in any theatre of war, there was no chance of ultimate victory. Even if we had overrun the whole of Africa and the Americans had been left with a suitable bridgehead through which they could transport their material, we must eventually have lost the continent.* Tactical skill at this stage could only postpone the collapse; it could not avert it in the long run. In Tunisia the aim must be to gain time, so as to bring as many as possible of the battle-tried veterans in safety to Europe. Because our experience had shown that there was no hope of maintaining a large army in Tunisia, our endeavour must be to reduce the fighting troops there to fewer but better-equipped formations. If the Allies tried to force a decision, we must constantly shorten the front and evacuate more and more troops by means of transport aircraft, barges and warships. The first stand must be in the hilly country extending round Tunis from Enfidaville, the second in the Cap Bon peninsula. When the Allies finally took Tunis they must find nothing there, or at most a few prisoners, and would thus be robbed of the fruits of their victory, as we were robbed at Dunkirk.

(d) From the troops scheduled for evacuation to Italy, a striking force would be formed. These troops were the best both in training and in battle experience that we could put against the British and Americans. Moreover, I was on such terms with them that their value under my command was not to be measured only by their actual numbers.

* This is only superficially a contradiction of Rommel's previous views and a confirmation of those of General Halder. Rommel remained convinced that, given support, he could have overrun the Middle East in the spring or summer of 1942 but he came to realise that American production must eventually prove decisive everywhere.

Index